sociology 337 minorities

majority & minority

Norman R. Yetman

Taken from
Majority and Minority
The Dynamics of Race and Ethnicity in American Life
Sixth Edition
Edited by Norman R. Yetman

Pearson
Custom
Publishing

Cover Art by Darryl L. Johnson

Taken from:

Majority and Minority: The Dynamics of Race and Ethnicity in American Life, Sixth Edition
by Norman R. Yetman
Copyright © 1999, 1991, 1985, 1982 by Allyn and Bacon
A Pearson Education Company
Boston, Massachusetts 02116

This special edition published in cooperation with Pearson Custom Publishing.

Printed in the United States of America

10   9

Please visit our web site at www.pearsoncustom.com

ISBN 0–536–67432–9

BA 994124

 PEARSON CUSTOM PUBLISHING
75 Arlington Street, Suite 300, Boston, MA 02116
A Pearson Education Company

CONTENTS

CHAPTER 1

CHAPTER 2

CHAPTER 3

CHAPTER 4

Introduction: Definitions and Perspectives

1

Among the most dramatic social phenomena of the past quarter century has been the resurgence of racial and ethnic rivalries, tensions, and hostilities throughout the world. Prejudice, discrimination, conflict, and violence based on racial and ethnic distinctions are widely found throughout the world today—among black, white, colored, and Indian in South Africa; between English-speaking and French-speaking people in Canada; between Islamic Arabs and black Christians in the Sudan; between East Indians and blacks in Guyana; between Kurds and Iraqis in Iraq; between Tamils and Sinhalese in Sri Lanka; between Chinese and Malays in Malaysia; between Hutu and Tutsi in Burundi and Rwanda; and between Krahn, Gio, and Mano ethnic groups in Liberia. In the last few decades, more people have died in ethnic conflicts around the world than in the Korean and Vietnam wars combined.

Indeed, the political ferment that was created by the dramatic political changes throughout eastern Europe during the late 1980s unleashed a resurgence of historic ethnic and national rivalries and antagonisms. The disintegration of the Soviet Union was reinforced by interethnic conflicts, such as those between the Armenians and Azerbaijanis, as well as by demands from numerous other nationalities, such as Lithuanians, Latvians, Estonians, Georgians, ethnic Poles, and Ukrainians, for greater ethnic autonomy and even independence. Even after the breakup of the Soviet Union, Russia has continued to be the site of numerous conflicts—in 1992 alone involving more than 180 ethnic clashes, and in 1994, 1995, and 1996 a bloody war to prevent nationalist rebels in the province of Chechnya from declaring their independence.

Slavic nationalism, which earlier in the century had provided the spark that ignited World War I, resurfaced with a vengeance. In the former Yugoslavia, conflicts among the country's several nationalities—Serbs, Croatians, Slovenes, Bosnians, Montenegrins, Macedonians, and Albanians—led to the nation's dissolution and to one of the most bitter and deadly conflicts among European peoples in the post–World War II era, resulting in the death of over 250,000 people and the displacement of more than 2 million (Cohen 1994). Since 1992, Bosnian Serbs have used a reign of terror, including rape, murder, torture, and intimidation, to expel forcibly hundreds of thousands of

Croats and, especially, Muslims from their homes and villages in Bosnia-Herzegovena. They characterized their efforts to eliminate non-Serbians from territories under their control as "ethnic cleansing," thereby adding a new and horrifically precise term to the lexicon of human ethnic conflict.

Prior to the fall of Rumanian strongman Nicolae Ceaușescu in 1989, approximately two million Hungarians living in Rumania were subject to forced assimilation, the closing of Hungarian schools and social organizations, the suppression of the Hungarian language, and discrimination against those Hungarians who tried to retain their ethnic identity. Similar accusations of forced assimilation were raised by the Turkish minority in Bulgaria, where ethnic tensions led to the forced removal of thousands of Muslim Turks to Turkey.

These examples demonstrate how widespread and deeply rooted ethnic conflict is throughout our world today. In this section we consider some basic definitions and some of the conceptual approaches that have been used to comprehend the dynamics of racial and ethnic relations, especially in the United States.

Ethnic, Racial, and Caste Categories

Ethnicity

The word *ethnic* is derived from the Greek word *ethnos,* meaning "people." An ethnic group is *socially defined* on the basis of its *cultural* characteristics. Ethnicity, the sense of identification with and membership in a particular ethnic group, implies the existence of a distinct culture or subculture in which people perceive themselves and are perceived by others to be bound together by a common origin, history, values, attitudes, and behaviors—in its broadest sense, a sense of peoplehood—and are so regarded by other members of the society. Ethnic groups may differ in cultural characteristics as diverse as eating habits, family patterns, sexual behaviors, modes of dress, standards of beauty, political orientations, economic activities, religions, languages, and recreational patterns. As Joane Nagel points out in Article 2 ("Constructing Ethnicity"), "ethnicity is constructed out of the material of language, religion, culture, appearance, ancestry, or regionality."

This conception of ethnicity resembles what Robert N. Bellah and his colleagues have termed "communities of memory," in which people share an identity rooted in a collective history, tradition, and experience that can be both heroic and painful. However, a community of memory is not simply cultural, involving shared beliefs and ideas; it is sustained through social relations, by participation in the life of the community. Such participation, which Bellah has termed "practices of commitment," "define the patterns of loyalty and obligation that keep the community alive" (Bellah et al. 1985:152–155). In American society, Mexican Americans, Italian Americans, Jewish Americans, Polish Americans, Filipino Americans, and white Anglo-Saxon Protestant Americans can all be considered ethnic groups, however broad and diverse their internal composition.

For example, in 1970 Lewis Killian argued that, because of their distinctive history, cultural characteristics, language, and identity, white Southerners represented an important ethnic category that had seldom previously been considered "ethnic." During Jimmy Carter's 1976 presidential campaign, Patrick Anderson, one of Carter's chief aides, described the ethnic dimensions of the Carter candidacy and the sense of ethnic identity it evoked.

> *Perhaps you have to be a Southerner to understand what [Jimmy Carter's candidacy] means to some of us. There is a great sense of personal pride and personal vindication involved, a sense that after losing for a long, long time, our side is finally going to win one. I imagine that Jews and blacks will feel the same way when one of their own finally gets a shot at the White House.*
>
> *The emotions involved run deep, and are hard to communicate, but I think they must be considered by anyone who wants to understand why young Southerners . . . are driving themselves so relentlessly on Governor Carter's behalf. They are motivated, I think, not only by the personal ambition that afflicts us all, but by personal affection for the candidate, by political commitment to certain goals, and by a regional pride that has its roots many generations in the past. (Anderson 1976:21, emphasis added)*

Ethnic groups are inherently ethnocentric, regarding their own cultural traits as natural, correct, and superior to those of other ethnic groups, who are perceived as odd, amusing, inferior, or immoral. Donald Noel (1968) has suggested that ethnocentrism is a necessary, but not sufficient, condition for the emergence of ethnic stratification. According to Noel, a dominant-subordinate relationship between two mutually ethnocentric groups cannot develop unless the groups are competing for the same scarce resources and, most important, one group possesses superior power to impose its will on the other.

Race

The terms *race* and *ethnicity* are often used interchangeably, but for analytic purposes they should be distinguished. Whereas an *ethnic group* is distinguished by *cultural* characteristics, *race* refers to a social category that is defined on the basis of *physical* characteristics. However, the term *race* is meaningless in a biological sense, because there are no "pure" races: the racial categories found in each society are social constructs or conventions; the characteristics that distinguish one racial group from another are arbitrary and thus are *socially defined and constructed*. As Berreman contends in Article 1 ("Race, Caste, and Other Invidious Distinctions"), "systems of 'racial' stratification are social phenomena based on social rather than biological facts." A group is defined as a race when certain physical characteristics are selected for special emphasis by members of a society. As Berreman notes, the definition of a group as a race is not a function of biological or genetic differences between groups, but of society's perceptions that such differences are real and that they are important—that they are related to or reflect other apparently innate mental, emotional, and moral differences, such as intelligence.

The term *race* has been an extremely loose, variable, and imprecise concept; it has been used to refer to linguistic categories (Aryan, English-speaking), to religious categories (Hindu, Jewish), to national categories (French, Italian), and to mystical, quasi-scientific categories (Teutonic). The wide range of social categories that have been considered "races" reinforces the notion that racial designations are artificial; they serve the function of separating certain social categories on the basis of an arbitrary selection or identification of specific physical or biologically transmitted characteristics. Because of the imprecision with which the term *race* has been used, some scholars have chosen to dispense with it, preferring to subsume what have previously been termed "races" under the broad category of ethnic groups.

Many groups possess physically identifiable characteristics that do not become the basis for racial distinctions. Thus, the criteria selected to make racial distinctions in one society may be overlooked or considered insignificant or irrelevant by another. For instance, in much of Latin America skin color and the shape of the lips—important distinguishing criteria in the United States—are much less significant than are hair texture, eye color, and stature. A person considered black in Georgia or Michigan might be considered white in Peru or the Dominican Republic (Pitt-Rivers 1967).

Many examples of the arbitrary, socially (and politically) defined nature of American racial categories can be found throughout American history. In 1926 three members of the National Association of Colored People (NAACP) asked the distinguished defense lawyer Clarence Darrow to defend a Detroit black man who had been accused of murdering a member of a white mob that was threatening his home. Arthur Spingarn, a dark-skinned man of Puerto Rican descent, described the case to Darrow, who replied,

> *"Yes. I know full well the difficulties faced by your race."*
> *"I'm sorry, Mr. Darrow," replied Spingarn, "but I'm not a Negro."*
> *Darrow turned to Charles Studin, another member of the committee, and said, "Well, you understand what I mean."*
> *"I am not colored either," replied Studin.*
> *The third man had blond hair and blue eyes. "I would not make that mistake with you," Darrow told him.*
> *"I am a Negro," replied Walter White, secretary of the NAACP.*
> *Darrow jumped out of bed. "That settles it," he cried. "I'll take the case." (Stone 1943:470, quoted in Katzman 1973:82)*

This example demonstrates that racial identity is not primarily a matter of skin color or is not based simply on physical appearance. It is, much more significantly, based on the social categories to which people are assigned. Although there may be some perceived biological basis for the distinctions we make, the criteria that we use and the range of people that we include in each category are arbitrary, irrational, and frequently illogical.

Marvin Harris (1964) has identified two socially defined "rules" that determine the racial categories into which people in the United States will be placed. First is the "one-drop rule," through which anyone who has *any* African ancestry, no matter how remote, will be classified as "black." The other is the "rule of hypodescent," by which people of multiracial backgrounds will be unable to claim membership in the dominant "race" but will automatically be placed in the minority racial category. As Barbara Fields has pointed out, these "rules" lead to the absurd racial convention "that considers a white woman capable of giving birth to a black child but denies that a black woman can give birth to a white child" (Fields 1982:149).

The operation of these "rules" and the socially defined nature of American racial categories are vividly demonstrated by laws in the United States prohibiting interracial marriages. Until 1967, when the Supreme Court ruled in *Loving v. Virginia* that such laws were unconstitutional, many states stipulated that any person with one-fourth or more African ancestry (that is, with one black grandparent) was legally defined as "black" and therefore prohibited from marrying someone "white."[1] However, some states enacted even more restrictive definitions of race. Indeed, the variability in state laws defining racial categories underscores the arbitrary nature of such classifications. If "race" is a "natural," invariable, and clearly biological phenomenon, then one's race should not change simply by crossing a state line into another state.

A recent court case in Louisiana illustrates the operation of the "one-drop rule" and the "rule of hypodescent." Susie Guillory Phipps, a light-skinned woman with Caucasian features and straight black hair, found that her birth certificate classified her as "colored." Mrs. Phipps, who contended that she had been "brought up white and married white twice," challenged a 1970 Louisiana law declaring that anyone with at least one-thirty-second "Negro blood" was legally black. Under this law an individual who had *one* great-great-great-grandparent who was black (and thus had one-thirty-second "black" and thirty-one–thirty-seconds "white" ancestry) was legally defined as black. Although the state's lawyer conceded that Phipps "looks like a white person," the state strenuously maintained that her racial classification was appropriate, and this interpretation was upheld by Louisiana's supreme court. However, Louisiana later repealed the law (Trillin 1986).

The arbitrary, irrational, and socially constructed nature of racial and ethnic categories and identities is also revealed by circumstances in which individuals change categories; if racial categories are "real," people should be unable to escape classification within them. The story of Gregory Howard Williams, the dean of the Ohio State University School of Law, is instructive in this regard. Williams grew up in Virginia believing that he was white. He was ten when his parents' marriage and his father's businesses failed, and he and his brother moved with their father to his hometown of Muncie, Indiana. On the bus ride to Muncie, his father told him and his brother, "Life is going to be different from now on. In Virginia you were white boys. In Indiana you're going to be colored boys. I want you to remember that you're the same today that you were yesterday. But people in Indiana will treat you differently" (Williams 1995:33). In Muncie he was thrust into the black segment of a racially segregated community, and his book describes the difficulties he encountered trying to negotiate "life on the color line" between black and white (Williams 1995). Thus, racial identity is not fixed, immutable, or unchanging.

The former South African system of apartheid, or racial separation, provides one of the most vivid examples of the way in which racial classifications are social, not biological, categories that are arbitrarily imposed. Under apartheid, which was established in 1950 and formally abolished in 1991, all people were required to be classified into one of four legally defined racial categories—white, black, colored, and Indian. The racial categories into which people were arbitrarily placed determined many features of their lives, including whether they could vote or own land, what jobs they could hold, which schools they could attend, where they could live, eat, or play, and whom they could love and marry. As in the case of Gregory Williams, the arbitrary and irrational nature of such categories is revealed in circumstances in which an individual's legal racial classification—and the entire range of opportunities that flowed from that classification—were changed. In 1988 a South African news-paper reported,

> Nearly 800 South Africans became officially members of a different race group last year. They included 518 coloreds who were officially reclassified as white, 14 whites who became colored, 7 Chinese [who are classified as "honorary whites"] who became white, 2 whites who became Chinese, 3 Malays [who are classified as colored] who became white, 1 white who became Indian, 50 Indians who became colored, 54 coloreds who became Indian, 17 Indians who became Malay, 4 coloreds who became Chinese, 1 Malay who became Chinese, 89 blacks who became colored, 5 coloreds who became black. (Usy 1988:27)

Because consciousness of race is so pronounced in the United States, most Americans are placed in a specific racial category by cultural conventions and everyday discourse—the "common sense" understandings that are widely shared among the American people. These categories are reinforced, as well, by discussions such as this one, which, by attaching labels to arbitrarily identified groups of people, serve to heighten the perception of the categories themselves and thus, ironically, to legitimize the notion that race is a "real"—biologically based—phenomenon and thus to obscure its socially constructed, contingent, and emergent nature.

The Variability of "Racial" Distinctions

Racial distinctions are not restricted to skin pigmentation alone but can involve other visible physical characteristics as well. An excellent example is found in the small African countries of Burundi and Rwanda, which during the past quarter century have experienced waves of intergroup violence and conflict in which the principal biological distinction between political antagonists has been stature.

Burundi and Rwanda are neighboring, landlocked countries of central Africa, situated between the republics of Zaire, Uganda, and Tanzania. During their colonial periods, which ended in 1962, both were controlled by the Belgians. As in several other African countries, independence from European colonialism brought deep-rooted ethnic rivalries to the surface. In 1972 a wave of government-sponsored violence swept through Burundi. An estimated 100,000 Hutus—3.5 percent of the population—were killed in 1972, and more than 100,000 more in subsequent massacres in 1988, 1993, and 1996 by the country's Tutsi-dominated military. A comparable annihilation in the American population would mean the deaths of about 9 million people. But the numbers killed in Burundi pale in comparison to the slaughter that occurred in neighboring Rwanda in 1994, where more than 750,000 people—nearly 10 percent of all Rwandans—were murdered by the Hutu-dominated Rwandan government, and over a million more were made homeless; subsequently, more than 2 million Hutus then fled Rwanda after Tutsi rebels gained power.

The genocide in Burundi and Rwanda reflects the rivalry of the countries' two major racial groups: the Tutsi and the Hutu. The Tutsi, originally a tall and slender people among whom men average six feet in height, make up only about 15 percent of Burundi's population and less than 10 percent of the population of Rwanda. For centuries before the arrival of European colonial powers, the Tutsi had held the Hutu, a people of shorter stature, in a form of serfdom (the term *Hutu* itself means "subject" or "servant"). During the colonial period the Belgians magnified and exaggerated the social divisions of a Tutsi aristocracy and a Hutu servant class. When independence was achieved in 1962, many Hutu were hopeful that, because they represented the overwhelming numerical majority of the populations of both countries, the promise of majority rule would bring an end to Tutsi domination. However, Hutu frustration in Burundi grew in the years following independence as the more politically powerful Tutsi effectively blocked Hutu efforts to change the status quo.

In 1972 the Tutsi-dominated government of Burundi responded with a wave of violence to allegations of a Hutu revolt against Tutsi control. In many villages, all Hutu of any wealth, community influence, or educational level above grade school were systematically shot or beaten to death. The killing was selective, aimed at all influential Hutu. The objective of the annihilation of the Hutu elites was to crush any Hutu threat to Tutsi power. The Tutsi sought to eliminate "not only the rebellion but Hutu society as well, and in the process lay the foundation of an entirely new social order" (Lemarchand 1975:575). This wave of genocide ensured Tutsi political and economic power in Burundi and led to the systematic exclusion of Hutu from the army, civil service, the university, and high schools. In 1988, 1993, and 1996 the long-simmering tension between these two groups flared once again into violent conflict. At least 5,000 more people were killed in another Hutu uprising and the Tutsi reprisal that followed, and more than 50,000 Hutu fled to the neighboring country of Rwanda, where Hutu are the tribal majority (Brooke 1988; Perlez 1988; Friedman 1996).

In Rwanda, on the other hand, freedom from colonial Belgian rule led to a bloody but successful Hutu-led revolt against Tutsi political domination. But exiled Tutsi leaders continued to seek to regain political power; and, fearful that they would succeed, Hutu extremists in the Rwandan government used Rwandan President Haabyarimana's death in a plane crash in April 1994 as a pretext to begin their campaign of genocide. Government-sponsored death squads roamed the country, using guns, clubs, and machetes to annihilate all opposition—primarily Tutsi but including any Hutus who protected Tutsi or protested against government policies (Smith 1995). The result was one of the most savage massacres of people since the Holocaust perpetrated by Nazi Germany during the 1930s and 1940s.

Although numerous writers have argued that racial and ethnic distinctions did not *cause* the waves of genocide that have swept Burundi and Rwanda, the savage conflict between Tutsi and Hutu in these two troubled countries not only demonstrates how racial and ethnic divisions continue to provide the basis for bloodshed and violence throughout the modern world but also suggests that, because of the principal criterion upon which the distinctions between Hutu and Tutsi were originally based—the physical characteristic of stature—this violent conflict between the two peoples can be considered racial.

As the racial/ethnic conflict in Burundi and the caste status of the *Burakumin* in Japan (which we will discuss more fully later) demonstrate, in real life, race, ethnicity, and caste are intimately related, and distinctions between them are difficult to make. Indeed, there has been considerable debate among social scientists concerning whether race relations are different in kind from ethnic relations or whether race relations can appropriately be subsumed under the broad rubric of ethnicity. Because in American society *racial* conflicts—those based on physical, rather than cultural, differences—have generally been more intense than ethnic conflicts, there has been a tendency to attribute a preeminence to the study of race relations. However, as many examples throughout the world in the past quarter century demonstrate—the enduring conflict between Protestants and Catholics in Northern Ireland or the violent tensions that have characterized the former Yugoslavia in the post-Soviet era, for example—ethnic differences are capable of eliciting antagonisms and loyalties comparable in intensity and tenacity to those based on racial distinctions. In an extensive comparative analysis of a wide range of ethnically divided societies in Asia, Africa, and the Caribbean, Horowitz (1985) has contested the assumption that *race* relations are somehow qualitatively different from intergroup relations based on language, religion, or putative common ancestry or origins. Such a notion, he contends, is based on two unwarranted premises—that racial distinctions arouse "uniquely intense emotions and loyalties" and that such distinctions "serve as unusually reliable signs of individual identity. . . . Neither of these assumptions," he argues, "can be supported" (Horowitz 1985:42).

Given that it is difficult to establish conclusively that *racial* and *ethnic* phenomena can be qualitatively distinguished, it is appropriate to adopt an inclusive definition of ethnicity that emphasizes the different criteria—physical differences, language, religion, and putative common ancestry or origins—used to distinguish groups. Such an inclusive definition is consistent with Berreman's emphasis that the crucial feature of such phenomena is that group differences are *attributed* to ascriptive characteristics. In other words, I am arguing that *racial* characteristics, which are perceived to be so crucial to the distinctions used in American society, represent only one of several possible criteria that can be used to allocate people to different ethnic categories. Therefore, in subsequent discussion, this book treats "racial" relations as one dimension of ethnic relations and uses the terms *ethnic* and *ethnicity* in this broader and more inclusive sense.

Primordial and Situational Explanations

Why have people used racial and ethnic distinctions so frequently throughout history to rank a society's members? Why have racial and ethnic differences so often demarcated the lines of intergroup conflict? Two broad explanatory models have been advanced: the primordialist (or nonrational) perspective and the social constructionist (or rational or situational) perspective. The former model conceptualizes racial and ethnic identities and distinctions as *essentialist*—that is, they are perceived to be biologically based, present at birth, instinctive, innate, and unchangeable, "attachments [that] seem to flow more from a sense of natural affinity than from social interaction" (Burgess 1978:266). A constructionist position, on the other hand, locates the sources of ethnicity in the structure and dynamics of human societies. From this perspective, race and ethnicity are functional, pragmatic, emergent, and constantly evolving and changing phenomena, "a rational group response to social pressures and a basis for group action, especially where no other exists. . . . Ethnicity [is] a strategy chosen to advance individual [and group] interest as the situation dictates" (Burgess 1978:267).

Pierre van den Berghe has been one of the most prominent and articulate advocates for what has been broadly termed a primordialist perspective, one that sees racial and ethnic distinctions as deeply rooted in the basic nature of human sociality. He contends that kin selection and its corollary, nepotism, are the basic principles on which societies have been based for most of human existence; and that ethnic and racial distinctions are merely extensions of kinship principles. The pervasiveness of ethnic distinctions and ethnocentrism in human societies suggests that these phenomena are instrumental in establishing group boundaries. Most preliterate societies, for example, employ cultural—ethnic—markers such as language or body adornment, rather than physical—racial—ones, for the simple reason that they rarely encounter other peoples who are physically distinguishable from themselves. Racial distinctions, van den Berghe argues, are the consequence primarily of large-scale migrations, which have occurred only relatively recently in human history:

> Humans, like other animals, are selected to favor kin, and whatever does a quick, easy and accurate job of differentiating kin and non-kin will be used. In most cases, and until recently, cultural criteria have been predominantly used. Physical criteria became salient only after large, strikingly different-looking populations found themselves in sudden and sustained contact. (van den Berghe 1978c:407–408)

A social constructionist approach to race and ethnicity, on the other hand, emphasizes that definitions of ethnic and racial categories are *socially* defined phenomena, the boundaries and content of which are constantly being renegotiated, revised, and redefined. From this perspective, an ethnic identity is neither "natural" nor inherent in the nature of the group itself; rather it is socially constructed, a reflection and product of broader social factors and competing individual and group interests. As Nagel points out in "Constructing Ethnicity" (Article 2), "Ethnicity is created and recreated as various groups and interests put forth competing visions of the ethnic composition of society and argue over which rewards or sanctions should be attached to which ethnicities." Nagel especially emphasizes the role of state and political factors in eliciting, heightening, and reinforcing ethnicity as an organizational resource around which competition for resources and power can be played out. She contends that ethnicity may be *resurgent* (involving the revitalization of historic identities) or *emergent* (involving the creation of newly formed groups). Her primary objective is to identify the conditions under which *ethnic mobilization,* "the process by which a group organizes along ethnic lines in pursuit of group ends," occurs. Her analysis suggests that the state possesses a capacity—one frequently ignored by students of race and ethnicity—to shape ethnic relations and to generate ethnic awareness and identification, either intentionally or unintentionally. Her basic thesis is that because ethnicity in the modern world is a largely political phenomenon, because it arises out of the political structures and policies of the modern nation-state, it is unlikely that its significance will diminish in the near future. The implication is that, as the power of the American state continues to expand and penetrate all sectors of modern life, the salience of ethnicity is unlikely to diminish in the future. The constructionist model, therefore, "constitutes an argument for the durability, indeed, the inevitability, of ethnicity in modern societies." Nagel's argument, therefore, has special relevance to Part 4, in which we shall consider more fully the future of race and ethnicity in American life.

As noted before, a constructionist perspective is useful not only in explaining the persistence of historic ethnic distinctions and conflicts but also in identifying the factors that contribute to both the *resurgence* of ethnic identities and the emergence of new forms of ethnic identity throughout the world. One of the most interesting of these has been the development of *panethnicity,* which refers to situations in which peoples of several previously distinct tribal, national, ethnic, or racial groups come to identify or be identified on the basis of a broader, more inclusive ethnic category.

For example, historians of European American ethnic groups have pointed out that a sense of national identity was in many instances not fully developed among many immigrants; rather, identity with a nation emerged only after they had lived in the United States for some time. For example, during the late nineteenth and early twentieth centuries people who emigrated from Italy to the United States often did not think of themselves as Italians; rather, they drew their primary identities from the villages or region of the country from which they hailed. Their consciousness of themselves as Italians emerged only as a consequence of their encounter with American society (Vecoli 1964). Similarly, William Yancey and his colleagues (1976) contend that among many European immigrant groups, a sense of ethnicity was produced, not as a result of the cultural baggage—shared cultural characteristics—or of a shared sense of ethnic identity that people brought with them, but rather by external factors—the conditions they confronted in their settlements in the United States. In such circumstances ethnic identity was always "emergent," that is, it represented a response to the common conditions in the cities in which the people settled. Among these conditions were "common occupational positions, residential stability and concentration, and dependence on common institutions and services, [which were] in turn directly affected by the process of industrialization."

Moreover, as both Doane (Article 3) and Barrett and Roediger (Article 6) argue, the very category of "white" has been socially constructed and has over time come to include groups (such as the Irish, Italians, Jews, Poles) that had previously been placed in other, or "inbetween," racial categories. In 1985 Lieberson identified from his analysis of 1980 census data, the emergence in American society of a new ethnic category: *unhyphenated whites,* whose European national origins are so obscure or so mixed that their only ethnic identity is in reference to American society. Since then, issues of ethnic identity among people of European descent and, in particular, the question of what it means to be "white"—seldom previously considered in studies of American race relations—have become the focus of a wide range of scholarly studies. These scholars see "whiteness" as a racial category that, like any other, has changed, acquired new meaning, and subsumed different groups over time. The basic questions with which these scholars (for example, Ignatiev 1995; Frankenberg 1993; Saxton 1990; Roediger 1991, 1994) are concerned are how to explain both the process by which these changes occurred and the social consequences of these changes for defining race in American life. Doane points out that the failure to consider the impact of "whiteness" "leaves the dominant group as the hidden center of race and ethnic relations in the United States [that] plays a key role in the persistence and reproduction of [dominant] group hegemony." This perspective was recently reinforced by the response of Derrick Bell, a prominent African American legal scholar, to President Bill Clinton's appointment of a national commission to initiate a national dialogue on race. The critical question that the commission—and, by implication, all Americans—should address, Bell argued, is, "What does it really mean to be white, not as a matter of pride in cultural heritage, but as social and economic facts of life in the United States?" (Bell 1997:19).

Thus each of the five broad categories that comprise what Hollinger (Article 4) has termed the American *"ethnoracial pentagon"* (American Indians, African Americans, Europeans, Asians, and Hispanics) are panethnic—that is, they subsume within them a broad range of cultural, national, linguistic, regional, tribal, religious, and generational groups. Although such categories give the illusion of cultural homogeneity (thus simultaneously reinforcing and redefining the structure of ethnic relations in American society), they ignore or obscure considerable internal diversity, conflict, and mutual antagonism within each category. For example, Espiritu (1992) notes that the Asian American category is comprised of diverse and often antagonistic national elements, including Chinese, Japanese, Korean, Vietnamese, Thai, Khmer, and Asian Indian. Joane Nagel points out in Article 2 how the terms *American Indian* and *Native American* are consequences of their minority status in American society and obscure the substantial tribal (ethnic) differences among them. Similarly, the terms *Hispanic* or *Latino,* which two decades ago were not even part of the common language, are increasingly employed to subsume into one category several extremely diverse ethnic categories. Although such distinctions are employed by social scientists, journalists, business people, and ultimately the people themselves, Cynthia Enloe (1981) has contended that the state has played a crucial role in defining these arbitrary social categories: "The state employs ethnic categories to suit its administrative-political needs. In so doing it requires individuals subject to certain laws to respond as 'Hispanics' or 'Indians' or 'Filipinos.'"

Examination of the U.S. census and the controversy over the categories to be used when the next decennial census is taken in 2000, reflect the fluid, arbitrary nature of American concepts of race and ethnicity. The racial categories used in each census, which the United States Constitution specifies is to be collected every ten years, are inevitably the result, not of a "scientific" and rational classification system but instead of arbitrary decisions that reflect primarily the social, cultural, and political assumptions of the day and governmental efforts to standardize them (see Wright 1994; Snipp 1997). The categories used in the 1980 and 1990 censuses were established by Statistical Directive 15, issued by the Office of Management and Budget in 1977. This bureaucratic definition officially recognizes four general racial categories in the United States: American Indian, Asian, Black, and White; people are also classified as Hispanic or non-Hispanic. As a consequence of this federal government definition, "the identities of Americans were fixed in five broad groupings. Those racial and ethnic categories that were dreamed up almost twenty years ago were not neutral in their effect. By attempting to provide a way for Americans to describe themselves, the categories actually began to shape those identities. The categories became political entities, with their own constituencies, lobbies, and vested interests. What was even more significant, they caused people to think of themselves in new ways—as members of 'races' that were little more than statistical devices" (Wright 1994:52–53).

Thus the census itself reflects the changing dynamics and meaning of race and ethnicity in American life. Because numerous governmental policies and practices address issues of racial classification, the racial categories to be used in the 2000 census has been the source of great acrimony and divisiveness. Numerous groups argued that the categories be changed to benefit their particular interests. For example, the National Council of La Raza urged that Hispanics be considered a race, not simply an ethnic group. Native Hawaiians have petitioned to be included under the category of American Indians/Native Americans rather than as Asians. And one of the heated controversies over the census to be administered in the year 2000 concerns pressures from an increasingly large group of people who are the children of interracial unions to have available a new category—"Multiracial"—a procedure that would have the effect of creating a new racial category in the United States (Wright 1994). Given the extent to which existing racial categories affect public policy (for example, in determining the boundaries for Congressional districts or in testing for racial discrimination in mortgage-lending practices), the consequences of any such change could be profound.

On the other hand, as intermarriage and the number of people acknowledging mixed racial ancestry have recently increased, the arbitrariness of racial categories has become increasingly apparent, as many people have recognized the difficulties of placing themselves or others in the existing categories. Indicative of this increasing recognition of the illogic of racial categories was the 1995 *Newsweek* cover story, "What Color Is Black?" in which it answered its own question with the assertion that "It is every conceivable shade and hue from tan to ebony—and suddenly a matter of ideology and identity as much as pigmentation" (*Newsweek* 1995:64).

As a result of demographic, cultural, social, and economic factors that we will explore throughout this book, increasing numbers of Americans, especially those with multiracial backgrounds, are rejecting requirements that they choose one single racial category on census forms, on school enrollment forms, and on job, loan, and mortgage applications. Increasingly, people are calling either for the elimination of official racial distinctions altogether or for the creation of a "multiracial" category that will not force individuals to choose between two or more racial identities. This situation has been epitomized by the golfing phenom Tiger Woods, whose 1997 victory at the prestigious Masters tournament was hailed by many sports commentators as the first such win by an African American. But because his mother was Thai, some Asian Americans contended that he was the first Asian American to win the tournament. Yet Woods, who also claims Caucasian and American Indian ancestry, coined the term "Cablinasian" to reflect his multiple backgrounds (Leland and Beals 1997; White 1997).

Some critics have gone even further and contend that, whatever public policy benefits may derive from having the Census Bureau continue to categorize the American people on the basis of race, those benefits are far outweighed by the negative consequences of continuing their use. One of the principal objections is that governmental racial categories contribute to a *self-fulfilling prophecy,* which refers to a situation that is inaccurately or falsely defined but, because it is believed to be true, produces behavior that makes the original belief come true. Thus, sociologist Orlando Patterson has criticized the Census Bureau decision to retain racial categories on the 2000 census, contending that, by contributing to the perception that these racial categories are real, the categories themselves only furthered racial division. "Distinguishing between race and ethnicity is an ingrained part of America's racial ideology. The racial categories maintained by the Census Bureau can only perpetuate the idea that there is such a thing as racial purity and that people in the United States have essential biological differences" (Patterson 1997:A21).

Ethnicity and Social Stratification

Societies differ in the extent to which they permit and encourage *social mobility*—the movement of persons from one social stratum to another. An *open system of stratification* is one in which few obstacles exist for people who are changing social positions;

achievement is unaffected either by the constraints of disadvantaged social origins or by the privileges of advantaged social rank. All people, regardless of birth status (sex, race, religion, ethnicity, social background), have genuinely equal opportunity to change positions and move up or down in the stratification. The greater the degree of social mobility, the more open the class system is. In an open class system, emphasis is placed on achievement.

By contrast, a *closed system of stratification* allows virtually no social mobility; children inherit their parents' social position. In a closed system, people's places in a social hierarchy are fixed or ascribed (that is, on the basis of qualities such as race, ethnicity, social background, or sex, over which they have no control). In a closed system, little possibility exists for social mobility. People are born into a position and cannot, under normal circumstances, move out of it.

The most rigid and closed of all stratification systems is a *caste system,* a system of social inequality characterized by rigidly separated social categories in which an individual's status is birth-ascribed, inherited, immutable, permanent, and fixed. A caste system is endogamous, which means that people must marry within their own caste. A person who does not marry within her or his caste will probably be punished severely. Intimate contact, such as eating with someone of a different caste, is prohibited. Typically elaborate systems of rituals and customs are developed to limit interaction between members of different castes. However, no stratification system is totally closed or totally open; virtually all societies display both ascription and achievement in some form (Tumin 1969).

The traditional Indian caste system, the basis of organizing Indian society since the fifth century B.C., is usually cited as the classic example of caste. The system can be divided into five broad strata, each of which contains thousands of internal distinctions based primarily on occupation. At the top of the hierarchy stand the *Brahmans,* the priests, scholars, and teachers of basic religious principles, who provided religious support and legitimation for the social order (Mayer and Buckley, 1970). Occupying the lowest and most despised position are the *Harijans,* a term meaning "people of God," which was popularized by Mohandas Gandhi. These people are the outcastes, whom Indians believe fall outside the caste system. They are frequently called "untouchables" because they are not permitted to touch members of the upper castes. Indians believe that they can be contaminated even if an outcaste's shadow touches their clothing, food, or person. Outcastes are so despised that in rural areas, they are frequently barred from villages during the parts of the day when they would cast long shadows and would therefore be more likely to contaminate other villagers.

Since 1949 discrimination on the basis of caste has been outlawed in India, and the coming of modernity to that nation has undermined and disrupted the traditional caste system, especially in large metropolitan areas. In the modern Indian world of bureaucracies, factories, and schools, contact among castes has increased. Despite these changes, however, the Indian caste system persists, especially in the rural areas, where 75 percent of the Indian population lives. In rural villages people still find it unthinkable to marry someone from another caste. How deeply the caste system is rooted and how harshly its rules are enforced is illustrated by a recent incident in a rural Indian village in which a sixteen-year-old girl, her eighteen-year-old lover, and a friend who had tried to help them elope were lynched by relatives and neighbors. The young woman was a *Jat,* the dominant caste in the region, while the young men were outcastes. The deaths of all three were decreed by the *Jat*-dominated village council after the young woman refused to give up her lover (Crossette 1991:60).

A caste system is not unique to India. For example, the Japanese *Burakumin*—Japan's "invisible race"—represent another excellent example of a caste system without apparent racial distinctions. Physically indistinguishable from other Japanese, the *Burakumin* are acknowledged to be completely Japanese, but of such lowly social origins that they are economically and socially discriminated against and are considered mentally inferior by the rest of Japanese society; marriages between *Burakumin* and members of the upper caste are considered a tragedy and are strongly discouraged (DeVos and Wagatsuma 1966).

The contemporary *Burakumin* are descendants of the untouchable *eta* caste. The degree to which the *eta* were despised by the rest of Japanese society is revealed in the name itself: *eta* means "filth abundant." Under the feudal system of Tokugawa Japan, from the seventeenth to the nineteenth centuries, the *eta* occupied an outcaste status below the four superior castes (the ruling caste of warriors and administrators, the peasants, the artisans, and the merchants) that constituted Japanese society. The *eta* were discriminated against in every aspect of their lives, and a number of laws were enacted to reinforce their inferior status. For example, as outcastes they were restricted to the dirtiest, most defiling, and least desirable occupations (such as being butchers, leatherworkers, grave tenders, and executioners). They were legally segregated from the rest of the Japanese people and forced to live in isolated ghettos. Moreover, they were required to walk barefoot and to wear special clothing that identified them as *eta*. Because they were considered innately inferior and "impure," their marriages were restricted to other *eta*; intermarriages with non-*eta* were virtually nonexistent.

The *eta* were legally "emancipated" during the mid–nineteenth century, and the laws that had formerly restricted their lives and discriminated against them were formally abolished. Although emancipation provided legal freedom, discrimination against the outcasts (subsequently known as *Burakumin*, or "village people") has persisted. Among the popular prejudices about the *Burakumin* that persisted well into the twentieth century were the following:

> One rib is lacking; they have a dog's bone in them; they have distorted sexual organs; they have defective excretory systems; if they walk in the moonlight their necks will not cast shadows, and, they being animals, dirt does not stick to their feet when they walk barefoot. (Quoted in Neary 1986:558)

Today there are an estimated one to three million *Burakumin* living in Japan, a nation of 123 million. During the past quarter century the status of the *Burakumin* has begun to change. The Japanese government has enacted legislation designed to end the cycle of poverty and discrimination against them and to improve their living conditions, and it has invested heavily in social programs designed to improve *Burakumin* neighborhoods. As a consequence, *Burakumin* are no longer restricted to their traditional occupations, and their access to housing outside traditional neighborhoods has increased.

Despite such signs of improvement, the socioeconomic status of *Burakumin* lags considerably behind that of the rest of the Japanese population. *Burakumin* family income is only 60 percent of the national average; they are often the "last hired and first fired." Single parent households are twice as common as in the nation as a whole, and *Burakumin* welfare rates are seven times those of the overall population. *Burakumin* children are characterized by lower IQ scores than are non-*Burakumin,* and their rates of college attendance are only about half that of other Japanese. And they are still more likely to live in overcrowded slum ghettoes (Kristoff 1995; Fallows 1990).

Although deeply ingrained prejudices against the *Burakumin* have begun to decline, traditional negative stereotypes persist. The *Burakumin* continue to be viewed by most Japanese as "mentally inferior, incapable of high moral behavior, aggressive, impulsive, and lacking any notion of sanitation or manners" (Wagatsuma 1976:245). The power of these stereotypes and the fear they elicit are reflected in the importance still attached to family registration records, which certify "proper" social backgrounds. Until recently, such records were frequently required in connection with applications for jobs, loans, and admissions to schools. Above all, it was not unusual for families to undertake exhaustive investigations of the lineages of their children's prospective spouses to ensure that their families would not be "contaminated" by *eta* origins. Although such searches have declined in recent years, few public figures are today willing to admit having had *Burakumin* ancestry (Kristoff 1995).

During the twentieth century, the *Burakumin* have organized social movements to protest the discrimination they have continued to encounter in employment, education, and housing. Recently, the militant *Burakumin* Liberation League has become a potent political force by using techniques of direct harassment and intimidation against those who do not share its views of the *Burakumin* plight. As a consequence, the publishers of Japanese books, magazines, and newspapers, fearful of disruptions of their offices and homes by *Burakumin* "direct action" squads, have adopted an unwritten policy of not mentioning the *Burakumin* in their publications (Fallows 1990).

The example of the *Burakumin* is instructive in two respects. First, upper-caste Japanese attribute the *Burakumin's* undesirable traits to biological—innate and inherited—factors, yet no physical characteristics can be detected between them. Second, there are remarkable similarities between the stereotypes of the *Burakumin* and those of subordinate groups in other racially stratified systems. As Donald Horowitz has pointed out, "Whether or not there is an attempt to deny the common humanity of the subordinate group, the stereotype of such a group generally depicts it as irremediably slow, violent, lazy, unmannered, and dirty" (Horowitz 1985:27). Thus, caste and racially stratified systems function in a similar manner. De Vos and Wagatsuma, on the basis of their analysis of the *Burakumin,* support Berreman's contention that racial and caste systems are analytically comparable: "From the viewpoint of comparative sociology or social anthropology, and from the viewpoint of human social psychology, racism and caste attitudes are one and the same phenomenon" (De Vos and Wagatsuma, 1966).

The Japanese *Burakumin* represent a caste system without racial distinctions as Americans usually think of them. However, as this example suggests, systems of racial stratification are closely related to caste systems. Indeed, Berreman contends that all systems of racial or ethnic stratification and caste are qualitatively comparable—that is, both are based on notions of birth-ascribed and immutable characteristics that are believed to determine one's status.

Racial factors—that is, physical characteristics such as skin color, hair texture, height, or the shape of the nose, eyes, or lips—can serve as the basis for status distinctions in a caste system; however, a caste system can also be organized without reference to distinguishable physical characteristics so long as social categories are distinguished on the basis of traits believed to be birth-ascribed.

As we will note more fully in Part 2, the structure of relations between blacks and whites in the United States historically—during more than two centuries of slavery and nearly a century and a half of "freedom"—has resembled a caste system in which hereditary factors (physical features such as skin color, hair texture, lip form) have determined one's status at birth; in which marriage between members of the different castes was legally prohibited; and in which opportunities for members of the lower caste have been circumscribed. African Americans have been relegated to an inferior status, and their access to political representation, education, employment, and housing has been restricted. Moreover, throughout the South especially, interpersonal relations between black and white were governed by what was known as the "etiquette of race relations," which required patterns of deference by the subordinate caste (blacks) to the dominant caste (whites). Although the legal basis for the caste system has been eliminated by judicial rulings and by federal legislation during the last half century, the issue of how closely black-white relations today resemble a caste system remains controversial.

Because ethnicity has frequently been associated with relations of dominance and subordination and thus to a society's system of stratification, there has been a tendency to equate ethnic relations with majority-minority relations. However, the relationship between ethnicity and a system of social ranking is not invariable or inevitable. In other words, it is possible for groups that are ethnically distinct and even in conflict to coexist without a system of dominant-subordinate relationships developing among them. However, because a ranking system involving relations of dominance and subordination has been so prominent a feature of ethnic relations, both today and in the past, in societies throughout the world, we will examine some of the key features of majority-minority relations.

Majority-Minority Relations

The centrality of ethnicity to many of the recent social and political upheavals in Eastern Europe serves as a reminder that the term *minority group* was originally derived from the European experience. Use of the term *minority* emerged in the context of the rise of nationalism and the nation-state in late-eighteenth-century and early-nineteenth-century Europe. In that context, it was used to characterize national or ethnic groups that had become subordinate to the peoples of another national or ethnic group through the imposition of, or the shifts in, political boundaries. Although in the past two centuries many commentators have predicted that "minority" concerns, issues, identities, and conflicts would wane as societies modernized, the extent to which long-simmering ethnic conflicts have emerged and resurfaced in the past decade reflects the tenacity of racial and ethnic identities, the significance of ethnic boundaries in organizing intergroup competition for scarce resources, and, hence, the continuing significance of majority-minority relations in human societies.

Although the term *minority* was widely used in Europe throughout the nineteenth century, it was adopted in the United States only after World War I, primarily in response to the publicity given to issues involving European minorities that were addressed in the negotiations that ended the war (Gleason 1991:393). However, in the United States the term developed a different meaning than in Europe. As Gunnar Myrdal commented in his monumental book *An American Dilemma,* "The minority peoples of the United States are fighting for status within the larger society; the minorities of Europe are mainly fighting for independence from it" (Myrdal 1944:50, quoted in Gleason 1991:397). Gleason contends that the way in which the social scientific concept of minority evolved in the United States reflected implicit American cultural and political assumptions about the nature of minorities—i.e., that minorities are the consequence of exclusion by majorities from the mainstream of American society and that, once tolerated and accepted as equals, minorities will (and should) ultimately disappear. Implicit in this conception is a notion of the majority's victimization of the minority and the idea that the goal of social policy should be to remove the barriers to their inclusion (Gleason 1991).

However, in numerous circumstances throughout the world, minorities do not seek inclusion into but rather separation from the society of which they are a part. What has typically characterized the definition of minority by American sociologists, however, is the assumption that members of a minority group seek inclusion into a society but are typically excluded from full participation in it; that they are the object of discrimination by the majority group; and that their life chances, when compared with those of the majority group, are circumscribed. Although many American minority groups have sought and do seek full admission to American society, it is important to recognize that the goal of minorities is not necessarily integration into a society's mainstream.

Nevertheless, American social scientists have generally used the terms *majority* and *minority* to refer to systems of structured social inequality in which racial and ethnic criteria play a critical role in the system's ranking system. The term *minority* has been applied with greatest frequency to subordinate groups characterized by hereditary membership and endogamy—racial, caste, and ethnic groupings (for example, Williams 1964:304; Wagley and Harris 1958:4–101). A minority or *subordinate group* occupies an inferior position of prestige, wealth, and power in a society.

However, it is important to recognize that the distinctive feature of majority-minority relations—group differences in power—is not restricted to racial and ethnic relations alone, but can characterize other forms of social relations. Therefore, a more inclusive definition of minority, one not restricted to racial and ethnic relations, is appropriate. Joseph B. Gittler's comprehensive definition is consistent with this approach: "Minority groups are those whose members experience a wide range of discriminatory treatment and frequently are relegated to positions relatively low in the status structure of a society" (Gittler 1956:vii). This definition retains the crucial elements of the term's original meaning: the reference to a distinct group or social category occupying a subordinate position of prestige, privilege, and power.

The term *minority* does not refer to the numerical size of a group. Occasionally a so-called minority group will represent a numerical majority of the total population. For example, in South Africa today, blacks are a numerical majority (69 percent) of the total population; but, despite the formal abolition of the repressive system of apartheid and the accession to political power by the predominantly black African National Congress, blacks are still dramatically underrepresented in higher-status occupations in the South African economy, while those individuals who have experienced occupational mobility and increased affluence still encounter social discrimination and exclusion from informal social networks that are frequently essential to economic advancement (Daley 1997). Similar situations existed historically in some areas of the American South and in most colonial situations. For example, in 1910, although African Americans represented more than 55 percent of the population of Mississippi and South Carolina, they were completely excluded from all political offices in these two states.[2] Numerical superiority, therefore, does not necessarily ensure majority status.

Many commentators have suggested that the terms *majority* and *minority* be replaced by *dominant* and *subordinate* to represent more accurately the differences in power. However, because *majority* and *minority* have been so widely used, I will use them here with the understanding that the crucial feature of the minority's status is its inferior social position, in which its interests are not effectively represented in the political, economic, and social institutions of the society. I will use the term *dominant* as a synonym for *majority,* and *subordinate* for *minority.*

Minorities and Conflict

Many different dimensions, such as race, ethnicity, and religion, have been used to distinguish a minority from the majority. However, ethnic, racial, or religious differences do not automatically generate conflict and social inequalities. Culturally, religiously, or racially distinct groups may coexist without a system of ethnic inequality developing (Horowitz 1985). Majority-minority relations do not appear until one group is able to impose its will on another. By definition, minority groups are subordinate segments of the societies of which they are a part. Once people perceive ethnic differences and ethnic groups and then compete against each other, the crucial variable is power.

Power is the ability of one group to realize its goals and interests, even in the face of resistance. This power may be derived from the superior size, weapons, technology, property, education, or economic resources of the dominant group. Hence, minority groups are categories of people that possess imperfect access to positions of equal power, prestige, and privilege in a society. Superior power is crucial not only to the establishment of a system of ethnic stratification but also to its maintenance and perpetuation. Having obtained control of a society's institutions, a majority group generally strives to solidify and consolidate its position.

Although conflict is not always overt, continuous, or apparent in a social system based on structured inequality, the potential for conflict is continually present. The extent to which conflict or stability are manifested itself is related to social structure. Pierre van den Berghe (1967) contrasted the patterns of race relations characteristic of two structurally different types of societies. Under the *paternalistic* type, characteristic of a traditional, preindustrial, predominantly agricultural society, race relations are highly stable, and conflict is submerged—a function of both the mechanisms of social control used by the dominant group and of the symbiotic nature of relations between dominant and subordinate groups. On the other hand, race relations in a *competitive* setting—an urbanized and highly industrialized society characterized by a complex division of labor—are less likely to remain stable. Overt conflict, initiated by both the dominant and the subordinate groups, frequently erupts.

However, even in the most stable situations, dominant groups view minority groups as potentially threatening to their position. This fact is nowhere more apparent than in the American slave system, which exemplifies van den Berghe's paternalistic type of race relations. Proponents of slavery—the so-called "peculiar institution" —frequently justified slaveholding on the grounds of the slave's docility, dependence, improvidence, and fear of freedom. Simultaneously, however, they saw slaves as "a troublesome presence" (Stampp 1956), they initiated elaborate mechanisms (such as patrols, passes, and legal prohibitions against literacy and the possession of weapons) to reduce resistance to the slave regime, and they employed brutal sanctions to discourage noncompliance with the prescribed subordinate roles.

The social inequalities inherent in majority-minority relations are, as Berreman points out in Article 1, symbolically expressed in the institutionalized patterns of interpersonal relations between dominant and subordinate group members. Social interaction among majority and minority group members is never among status equals; as noted above, it consistently involves what was known in the American context as "the etiquette of race relations," which involved restrictions on such activities as eating, touching, terms of address, marriage, sexual conduct, and social contact generally. Although the patterns of deference that the slave system demanded persisted long after slavery was legally abolished, the American slave regime vividly exemplified this point. One primary objective of slave socialization was to implant in slaves a sense of personal inferiority. Slaves were taught to "know their place," to recognize the difference between the status of master and slave. Whites interpreted any impudence on the part of slaves as an effort to reject their subordinate role. Frederick Douglass, the great nineteenth-century African American leader, recalled that slaves could be labeled disobedient and punished for a variety of actions, including "the tone of an answer; in answering at all; in not answering; in the expression of countenance; in the motion of the head; in the gait, manner and bearing of the slave" (Stampp 1956:145).

As events during the Black Protest Movement of the 1960s in the United States demonstrated, attempts by a minority group to alter traditional relationships between dominant and subordinate groups and to achieve autonomy and equality of status are strenuously resisted by the majority group. Allen D. Grimshaw has summarized the history of changes in black-white relations by pointing out that

> The most savage oppression, whether expressed in rural lynching and pogroms or in urban race riots, has taken place when the Negro has refused to accept a subordinate status. The most intense conflict has resulted when the subordinate minority group has attempted to disrupt the accommodative pattern or when the superordinate group has defined the situation as one in which such an attempt is being made. (Grimshaw 1959:17)

Efforts to alter the relative power of the majority and the minority thus inevitably involve conflict between the two groups, with the subordinate group attempting to decrease the inequalities in the system through a wide variety of means, including violence; and with the dominant group resorting to a multiplicity of techniques, also including violence (both legal and extralegal) to prevent such changes from occurring.

Majorities and Institutional Power

The discussion thus far has suggested that the concept of minority group must always be considered in relation to a majority, or dominant, group. Although this conclusion may appear self-evident, until the 1970s only a meager amount of the voluminous research on racial and ethnic relations had been devoted to the characteristics and attributes of the majority group and the mechanisms by which the relationships between majority and minority are created, maintained, and altered. A notable exception was the work of Robert Bierstedt. In "The Sociology of Majorities," published half a century ago, Bierstedt wrote the following:

> It is the majority . . . which sets the culture pattern and sustains it, which is in fact responsible for whatever pattern or configuration there is in a culture. It is the majority which confers upon folkways, mores, customs, and laws the status of norms and gives them coercive power. It is the majority which guarantees the stability of a society. It is the majority which requires conformity to custom and which penalizes deviation—except in ways in which the majority sanctions and approves. It is the majority which is the custodian of the mores and which defends them against innovation. And it is the inertia of majorities, finally, which retards the processes of social change. (Bierstedt 1948:709)

Writing nearly fifty years later, Doane (Article 3) similarly emphasizes the "hidden" nature of dominant group identity, assumptions, and privilege:

> The hidden nature of dominant group identity and the normalization of cultural, political, and economic dominance tend to obscure the advantages that accrue to dominant group members. This taken-for-granted aspect of dominant group privilege, when coupled with the removal of formal barriers to subordinate group advancement, leads to the denial of ethnicity or race as a meaningful social force amid the promotions of ideologies of individualism.

Bierstedt's and Doane's insistence that the analysis of majority-minority relations focus on the characteristics of the dominant group, not on those of the minority, reflects one of the major themes of this book. From this perspective, the principal focus of inquiry should be on the nature of "white" ethnic identity and the manner in which the dominant group controls the institutions of the society. As Preston Wilcox has argued, "Much of what has been written as sociology would suggest that . . . minorities suffer problems because of their unique characteristics rather than [because of] the systems which impinge upon them and the sanctioning of these systems by dominant groups" (Wilcox 1970:44).

Lack of recognition of the importance of societal patterns of institutional control has meant that, as John Horton (1966) has pointed out, sociologists and laypeople alike frequently define social problems as a minority group's deviation from dominant societal norms and standards; seldom do they themselves critically examine the society's institutions, values, and social processes. The importance of an institutional approach to the analysis of mass protest and violence in America was forcefully articulated in 1969 by the Violence Commission, which was appointed by President Lyndon Johnson to examine and explain the mass protest that swept the country during the turbulent 1960s. Mass protest, the Commission contended,

> must be analyzed in relation to crises in American institutions. . . . [It] is an outgrowth of social, economic, and political conditions. Recommendations concerning the prevention of violence which do not address the issue of fundamental social, economic, and political change are fated to be largely irrelevant and frequently self-defeating. (Skolnick 1969:3)

In other words, both the sources of, and the solutions to, problems of majority-minority conflict are institutional. Thus, the most realistic approach to their analysis must focus primarily on the majority group and the institutional structures that they created, and continue to operate and control.

Examination of the ways that majority group members typically approach inter-group conflict demonstrates the importance of an institutional perspective. As noted before, the majority determines whether a problem even exists—witness the classic statement advanced by proponents of the status quo in communities throughout America: "We have no problems here. Our [insert appropriate minority group residing in the community] are happy." Whether or not one perceives social conditions as a problem depends on one's position within the social structure. As the Violence Commission noted, whether or not one classifies behavior as violent depends on whether one is challenging the existing institutional arrangements or is seeking to uphold them (Skolnick 1969:3–4).

In an important article examining the functions of racial conflict, Joseph Himes (1966) has pointed out that conflict may have positive consequences: it can force the dominant group to be aware of, come to grips with, and respond to societal inequities. Himes argues that organized social conflict alters traditional power relations and the traditional etiquette of race relations. As the minority group develops the ability to mobilize power against the dominant group's interests, traditional race relations change to the point where minority grievances can be more realistically discussed and addressed. During the late 1950s and early 1960s, African Americans, denied change through institutionalized political channels (voting, for example), used mass protest to mobilize power against the dominant group's entrenched interests. Nonviolent protest and conflict were integral strategies of power in the civil rights movement. Martin Luther King, Jr., one of history's most articulate advocates of the weapon of nonviolence, perceived that it represented a means of effecting a redistribution of power:

> Nonviolent direct action seeks to create such a crisis and foster such a tension that a community which has constantly refused to negotiate is forced to confront the issue. It seeks so to dramatize the issue that it can no longer be ignored. (King 1964:81)

If the dominant group acknowledges social problems at all, they invariably ascribe them to the characteristics of the subordinate group rather than to defects in the social system controlled by the majority group. For many years, discussion of black-white relations in America was described as the "Negro problem," a stance explicitly challenged by Gunnar Myrdal in his classic work, *An American Dilemma* (1944). Today, most white Americans deny that opportunities for black Americans are limited, and perceive that blacks themselves are primarily responsible for the conditions in which they find themselves (Schumann 1969; Kluegel and Smith 1982; Schuman, Steeh, and Bobo 1985).

This interpretation is also implicit in the idea of cultural deprivation (Baratz and Baratz 1970), or what Maxine Baca Zinn (1989) has termed the "cultural deficiency model" for explaining poverty and, especially, what has recently been termed the *underclass*—the most impoverished segment of American society. Found primarily in the nation's inner cities, the underclass is characterized by high unemployment, school dropouts, academic failures, out-of-wedlock births, female-headed families, welfare dependence, homelessness, and serious crime. According to the cultural deficiency model, these characteristics are attributable primarily to the internal deficiencies and instabilities of the minorities—primarily black and Hispanic—that make up the underclass. That is, cultural, family, and community and neighborhood factors, not the inadequate economic and educational opportunities, are the primary causes of the social dislocations experienced by the underclass. The cultural deficiency model focuses on the characteristics of minorities and deflects attention from the institutional factors that impinge upon them. In short, the emphasis in such a model is on the symptom rather than on the disease.

The resolution of intergroup conflict also reflects power differentials, for conflicts tend to be resolved within limits acceptable to the majority group. Efforts to alter the pattern of inequalities are therefore restricted to methods defined as legitimate or appropriate by the majority group, a requisite that seldom poses a threat to the continued functioning of the existing system. The history of American Indian encounters with white Americans provides an excellent example of this pattern. Indian-white problems were almost invariably defined from the perspective of whites and generally involved the refusal of Native Americans to accede to white demands for cultural assimilation or for the cession of their lands. Native American values, needs, and desires were seldom, if ever, a consideration in the solution of such confrontations. According to the humanitarian Thomas Jefferson, if Indians did not conform to white cultural patterns, the only viable solution was their forcible removal.

The role of the majority group in delimiting the context within which solutions to problems of intergroup conflict can be reached is exemplified by the analysis and recommendations of the 1968 Kerner Commission report and the nation's reactions to it. Charged by President Lyndon Johnson with investigating the causes of the civil disorders that rent the nation for several years during the 1960s, the Commission concluded, as we shall note later, that the primary explanation was white racism. Moreover, it argued that, given the sustained and pervasive effects of racism, "there can be no higher priority for national action and no higher claim on the nation's conscience" than the elimination of racism from American society (National Advisory Commission on Civil Disorders 1968:21, 203). However, it warned that implementation of its recommendations would necessitate "unprecedented levels of funding and performance." Because implementation of these terms were politically unpopular with the dominant group, the response to the Kerner report—both officially and unofficially— was to discredit or (perhaps more significant) to ignore its findings.

Because the conclusion that white racism was primarily responsible for the intense racial conflicts of the 1960s was unacceptable to most white Americans, the Commission's report demonstrated that majority solutions to social problems seldom entail basic alterations of the society's institutional patterns. On the one hand, the Kerner Commission indicted American institutions as the primary source of the racism that permeates the society. On the other hand, most of its recommendations involved changing blacks to conform to these institutions rather than substantially altering the institutions themselves. Such an approach, involving what Horton (1966) has termed an *order model* of social problems, slights the basic institutional sources of racial inequality in American society, a subject that we will explore more fully in Parts 3 and 4.

Prejudice, Discrimination, and Racism

Prejudice and discrimination are important elements in all majority-minority relations. The term *prejudice* derives from two Latin words, *prae* "before" and *judicum* "a judgment." It denotes a judgment before all the facts are known. According to Gordon Allport, *prejudice* is "an avertive or hostile attitude toward a person who belongs to a group, simply because he [or she] belongs to that group, and is therefore presumed to have the objectionable qualities ascribed to the group" (Allport 1958:8). Prejudice thus refers to a set of rigidly held negative attitudes, beliefs, and feelings toward members of another group.

Prejudice often involves an intense emotional component. Thus, many white Americans consciously and rationally reject the myths of African American inferiority but react emotionally with fear, hostility, or condescension in the presence of African Americans. The forms of prejudice range from unconscious aversion to members of the out-group to a comprehensive, well-articulated, and coherent ideology, such as the ideology of racism.

Discrimination, on the other hand, involves unfavorable treatment of individuals because of their group membership. Prejudice and discrimination should not be equated. Prejudice involves attitudes and internal states, whereas discrimination involves overt action or behavior. Discrimination may be manifested in a multitude of ways: mild slights (such as Polish jokes); verbal threats, abuse, and epithets; intimidation and harassment (such as threatening phone calls); defacing property with ethnic slurs, graffiti, or symbols; unequal treatment (such as refusing to hire or promote qualified applicants); systematic oppression (such as slavery); or outright violence (vandalism, arson, terrorism, lynching, pogroms, massacres).

Because sociologists are primarily concerned with human behavior, the focus in this book is on discrimination. Clearly, however, a close relationship frequently exists between prejudice and discrimination. Consequently, an extensive amount of research has been carried out concerning the nature and causes of prejudice. Attitude surveys conducted in the United States since the 1940s have shown a significant decline in antiblack prejudice; increasingly, white Americans have come to support broad principles of racial integration and equal treatment in public accommodations, employment, public transportation, schools, housing, and marriage. For example, in 1942, 32 percent of whites agreed that whites and blacks should attend the same schools; by 1982, this figure was 90 percent. When asked in 1958 whether they would object to sending their children to schools in which half the children were black, nearly half (47 percent) responded affirmatively; by 1997, this figure had declined to 12 percent. In 1944, 45 percent thought that blacks should have as good a chance as whites to get any kind of job; and by 1972, 97 percent agreed. The percentage approving integration in public transportation rose from 46 percent in 1942 to 88 percent in 1970. Moreover, whites have indicated increasing willingness to participate personally in desegregated settings. In 1958, four-fifths of whites said they would move if blacks moved into their neighborhood "in great numbers"; in 1997, those indicating they would move declined to 12 percent. Finally, whereas only 4 percent of whites said they approved of interracial marriages in 1958, more than three-fifths (61 percent) expressed their approval in 1997 (Schuman, Steeh, and Bobo 1985; Hochschild

1995; Gallup Poll Social Audit 1997). These changes are a result of two factors. First, they reflect attitude changes among individuals over their lifetimes. Second, younger people generally exhibit less racial prejudice than their elders, and as younger, more tolerant cohorts have replaced older, more prejudiced ones, overall racial prejudice has declined (Firebaugh and Davis 1988).

However, among white Americans, the same striking agreement on how to combat discrimination or segregation does not appear. Although today white Americans endorse broad principles of nondiscrimination and desegregation in important areas of American life, they are much less likely to support policies for translating these principles into practice. For example, despite the strong support among white Americans for the principle of integrated education, the percentage of whites who felt that the federal government should ensure that black and white children attend the same schools declined between the 1960s and 1980s. Moreover, widespread white opposition was raised to busing as a means of desegregating schools (Schuman, Steeh, and Bobo 1985).

The substantial gap between white people's support for broad principles of equality and their support for specific programs to implement these principles indicates the complexity of racial attitudes. The relationship between prejudicial attitudes and discriminatory behavior is equally complex. Prejudice does not always produce discrimination, although it has frequently been treated as the cause of discrimination. An individual, however, may be prejudiced without *acting* in a discriminatory manner. In recent years it has become less fashionable to express racial prejudice publicly. Overt forms of discrimination, such as exclusion from public accommodations, jobs, and colleges and universities—behaviors that in the past were tolerated by most whites—are now often prohibited by law and condemned by public opinion.

The distinction between prejudice and discrimination and the interrelationship between these two phenomena were first systematically developed by Robert Merton (1949) in his classic article, "Discrimination and the American Creed." "Prejudicial attitudes," Merton argued, "need not coincide with discriminatory behavior." Merton demonstrated the range of possible ways in which prejudice and discrimination interact by distinguishing among four types of individuals:

1. The unprejudiced nondiscriminator—the all-weather liberal
2. The unprejudiced discriminator—the fair-weather liberal
3. The prejudiced nondiscriminator—the fair-weather bigot
4. The prejudiced discriminator—the all-weather bigot

The unprejudiced nondiscriminator consistently adheres to the American creed of equality for all in both belief and practice. The unprejudiced discriminator, on the other hand, internalizes and may even articulate the ideals of the American creed but may acquiesce to group pressures to discriminate. Similarly, the prejudiced nondiscriminator conforms to social pressures not to discriminate despite harboring prejudices toward ethnic minorities. Finally, the prejudiced discriminator is, like the unprejudiced nondiscriminator, consistent in belief and practice, rejecting the American creed and engaging in personal discrimination.

Merton's discussion was critical to the recognition that whether prejudice becomes translated into discriminatory behavior depends on the social context. From this perspective it becomes impossible to understand the dynamics of majority-minority relations by examining prejudice alone; prejudice is most appropriately considered not as a causal factor but as a dependent variable. As Richard Schermerhorn has cogently suggested, prejudice "is a product of situations, historical situations, economic situations, political situations; it is not a little demon that emerges in people because they are depraved" (Schermerhorn 1970:6).

Thus, discrimination is much more likely to occur in a social setting in which acts of ethnic and racial bias are accepted or are not strongly condemned. This principle was underscored in a study undertaken at Smith College, where in 1989 racial tensions erupted after four black students received anonymous hate messages. Researchers asked students how they felt about these incidents. Before a student could answer, a confederate, arriving at the same time, would respond by strongly condemning or strongly justifying the incidents. The researchers found that the students' opinions were strongly influenced by the opinions they heard expressed by the confederates. Hearing others express strongly antiracist opinions produced similar sentiments, whereas students who first heard expressions more accepting of racism offered "significantly less strongly antiracist opinions" (Blanchard, Lilly, and Vaughn 1991:105). Clearly, the social climate affects whether personal prejudices are translated into discriminatory acts; to explain the dynamics of ethnic and racial relations fully, it is necessary to analyze the historical, cultural, and institutional conditions that have preceded and generated them.

During the past quarter century, the conceptualization of American race relations has undergone several significant changes. These changes have been profoundly influenced by the changing nature of race relations in the United States. Before the advent of the Black Protest Movement during the 1950s, social scientists focused their attention primarily on racial attitudes, because prejudice was thought to be the key to understanding racial and ethnic conflict. This perception of the essential dynamics of race relations is perhaps best illustrated in Myrdal's classic *An American Dilemma,* in which he defined race prejudice as "the whole complex of valuations and beliefs which are behind discriminatory behavior on the part of the majority group . . . and which are contrary to the egalitarian ideals in the American Creed" (Myrdal 1944:52). This model of race relations was predicated on the assumption that racial conflict in the United States was a problem of ignorance and morality that could best be solved by changing—through education and moral suasion—the majority's prejudicial attitudes toward racial minorities. "A great majority of white people in America," Myrdal wrote, "would be better prepared to give the Negro a substantially better deal if they knew the facts" (Myrdal 1944:48).

The black protest era of the 1950s and 1960s challenged the assumption that change in the patterns of racial inequality in American society could be brought about through a reduction in prejudicial attitudes alone. Sociologists and social activists focused increasingly on the dynamics of discrimination and sought means of eliminating discriminatory behavior. The numerous forms of direct protest, such as nonviolent sit-ins, boycotts, and voter registration drives, were tactics designed to alter patterns of discrimination. In keeping with this emphasis on discrimination were the legislative efforts undertaken to secure enactment of the Civil Rights Act of 1964, which outlawed discrimination in public accommodations and employment, and the 1965 Voting Rights Act, which provided federal support to ensure that African Americans had the right to vote throughout the South.

However, the greatest racial unrest of the black protest era occurred after these legislative victories had been achieved. Whereas the earlier civil rights phase of the Black Protest Movement had been directed primarily against public discrimination and especially its manifestations in the South, the outbreak of urban riots in northern cities focused attention on the nature of racial inequalities affecting African Americans throughout the entire nation. For several summers during the late 1960s, the nation was torn with racial strife. Parts of cities were burned, property damage ran into the millions of dollars, and the toll of dead—primarily, although not exclusively, blacks—numbered almost a hundred (National Advisory Commission on Civil Disorders 1968:116). In July 1967 President Lyndon Johnson appointed a national commission (the Kerner Commission) to investigate the causes of these urban riots. In 1968 the commission issued its report, which concluded the following:

> What white Americans have never fully understood—but what the Negro can never forget—is that white society is deeply implicated in the ghetto. White society condones it. . . . Race prejudice has shaped our history decisively in the past; it now threatens to do so again. White racism is essentially responsible for the explosive mixture which has been accumulating in our cities since the end of World War II. (National Advisory Commission on Civil Disorders 1968:203)

Racism

Especially because the Kerner Commission concluded that the ultimate responsibility for the racial disorders of the 1960s should be attributed to "white racism," the term has been widely invoked to explain racial inequalities and conflict in American society. However, the term is extremely imprecise and ambiguous. This imprecision enabled President Johnson, who had created the Kerner Commission, to ignore its findings, and his successor, Richard Nixon, to condemn and deny them. Consequently, the term *racism* is in urgent need of clarification.

First, *racism* is a general term, subsuming several analytically distinct phenomena —prejudice and several forms of discrimination. Stokely Carmichael and Charles Hamilton distinguished between *individual* racism and *institutional* racism:

> Racism is both overt and covert. It takes two closely related forms: individual whites acting against individual blacks and acts by the total white community against the black community. . . . The second type is less overt, far more subtle, less identifiable in terms of specific individuals committing the acts. But it is no less destructive of human life. . . . When white terrorists bomb a black church and kill five black children, that is an act of individual racism, widely deplored by most segments of the society. But when in that same city, Birmingham, Alabama—five hundred black babies die each year because of the lack of proper food, shelter, and medical facilities, and thousands more are destroyed and maimed physically, emotionally, and intellectually because of the conditions of poverty and discrimination in the black community, that is a function of institutional racism. (Carmichael and Hamilton 1967:4)

However, as I will note more fully later, prejudicial attitudes are causal factors in Carmichael and Hamilton's conceptualization of institutional racism. Moreover, they do not distinguish between psychological and sociological factors in its operation.

Another problem in the use of the word *racism* is that although it lumps together all forms of racial oppression, it is not sufficiently inclusive. It does not encompass majority-minority situations based on criteria other than race—criteria such as religion, tribal identity, ethnicity, or gender. Therefore, in the following discussion, I have analytically distinguished the terms *racism, prejudice,* and *discrimination.*

The term *racism* has traditionally referred to an *ideology*—a set of ideas and beliefs—used to explain, rationalize, or justify a racially organized social order. There are two essential parts of racism: its content and its function. Racism is distinguished from ethnocentrism by insistence that differences among groups are biologically based. The in-group is believed to be innately superior to the out-group, and members of the out-group are defined as being "biogenetically incapable of ever achieving intellectual and moral equality with members of the ingroup" (Noel 1972:157). Howard Schuman has offered a commonly accepted definition of racism:

> The term racism is generally taken to refer to the belief that there are clearly distinguishable human races, that these races differ not only in superficial physical characteristics, but also innately in important psychological traits; and finally that the differences are such that one race (almost always one's own, naturally) can be said to be superior to another. (Schuman 1969:44)

Racism's primary function has been to provide a rationale and ideological support —a moral justification—for maintaining a racially based social order. In other words, the assertion of the innate "natural" superiority or inferiority of different racial groups serves to justify domination and exploitation of one group by another. As Manning Nash has written, "no group of [people] is able systematically to subordinate or deprive another group of [people] without appeal to a body of values which makes the exploitation, the disprivilege, the expropriation, and the denigration of human beings a 'moral' act" (Nash 1962:288). In addition, not only does an ideology of racism provide a moral justification for the dominant group of their positions of privilege and power, but it also discourages minority groups from questioning their subordinate status and advancing claims for equal treatment.

Van den Berghe (1967:16–181) has suggested three major sources of Western racism. First, racism developed as a justification of capitalist forms of exploitation, particularly slavery in the New World. As Noel has argued, "As slavery became ever more clearly the pivotal institution of Southern society, racism was continually strengthened and became an ever more dominant ideology" (Noel 1972:162).

Second, racism was congruent with late nineteenth-century Darwinian notions of stages of evolution and survival of the fittest, and with the idea of Anglo-Saxon superiority. According to these doctrines, those people in inferior social positions were destined to their station because they were least evolved or least fit in the struggle for existence. In 1870 Francis A. Walker, United States Commissioner of Immigration, characterized the immigrants from southern and eastern Europe in the following manner:

> They are beaten men from beaten races: representing the worst failures in the struggle for existence. Centuries are against them, as centuries were on the side of those who formerly came to us. They have none of the ideas and aptitudes which fit men to take up readily and easily the problem of self-care and self-government. (Quoted in Saveth 1948:40)

The third explanation of racism, van den Berghe argues, is paradoxically related to the egalitarian ideas of the Enlightenment, which were expressed in the Declaration of Independence:

> *Faced with the blatant contradiction between the treatment of slaves and colonial peoples and the official rhetoric of freedom and equality, Europeans and white North Americans began to dichotomize humanity between men and submen (or the "civilized" and the "savages"). The scope of applicability of the egalitarian ideals was restricted to "the people," that is, the whites, and there resulted . . . regimes such as those of the United States or South Africa that are democratic for the master race but tyrannical for the subordinate groups. The desire to preserve both the profitable forms of discrimination and exploitation and the democratic ideology made it necessary to deny humanity to the oppressed groups. (van den Berghe 1967:17–18)*

As noted before, there has been a substantial decline in professions of racist attitudes among white Americans in the past half century; especially since 1970, white Americans have increased their approval of racial integration (Schuman, Steeh, and Bobo 1985; Gallup Poll Social Audit 1997). In 1942 only 42 percent of a national sample of whites reported that they believed blacks to be equal to whites in innate intelligence; since the late 1950s, however, around 80 percent of white Americans have rejected the idea of inherent black inferiority. The Kerner Commission was therefore misleading in lumping all white antipathy toward blacks into the category of racism.

Rather than believing that African Americans are genetically inferior, whites often employ a *meritocratic ideology* to explain the substantial gap that continues to separate black and white income, wealth, and educational attainment. The basic element in a meritocratic ideology is the assumption of equality of opportunity—that all people in the United States have equal chances to achieve success, and that inequalities in the distribution of income, wealth, power, and prestige reflect the qualifications or merit of individuals in each rank in society. In other words, in a meritocratic society, all people are perceived to have an equal opportunity to succeed or fail—to go as far as their talents will take them—and the system of social ranking that develops is simply a "natural" reflection of each person's abilities or merit. Affluence is perceived as the result of the personal qualities of intelligence, industriousness, motivation, and ambition, while the primary responsibility for poverty rests with the poor themselves. Therefore, in this aristocracy of talent, those in the upper strata deserve the power, prestige, and privileges that they enjoy, while those lower in the social ranking system are placed according to their ability. Such a belief system is not inherently racist, but rather is a general judgment about human nature that can be applied to all sorts of human conditions or groups. However, it can have racist effects when it is used to explain racial inequalities in the United States without recognizing or acknowledging the external disabilities (such as prejudice and discrimination) that racial minorities experience. Thus, by this definition, African Americans are still considered inferior people; otherwise, they would be as well-off as whites. (See Hochschild 1995 for an excellent discussion of the conflicting perceptions of whites and blacks regarding opportunity in American society.)

If the term *racism* referred merely to the realm of beliefs and ideology and not to behavior or action, its relevance for the study of race relations would be limited. To restrict the meaning of racism to ideology would be to ignore the external constraints and societally imposed disabilities—rooted in the power of the majority group—confronting a racial minority. If one group does not possess the power to impose its belief system on another, ethnic stratification cannot occur (Noel 1968). During the late 1960s and 1970s, when critics charged that the ideology of Black Power was "racism in reverse," African American spokespersons responded that their critics failed to consider the components of differential power that enabled the ideology of white supremacy to result in white domination:

> There is no analogy—by any stretch of definition or imagination—between the advocates of Black Power and white racists. Racism is not merely exclusion on the basis of race but exclusion for the purpose of subjugating or maintaining subjugation. The goal of the racists is to keep black people on the bottom, arbitrarily and dictatorially, as they have done in this country for over three hundred years. (Carmichael and Hamilton 1967:47)

Recently Feagin and Vera (1995) have taken a similar stance against the contention that "black racism" is equally as critical an issue as white racism. They contend that "black racism does not exist" because

> Racism is more than a matter of individual prejudice and scattered episodes of discrimination. There is no black racism because there is no centuries-old system of racialized subordination and discrimination designed by African Americans to exclude white Americans from full participation in the rights, privileges and benefits of this society. Black (or other minority) racism would require not only a widely accepted racist ideology directed at whites but also the power to systematically exclude whites from opportunities and rewards in major economic, cultural, and political institutions. (Feagin and Vera 1995:ix–x)

Therefore, the crucial component of a definition of racism is behavioral. Racism in its most inclusive sense refers to actions on the part of a racial majority that have discriminatory effects, preventing members of a minority group from securing access to prestige, power, and privilege. These actions may be intentional or unintentional. This broader conception of racism therefore entails discrimination as well as an ideology that proclaims the superiority of one racial grouping over another.

As noted earlier, *discrimination* refers to the differential treatment of members of a minority group. Discrimination in its several forms comprises the means by which the unequal status of the minority group and the power of the majority group are preserved. In the ensuing discussion, I distinguish between *attitudinal* discrimination, which refers to discriminatory practices attributable to or influenced by prejudice, and *institutional* discrimination, which cannot be attributed to prejudice, but instead is a consequence of society's normal functioning. Both of these types can be further elaborated according to the sources of the discriminatory behavior. In reality, these types are at times interrelated and reinforce each other. Seldom is discrimination against a minority group member derived from one source alone.

Attitudinal Discrimination

Attitudinal discrimination refers to discriminatory practices that stem from prejudicial attitudes. The discriminator either is prejudiced or acts in response to the prejudices of others. Attitudinal discrimination is usually direct, overt, visible, and dramatic. Despite increasing white acceptance of principles of nondiscrimination and racial segregation, ethnic minorities, especially African Americans, continue to be confronted with incidents of attitudinal discrimination. In "The Continuing Significance of Race" (Article 20), Feagin distinguished five categories of such discrimination: avoidance, rejection, verbal attacks, physical threats and harassment, and physical attacks. Despite increasing verbal acceptance by whites of the principles of nondiscrimination and racial integration, African Americans have been confronted with attitudinal discrimination in almost every public aspect of their lives. Many of these discriminatory acts appear trivial, insignificant, and unimportant to white observers: a white couple's crossing the street to avoid walking past a black male, a "hate stare," receiving poor service at restaurants, stores, and hotels. Many whites also trivialize discrimination that takes the form of racial and ethnic slurs and epithets. Incidents of this kind are seldom reported in the press, yet they are demeaning realities to which minorities of all social classes are consistently exposed.

Much more dramatic incidents of discrimination are reported almost daily in the news media. For example, the brutal beating of Rodney King, a black motorist, by members of the Los Angeles Police Department in 1991 was captured on videotape, was widely publicized, and drew widespread attention to the vulnerability of blacks to police harassment. The subsequent acquittal of four police officers who had been videotaped beating him unleashed the most destructive American urban disorders of the twentieth century. Yet the King incident was only one of 15,000 complaints of police brutality filed with the federal government between 1985 and 1991 (Lewis 1991). Moreover, during the 1980s and 1990s hundreds of incidents of discrimination, intimidation, harassment, and vandalism as well as physical attacks against racial and religious minorities were reported. These included the burning of over 65 black churches in 1995 and 1996 alone; although investigators concluded that there was no evidence of an organized national racist conspiracy, they did find that racial hatred was a motive in most cases (Sack 1996; Butterfield 1996).

Similarly, cases of racial discrimination in education, in housing, in public accommodations, and in the workplace continue to be widely reported. Some of the most widely publicized cases of discrimination in the workplace and in public accommodations involved nationally prominent corporations—Denney's, Shoney's, Avis, Circuit City, and Texaco (*Time* 1987; Ehrlich 1990; U.S. Commission on Civil Rights 1990; Jaffe 1994; Feagin and Vera 1995; Eichenwald 1996; Myerson 1997). Yet these cases were among only the most widely publicized; between 1990 and 1993 the Equal Employment Opportunity Commission (EEOC), the federal agency responsible for enforcing civil rights laws in the workplace, resolved an average of 4,636 cases in favor of individuals charging racial discrimination. In most instances, however, discrimination is extremely difficult to prove, and the burden of filing charges and the recourse to legal remedies are so cumbersome and time-consuming that many people are discouraged from pursuing them. Nevertheless, by 1995 the EEOC had a back log of about 100,000 cases charging racial discrimination in employment alone (Kilborn 1995; Myerson 1997).

Thus, despite the enactment of antidiscrimination legislation and contrary to white perceptions that discrimination has been eradicated and that, as a consequence of affirmative action programs, minorities receive preferential treatment in hiring, recent "bias studies" have demonstrated that African Americans and Hispanics continue to experience discrimination. In a study of employment discrimination, for example, pairs of white and black men with identical qualifications applied for 476 jobs advertised in Washington and Chicago newspapers. Whereas 15 percent of the white applicants received job offers, only 5 percent of the black applicants did. Moreover, white applicants advanced further in the hiring process and in the Washington area were much less likely to receive rude, unfavorable, or discouraging treatment than were their black counterparts. These findings were similar to an earlier study of the hiring experiences of Hispanics and Anglos in Chicago and San Diego in which whites were three times as likely both to advance further in the hiring process and to receive job offers as were Hispanic applicants (Turner, Fix, and Struyk 1991).

What are the consequences of these continuing encounters with attitudinal discrimination? In his study involving interviews with African Americans throughout the United States (Article 20), Feagin found that despite antidiscrimination legislation and changing white attitudes, even middle-class blacks remain vulnerable to discrimination and that incidents of discrimination against them are far from isolated. Instead, they are *cumulative;* that is, a black person's encounters with discrimination are best described as a "lifelong series of such incidents."

The cumulative impact of constant experiences of discrimination—what writer Ellis Cose (1993) has characterized as "soul-destroying slights"—and the energy expended in dealing with them was clearly articulated by one of the respondents in Feagin's study:

> . . . *if you can think of the mind as having one hundred ergs of energy, and the average man uses fifty percent of his energy dealing with the everyday problems of the world—just the general kinds of things—then he has fifty percent more to do creative kinds of things that he wants to do. Now that's a white person. Now a black person also has one hundred ergs: he uses fifty percent the same way a white man does, dealing with what the white man has [to deal with], so he has fifty percent left. But he uses twenty-five percent fighting being black, [with] all the problems of being black and what it means. Which means he really only has twenty-five percent to do what the white man has fifty percent to do, and he's expected to do just as much as the white man with that twenty-five percent. . . . So, that's kind of what happens. You just don't have as much energy left to do as much as you know you really could if you were free, [if] your mind were free.*

Anthony Walton, an African American who grew up in a comfortable middle-class home in the Chicago suburbs, has referred to these "petty, daily indignities that take such a toll on the psyches of American blacks" as a "black tax," "the tribute to white society that must be paid in self-effacement and swallowed pride" (Walton 1996:7).

Attitudinal discrimination does not always occur in so virulent or so direct a manner. It may be manifested less dramatically merely by the acceptance by members of the dominant group of social definitions of traditional subordinate group roles. Malcolm X, the charismatic black protest leader who was assassinated in 1965, recalled how his well-intentioned white high school English teacher, Mr. Ostrowski, was bound by cultural norms concerning the "proper" caste roles for blacks:

> *I know that he probably meant well in what he happened to advise me that day. I doubt that he meant any harm. . . . I was one of his top students, one of the school's top students—but all he could see for me was the kind of future "in your place" that almost all white people see for black people. . . . He told me, "Malcolm, you ought to be thinking about a career. Have you been*

giving it any thought?" . . . The truth is, I hadn't. I have never figured out why I told him, "Well, yes, sir, I've been thinking I'd like to be a lawyer." Lansing certainly had no lawyers—or doctors either—in those days, to hold up an image I might have aspired to. All I really knew for certain was that a lawyer didn't wash dishes, as I was doing.

Mr. Ostrowski looked surprised, I remember, and leaned back in his chair and clasped his hands behind his head. He kind of half-smiled and said, "Malcolm, one of life's first needs is for us to be realistic. Don't misunderstand me, now. We all here like you, you know that. But you've got to be realistic about being a nigger. A lawyer—that's no realistic goal for a nigger. You need to think about something you can be. You're good with your hands—making things. Everybody admires your carpentry shop work. Why don't you plan on carpentry? People like you as a person—you'd get all kinds of work." (Malcolm X 1966:36)

Here we should recall Merton's distinction between the prejudiced discriminator and the unprejudiced discriminator. According to the definition advanced earlier, discrimination involves differential treatment of individuals because of their membership in a minority group. The term has traditionally referred to actions of people who arbitrarily deny equal treatment (for example, equal opportunity to obtain a job or to purchase a home) to minority group members because of their own personal prejudices. Such is the behavior of the prejudiced discriminator or all-weather bigot.

But discrimination can occur without the discriminator's necessarily harboring prejudices. As Merton points out, an unprejudiced discriminator—the fair-weather liberal—can discriminate simply by conforming to existing cultural patterns or by acquiescing to the dictates of others who are prejudiced. Such discrimination can be attributed to the actor's conscious or unconscious perception of the negative effects that nondiscriminatory behavior will have. An employer or a realtor may genuinely disclaim any personal prejudice for having refused a minority group member a job or home. Perhaps the person felt constrained by the negative sanctions of peers, or by the fear of alienating customers. In this case, the discriminatory actor's judgment would be based on the prejudicial attitudes of a powerful reference group. Although the heart and mind of the actors in our hypothetical situations may be devoid of any personal prejudice, nevertheless, the consequences—no job, no home—for the minority-group applicant are no different than if they were old-fashioned, dyed-in-the-wool bigots.

Attitudinal discrimination remains an important component of intergroup relations. One of the most prominent examples is the world of sports, which is perceived by most Americans to be devoid of racism. Although there have been substantial—even overwhelming—changes in the racial composition of sports teams during the past half century, the persistence of racial stacking (the placement of black and white players in certain positions, such as quarterback or wide receiver, in which they are stereotyped as best suited), the omission of African Americans from leadership and outcome-control positions, and the relative dearth of African Americans in second-team positions, indicate that discrimination is still a factor in player selection. The effects of attitudinal discrimination are even more pronounced at management levels: while African Americans are overrepresented in player roles, there is still a dearth of African-American executives, managers, and coaches (Yetman and Eitzen 1982; Jaynes and Williams 1989:95–98; Center for the Study of Sport in Society 1998).

Communication, including the mass media and everyday conversation, provides one of the most important means by which negative images and the powerlessness of minorities are (often unconsciously) perpetuated. Geneva Smitherman-Donaldson and Teun van Dijk contend that the process of communication and discourse "essentially reproduces and helps produce the racist cognitions and actions of and among the white majority" (1988:18). They use the term *symbolic racism* to refer to communications that preserve or justify racist acts and policies:

> *Even more than physical racism (or sexism for that matter), symbolic racism allows for subtlety, indirectness, and implication. It may, paradoxically, be expressed by the unsaid, or be conveyed by apparent "tolerance" and egalitarian liberalism. Whereas the racial slur, the graffiti, or the old movie may be blatantly racist, many other present-day types of talk may communicate racism in a more veiled way.*
>
> *In everyday talk, underlying ethnic prejudices may indirectly appear in "innocent" stories about a black neighbor, or about a Turkish immigrant worker cleaning the office. Although such stories claim to tell the "facts," describe how "they" did it (wrong) again, or generally imply that "they" are stupid, lazy, welfare-cheats, criminal, or lack motivation to learn, the storyteller may, at the same time, emphasize that he has nothing against "them," and they are his "best friends." Yet the stories, spreading quickly in families, schools, or neighborhoods, and occasionally greatly magnified by media reproduction, contribute to the fundamental communication and reproduction of racism in society. (Smitherman-Donaldson and van Dijk 1988:18)*

Symbolic racism is manifested in a variety of communication contexts. Popular magazines and children's literature have been among the most conspicuous purveyors of racial stereotypes. Although social scientists have pointed out the racially biased nature of these publications for decades, a 1965 study found that of 5,206 children's trade books published from 1962 through 1964, only 349, or 6.7 percent, included one or more blacks (Larrick 1965:63–65; Berelson and Salter 1946; Klineberg 1963; Teague 1968). Moreover, Tom Engelhardt (1971) has shown that the cultural stereotypes in American movies reinforce those found in other media forms. All positive, humanitarian virtues remain with whites: even if they represent the dregs of Western society, "any White is a step up from the rest of the world." Nonwhites, on the other hand, are depicted as alien intruders, helpless, dependent, or less than human. When they do assume center stage, they do so as villains—"the repository for evil." Hune (1977) has demonstrated how stereotypes of Asian Americans have been reinforced and legitimated by the omission, distortion, or misrepresentation of the role of racial and ethnic minorities in the nation's history books (see also Henry 1967 and Stampp et al. 1968). Hune argues the assumptions of leading intellectuals—social scientists and historians in particular—have influenced policies and practices toward both European and Asian immigrants. Therefore, whether undertaken consciously or unconsciously, intentionally or unintentionally, perpetuation of these symbolic biases serves to reflect and reinforce cultural beliefs in the racial inferiority of nonwhites.

Institutional Discrimination

Both forms of attitudinal discrimination just defined are ultimately reducible to psychological variables: the actor is prejudiced, defers to, or is influenced by the sanctions of a prejudiced reference group or the norms of a racially biased culture. Institutional discrimination, on the other hand, refers to organizational practices and societal trends that exclude minorities from equal opportunities for positions of power and prestige. This discrimination has been labeled "structural" by some scholars (*Research News* 1987:9). Institutional or structural discrimination involves "policies or practices which appear to be neutral in their effect on minority individuals or groups, but which have the effect of disproportionately impacting on them in harmful or negative ways" (Task Force on the Administration of Military Justice in the Armed Forces 1972:19). The effects or consequences of institutional discrimination have little relation to racial or ethnic attitudes or to the majority group's racial or ethnic prejudices.

The existence of institutional inequalities that effectively exclude substantial portions of minority groups from participation in the dominant society has seldom been considered under the category of discrimination. According to J. Milton Yinger, discrimination is "the persistent application of criteria that are arbitrary, irrelevant, or unfair by *dominant standards*, with the result that some persons receive an undue advantage and others, *although equally qualified*, suffer an unjustified penalty" (Yinger 1968:449, italics added). The underlying assumption of this definition is that if all majority-group members would eliminate "arbitrary, irrelevant, and unfair criteria," discrimination would, by definition, cease to exist. However, if all prejudice—and the attitudinal discrimination that emanates from it—were somehow miraculously eliminated overnight, the inequalities rooted in the normal and impersonal operation of existing institutional structures would remain. Therefore, the crucial issue is not the equal treatment of those with equal qualifications but rather is the access of minority-group members to the qualifications themselves.

Consider the following additional examples of institutional discrimination:

- An employer may be genuinely willing to hire individuals of all races but may rely solely on word-of-mouth recommendations to fill job vacancies. If Hispanics had previously been excluded from such employment, they would be unlikely to be members of a communications network that would allow them to learn about such vacancies.
- Jury selection is supposedly color-blind in most states, with jurors randomly selected from lists of registered voters. However, because they are more likely to be poor and geographically mobile (and thus ineligible to vote), blacks are less frequently selected as jurors. Similarly, a recent study found that, because a disproportionate number of black males are in prison or have been convicted of a felony, 14 percent of black men—nearly 1.5 million of a total voting age population of 10.4 million—are ineligible to vote, thus substantially diluting African American political power (Butterfield 1997).
- City commissions are often selected on either an at-large or a district basis. In at-large elections, all voters select from the same slate of candidates. By contrast, when elections are conducted on a district basis, the city is divided into geographically defined districts, and a resident votes only for candidates within his or her district. When an ethnic or a racial group constitutes a numerical minority of a city's population, its voting power is likely to be diluted and its representation in city government is likely to be lower than its proportion of the population under an at-large system of voting. Thus, under an at-large system, a city with a population that is 40 percent black could have no black representation on the city commission if voting followed racial lines. Because of patterns of residential seg-

regation, this situation would be much less likely in a system organized on a district basis.

- In Minnesota a judge ruled unconstitutional a law that punished possession of crack more severely than possession of comparable amounts of powdered cocaine. Testimony indicated that crack is used mainly by blacks, whereas whites are much more likely to use cocaine. Although there was general agreement that the Minnesota legislature had enacted the penalties for the two crimes without any intent of targeting a specific minority group, the judge contended that the absence of racial prejudice or negative intent in the law's enactment was less relevant in considering the constitutionality of the crack law than whether enactment affected blacks disproportionately and thus had the practical effect of discriminating against them. "There had better be a good reason for any law that has the practical effect of disproportionately punishing members of one racial group. If crack was significantly more deadly or harmful than cocaine that might be a good enough reason. But there just isn't enough evidence that they're different enough to justify the radical differences in penalties" (London 1991).

The issue of racial disparities in sentencing for crack and powdered cocaine has become a hotly contested part of the national debate over mandatory federal sentences for drug offenses, where blacks were 90 percent of those convicted in Federal court crack offenses but only 30 percent of those convicted for cocaine. Studies show that the physiological and psychoactive effects of crack and powered cocaine are similar, and the independent U.S. Sentencing Commission recommended that Congress scrap laws that establish dramatically harsher sentences (by a ratio of 100 to 1) for possession of crack than for possession of cocaine. Nevertheless, in 1995 both the Clinton Administration and Congress refused to modify the disparate sentences given for possession of the two drugs, and in 1996 the Supreme Court rejected the argument that the dramatic racial differences in prosecution and penalties for crack possession reflected racial discrimination. However, the consequence of these decisions was to reinforce and maintain the dramatically disproportionate number of African Americans under the control of the criminal justice system (Morley 1995; Jones 1995; Greenhouse 1996; Wren 1996).

Institutional discrimination is central to two important recent interpretations of inequalities in American life that focus on opportunities in two institutions in American life—the economy and education. In a series of books—*The Declining Significance of Race* (1978a), *The Truly Disadvantaged* (1987), and *When Work Disappears* (1996), William Julius Wilson has identified several broad social structural factors that have dramatically transformed the economic opportunity structure for African Americans. He contends that the overall economic and social position of the inner-city poor has deteriorated in the past quarter century not only because of attitudinal discrimination but also because of impersonal structural economic changes—the shift from goods-producing to service-producing industries, increasing labor market segmentation, increased industrial technology, and the flight of industries from central cities—that have little to do with race. Earlier in the twentieth century, relatively uneducated and unskilled native and immigrant workers were able to find stable employment and income in manufacturing. Today, however, deindustrialization has created an economic "mis-match" between the available jobs and the qualifications of inner-city residents. On the one hand, manufacturing jobs, which in the past did not require highly technical skills, have either been mechanized or have moved from the inner cities to the sub-urbs, the sun belt, or overseas. Unskilled blacks in central cities are especially vul-nerable to the relocation of high-paying manufacturing jobs. On the other hand, the jobs now being created in the cities demand highly technical credentials that most inner-city residents do not have. The economic opportunities of the African American urban poor, who lack the educational and occupational skills necessary for today's highly technological jobs, are therefore rapidly diminishing. The result is extremely high levels of unemployment.

These broad structural changes have triggered a process of "hyperghettoization" in which the urban poor are disproportionately concentrated and socially and economi-cally isolated. As many stable working-class and middle-class residents with job quali-fications have moved from inner-city neighborhoods, the stability of inner-city social institutions (churches, schools, newspapers, and recreational facilities) has been un-dermined, and the social fabric of neighborhoods and the community has deteriorated. As Wilson argues in Article 19 ("Work"), "A neighborhood in which people are poor but employed is different from a neighborhood in which people are poor and jobless."

Although the lack of educational and occupational skills among the African Amer-ican urban poor reflects a historical legacy of attitudinal discrimination, institutional factors—the broad structural changes in the economy that were just mentioned—play a crucial role in sustaining black economic inequality. Even if all racial prejudice were eliminated, inner-city African Americans would still lack access to high-paying jobs that provide security and stability for both families and the black community (Wilson 1987; 1996).

Similar impersonal factors play a critical role in creating and sustaining dramatic racial disparities in educational opportunities. In his powerful book, *Savage Inequali-ties,* Jonathan Kozol (1991) has focused on the dramatic differences in the quality of public education in poor and in wealthy school districts in the United States and on the way in which these differences—these "savage inequalities"—affect educational oppor-tunity. Focusing on the vast disparities in the quality of facilities, programs, and cur-ricula that typically distinguish inner-city and suburban schools, Kozol contends that what is most glaringly apparent are the dramatic financial inequities among schools serving poor and affluent students, often in neighboring school districts; schools at-tended by poor students are invariably the most poorly funded, while those attended by students from affluent backgrounds have the highest per-pupil expenditures. Kozol reports that a study

of 20 of the wealthiest and poorest districts of Long Island [New York], for example, matched by location and size of enrollment, found that the differences in per-pupil spending were not only large but had approximately doubled in a five-year period. Schools in Great Neck, in 1987, spent $11,265 for each pupil. In affluent Jericho and Manhasset the figures were, respectively, $11,325 and $11,370. In Oyster Bay the figure was $9,980. Compare this to Levittown, also on Long Island but a town of mostly working-class white families, where per-pupil spending dropped to $6,900. Then compare these numbers to the spending level in the town of Roosevelt, the poorest district in the county, where the schools are 99 percent non-white and where the fig-

ure dropped to $6,340. Finally, consider New York City, where in the same year, $5,590 was invested in each pupil—less than half of what was spent in Great Neck. The pattern is almost identical to that [in the Chicago and many other metropolitan areas] [Kozol 1991:120].

The principal source of these glaring financial inequities is the mechanism—local property taxes—that traditionally has been used to fund public schools. Reliance upon local property taxes to fund public schools, although perhaps initiated as public policy with no racial considerations in mind, has, given the history of racial residential segregation in American society, created dramatically different educational opportunities for white and for minority children. Recently these disparities have increased at precisely the same time that cities have undertaken extensive urban redevelopment programs; by offering tax abatements to businesses and corporations that locate in central city locations, the tax bases from which inner-city schools are funded lose an estimated $5 to $8 billion annually (Lewin 1997). Kozol contends that, because states require school attendance but allocate their resources inequitably, they "effectively require inequality. Compulsory inequity, perpetuated by state law, too frequently condemns our children to unequal lives" (Kozol 1991:56).

Similarly, in an analysis of school desegregation within and between American cities and their suburbs, David James (Article 21; 1989) has shown that the state, by creating political boundaries that separate school districts and by refusing to accept interdistrict desegregation, has been instrumental in creating school segregation, thereby reinforcing patterns of social inequality. Suburban rings surrounding major American cities tend to have multiple school districts, and black suburbanites tend to be concentrated in areas close to the central cities. Therefore, because the Supreme Court has ruled that racial segregation *within* school districts is unconstitutional but that segregation *between* districts is not, whites can avoid living in school districts with large proportions of black students. They are able to implement a form of attitudinal discrimination precisely because the structure of school districts (in many instances created without racial intent) provides such opportunities.

Institutional discrimination, although not intended to victimize racial groups directly, is thus more subtle, covert, complex, and less visible and blatant than attitudinal discrimination. Because it does not result from the motivations or intentions of specific individuals, but rather from policies that appear race-neutral, institutional discrimination is more impersonal than attitudinal discrimination, and its effects are more easily denied, ignored, overlooked, or dismissed as "natural," inevitable, or impossible to change. Nevertheless, institutional discrimination has the same discriminatory consequences for minority group members. In examining institutional discrimination, therefore, it is more important to consider the *effect* of a particular policy or practice on a minority group than it is to consider the *motivations* of the majority group.

ENDNOTES

1. Reflecting the dynamic, fluid, and socially defined nature of racial and ethnic categories, both the categories and the terms used to identify them frequently change. For example, over the last two hundred years, a variety of terms—colored, Negro, Afro-American, black—have been used to refer to Americans of African descent. Recently, many black leaders have urged adoption of the term *African American*. However, although that term has gained increasing acceptance among both black and white Americans, no

consensus on terminology has emerged. Therefore, we will use both *African American* and *black American* throughout this book. Similarly, there is no consensus today concerning the appropriate terminology for two other important racial and ethnic categories in the United States: American Indian, Native American, or Native peoples, on the one hand, or Hispanic or Latino, on the other. In each case we will use the terms interchangeably.

2. This situation of black numerical superiority and complete political exclusion was explicitly prohibited by the 14th Amendment of the Constitution, which includes a provision that required a reduction of Congressional representation for states that practiced such exclusion. "When the right to vote at any election for . . . President and Vice-President of the United States, Representatives in Congress, the executive and judicial officers of a State, or the members of the legislature thereof, is denied . . . or in any way abridged . . . , the basis of representation therein shall be reduced in the proportion which the number of such male citizens shall bear to the whole number of male citizens twenty-one years of age in such State" (*Constitution of the United States* 1996:520). Reflecting the *majority* power of whites in these two (and numerous other) states, this Constitutional provision was never implemented; no state's representation was ever thus reduced, despite the wholesale disfranchisement of African Americans for well over half a century.

Historical Perspectives

2

The United States, which has been called a "nation of nations," is one of the most ethnically diverse societies in the modern world (Table 1). Despite an ideology—the "American Creed"—formally committed to human equality, racial and ethnic criteria have frequently determined social status in American society, and conflict for economic, social, and political preeminence among its numerous racial and ethnic groups has been one of the most salient features of the American experience. Figure 1 presents data on the distribution of major racial and ethnic groups in the United States. Presently, members of the largest racial and ethnic minorities (African Americans, Latinos, Asians, and American Indians comprise more than one-quarter (28.5 percent) of the population. This section provides a brief overview of the history of American ethnic relations. Because they are so numerous, it would be impossible to examine the experience of all American ethnic groups in this brief section (for a comprehensive survey, see the superb essays in the *Harvard Encyclopedia of American Ethnic Groups* [Thernstrom 1980] and the *Gale Encyclopedia of Multicultural Groups* [Galens, et al. 1995]). The articles included here provide conceptual and substantive continuity to the volume as a whole. This survey of several of the major ethnic and racial categories that collectively comprise the American people—what Hollinger (Article 4) terms the American "ethnoracial pentagon"—is organized in roughly the chronological order of their migration to North America. We begin by sketching some key features of the experience of the earliest inhabitants—American Indians—and conclude with a discussion of some of the most recent immigrants to the United States.

American Indians/Native Americans

The first Americans migrated from Asia between 12,000 to 40,000 years ago, slowly dispersing throughout North, Central, and South America. Although the length of time that they have inhabited the American continents is brief when compared with human societies elsewhere in the world, American Indian peoples developed a great diversity of cultures with widely different levels of technology, cultural complexity, and languages. The large and highly sophisticated Aztec, Inca, and Mayan civilizations contrast

TABLE 1   *Racial Populations in the United States, 1970–1998*

	NUMBER (THOUSANDS)				PERCENT OF THE POPULATION			
	1970	*1980*	*1990*	*1998*	*1970*	*1980*	*1990*	*1998*
Total	203,212	226,546	249,398	269,073	100.0	100.0	100.0	100.0
White	177,749	188,341	209,173	222,304	87.5	83.2	83.9	82.6
Black	22,580	26,488	30,598	34,200	11.1	11.7	12.3	12.7
American Indian, Eskimo, and Aleut	827	1,418	2,073	2,343	0.4	0.6	0.8	0.9
Asian and Pacific Islander	1,539	3,501	7,554	10,225	0.8	1.5	3.0	3.8
Chinese	435	806	1,645	*	0.2	0.4	0.7	*
Filipino	343	775	1,407	*	0.2	0.3	0.6	*
Japanese	591	701	848	*	0.3	0.3	0.3	*
Asian Indian	*	362	815	*	*	0.2	0.3	*
Korean	69	355	799	*	0.0	0.2	0.3	*
Vietnamese	*	262	615	*	*	0.1	0.2	*
Hispanic[†]	9,073	14,609	22,558	29,960	4.5	6.4	9.0	11.1
Mexican American	4,532	8,740	13,496	*	2.2	3.9	5.4	*
Puerto Rican	1,429	2,014	2,728	*	0.7	0.9	1.1	*
Cuban	544	803	1,044	*	0.3	0.4	0.4	*
Other Hispanic	2,566	3,051	5,086	*	1.2	1.3	2.0	*

Sources: U.S. Bureau of the Census, *U.S. Census of the Population: 1970*, vol. 1, Part I: *Characteristics of the Population*, Summary Section 2, Washington, D.C.: U.S. Government Printing Office, 1973; U.S. Bureau of the Census, *U.S. Census of the Population: 1970*, Subject Reports PC(2)-1G; *Japanese, Chinese, Filipinos*, Washington, D.C.: U.S. Government Printing Office, 1973; U.S. Bureau of the Census, *Census of the Population*: 1980, vol. 1: *Characteristics of the Population*, "Detailed Population Characteristics, Part I: U.S. Summary," PC80-1-D1-A, Washington, D.C.: U.S. Government Printing Office, 1984; U.S. Bureau of the Census, *Census and You*, Washington, D.C.: U.S. Government Printing Office, 1991. U.S. Bureau of the Census, Population Division, [online] "United States Population Estimates, by Age, Sex, Race, and Hispanic Origin," (1997). Available: http://www.census.gov/population/estimates/nation/intfile3-1.txt [1998, April 16].

*Not available.

[†]Hispanics are also included in "White," "Black," and "Other Hispanic."

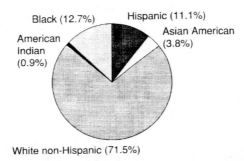

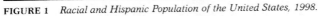

FIGURE 1   *Racial and Hispanic Population of the United States, 1998.*

Source: U.S. Bureau of the Census, [Online], "Resident Population of the United States: Estimates by Sex, Race, and Hispanic Origin, with Median Age," (1998). Available: http://www.census.gov/population/estimates/nation/intfile3-1.txt [1998, April 16].

sharply with the simpler societies of the Yavapai, Onondaga, and Kansa. As Cynthia Enloe has written, even "before the arrival of Europeans the American continent was already ethnically plural" (Enloe 1981:126). Today the U.S. government officially recognizes 554 Indian tribes and Alaska Native groups (U.S. Department of the Interior, 1997).

A bewildering diversity of native peoples was present when Europeans first invaded the Americas. Perhaps the best index of this extraordinary cultural diversity is the myriad number of languages found in the Americas; as Ruhlen (1987) has pointed out, the Americas were linguistically as diverse as the Eurasian land mass. Native American languages can be classed into about a dozen different stocks (each as distinct from the other as the Semitic from the Indo-European) and within each stock into languages as distinct as English from Russian. Despite a dramatic decline of native languages, about two-hundred distinct languages are still spoken among American Indian peoples in North America. Although Indians represent less than 1 percent of the American people, this number is equal to the number spoken among the other 99 percent of the population combined (Hodgkinson 1990:1). This cultural diversity persists among American Indians to the present day, despite the popular perception among outsiders that they are a single distinct ethnic group.

The European invasion of North America had a pervasive and enduring impact on American Indian peoples and cultures. Examination of the effects of Indian-white contact illustrates the process by which a system of ethnic stratification develops. As we noted in Part 1, *ethnic stratification* is a system of social ranking in which one ethnic group acquires greater power, privilege, and prestige than another (or others). An unequal relationship between two or more ethnic groups is not inevitable, however. In other words, some groups are not inherently dominant and others inherently subordinate; the establishment of a system of ethnic inequalities is the result of a historical process.

As mentioned in Part 1, Donald Noel (1968) has suggested that three conditions are necessary for a system of ethnic stratification to be created: *ethnocentrism, competition,* and differences in *power.* Noel applied these conditions to the development of the caste system of black-white relations in the United States, but let us here examine how these variables influenced patterns of Indian-white relations.

Ethnocentrism is the idealization of the attributes of the group to which an individual belongs. People of all societies tend to think of themselves as the chosen people or, at the very least, as those at the center of humanity. People of any society tend to think that their ways of doing things are correct, just, righteous, and virtuous—the way God intended. On the other hand, people tend to perceive the ways of other people as odd, incorrect, or immoral, and to reject or ridicule groups from which they differ. Ethnocentrism seems to be an inevitable outgrowth of the socialization process, during which cultural values and standards of right and wrong, beauty and ugliness, and so forth, are internalized.

Most European settlers regarded Native Americans as heathen savages, possessing cultures vastly inferior to their own. Indeed, among many Puritans of New England, Indians were regarded as agents of Satan, to be exterminated by gunfire or disease. The European invaders considered agriculture a superior economic activity and an index of their own cultural superiority. Therefore, they perceived the lands they entered to be "wilderness"—in their eyes, wild, unoccupied, and unused territory. Europeans also sought to Christianize the Indians and to eliminate their traditional religious practices. The ethnocentrism that underlay the missionary impulse is exemplified by the following speech by a Boston missionary to a group of Seneca Indians:

> There is but one religion, and but one way to serve God, and if you do not embrace the right way, you cannot be happy hereafter. You have never worshiped the Great Spirit in a manner acceptable to him; but have all your lives been in great errors and darkness. To endeavor to remove these errors, and open your eyes, so that you might see clearly, is my business with you. (quoted in Washburn 1964:210)

When two different ethnic groups come into initial contact, ethnocentrism is not restricted to one group. Rather, both sides respond with mutual ethnocentrism. Noel has noted this reciprocal process when he cites the reply of representatives of the Six (Indian) Nations to an offer by the Virginia Commission in 1744 to educate Indian youth at the College of William and Mary:

> Several of our young people were formerly brought up at Colleges of the Northern Provinces; they were instructed in all your sciences; but when they came back to us, they were bad runners, ignorant of every means of living in the woods, unable to bear either cold or hunger, knew neither how to build a cabin, take a deer, or kill an enemy, spoke our language imperfectly, were therefore neither fit for hunters, warriors, or counselors; they were totally good for nothing. We are, however, not the less obliged by your kind offer, though we decline accepting it; and to show our grateful Sense of it, if the Gentlemen of Virginia will send us a Dozen of their Sons we will take great care of their education, instruct them in all we know and make Men of them. (quoted in Noel 1968)

It is clear that the American Indian leaders felt their ways to be superior to those of the Virginians.

The second condition necessary for a system of ethnic stratification to develop is *competition;* that is, two or more individuals or groups must strive for a goal or objective that only one can achieve. From the beginning of Indian-European contacts, competition between the two groups centered around land. American Indian and white looked on land differently. The former emphasized the notion of *usufruct*, or user's rights. The land could be occupied, hunted, cultivated, and otherwise used as long as a group wished. Once it was abandoned, it became available for use by others. To most Indian peoples, land was not something that could be individually owned or bought or sold, as Europeans conceived of it. Many land transactions between Native Americans and Europeans were based on radically different conceptions of what rights were being conveyed.

A system of ethnic stratification ultimately rests on differences in *power*. Initial contacts between Indians and whites usually took place in a context of equality and were not necessarily destructive of Indian cultures and societies. In fact, many items of white technology—especially guns, knives, cloth, fishhooks, pots, and other tools—were eagerly sought. For instance, it was only after the introduction of the horse by Europeans that the Plains Indian cultures flourished (Washburn 1964:66–70). The posture of equality is reflected by the white recognition of American Indian peoples as independent powers—nations (like the Cherokee Nation and the Navajo Nation)—and by numerous diplomatic treaties, gifts, and even politically arranged marriages. (The marriage of Pocahontas and John Rolfe, for example, was primarily a political match to ensure the survival of early Virginia colonists.)

Initially, the desire of Europeans for land they could cultivate did not strain Indian-white relationships; but as the number of Europeans increased throughout the seventeenth, eighteenth, and nineteenth centuries, their demand for land became the primary source of conflict with American Indians. Moreover, cultivation soon reduced the supply of game and forced an Indian retreat. The advance of European settlement eventually overwhelmed even the most resolute Indian resistance. Armed with superior military technology and bolstered by increasing numbers, Europeans moved inexorably westward. As the whites expanded westward, American Indian peoples were frequently expelled from their traditional settlements to lands beyond the immediate frontier. Removal was frequently legitimated by an underlying Anglo-Saxon ethnocentrism, exemplified by President Theodore Roosevelt's assertion that "this great continent could not have been kept as nothing but a game preserve for squalid savages" (quoted in Lurie 1968:66).

As control of lands they had formerly occupied increasingly passed to whites, the status of American Indians came increasingly to resemble what C. Matthew Snipp (1986) has called "captive nations." The Native American land base, which initially had been over 2 billion acres, dwindled to 155 million acres in 1871 and to 54 million acres in 1997 (Dorris 1981; U.S. Department of the Interior 1997). Diseases carried by the Europeans, such as smallpox, scarlet fever, measles, and cholera, were fatal to large numbers of native peoples, who for centuries had been physically isolated from the Old World and had developed little or no resistance to these diseases. Epidemics ravaged American Indian peoples throughout American history, frequently killing more than half of a tribe. Washburn concludes that "unwittingly, disease was the white man's strongest ally in the New World" (1975:107). Moreover, substantial numbers of Indians died as a result of warfare with Europeans, policies of removal from ancestral lands, and deliberate extermination. The American Indian population, which had numbered between 5 and 6 million when Columbus reached the New World, dwindled to 237,000 by 1900 (Thornton 1987:32). American Indians experienced a decline not only in their numbers but also in the number of tribes or ethnic groups—from an estimated 1,000 at the time of initial European contact to 318 officially recognized tribes residing in the lower 48 states in 1992 (Nagel 1996:4, 14).[1]

The reservation system that developed most fully during the nineteenth century symbolized both the end of the era of Indian-white equality and the relegation of native peoples to a minority status. Most Indians had to obtain passes to leave the reservation, were denied the vote, and were forcefully prohibited from engaging in native religious and ceremonial practices. Traditional Indian cultures and patterns of authority were undermined as their economic resources eroded, their numbers plummeted, and the administration and control of the reservation were placed in the hands of white agents. Reservation peoples lost control over their fate. As a consequence, they came to resemble a "captive nation" characterized by white political domination.

In the last quarter of the nineteenth century, most white Americans agreed that Native Americans were a vanishing race and that forced assimilation—socialization to white culture—represented the most "humane" means of dealing with the dilemma of the American Indian's continued existence. Whites employed a strategy of destroying tribal governments, breaking up the reservations, and granting land to Indians on an individual basis. The federal government subsidized American Indian schools, many of which were controlled by white religious groups. In many instances, Indian children were forcibly taken from their families and enrolled in boarding schools, where they were compelled to adopt white styles of dress and were punished for speaking their own native languages (see Adams 1988). The underlying assumption of these policies was that Indians should be forced to give up their cultural heritages and to adopt the European values of rugged individualism, competition, and private enterprise. To ethnocentric whites, these values represented more "civilized" forms of behavior, in contrast to the "savage" practices of American Indians. In 1887 Carl Schurz, the German-born Secretary of the Interior, justified these practices: "The enjoyment and pride of individual ownership of property is one of the most effective civilizing agencies" (U.S. Commission on Civil Rights 1961:122). Theodore Roosevelt, reflecting the late nineteenth-century Social Darwinist theory that emphasized the "survival of the fittest," agreed: "This will bring the whites and Indians into close contact, and while, of course, in the ensuing struggle and competition many of the Indians will go to the wall, the survivors will come out American citizens" (Quoted in Washburn 1975:242).

Nevertheless, the striking feature of Native American Indian life in the twentieth century has been the ability of Indian cultures to endure. Despite intense pressures to assimilate into the mainstream of American society, American Indians have clung tenaciously to their cultural values, standards, and beliefs. Although plagued by the nation's poorest health standards, the American Indian population increased by 1990 to nearly 2 million, better than a 40 percent increase over 1980. Census Bureau estimates place the Native American population in 1998 at more than 2.3 million, nearly ten times the number a century ago. Moreover, Census Bureau projections estimate that by 2050 the American Indian population will reach 4.6 million (1.2 percent of the population) (Day 1993; Harris 1994b). This dramatic increase in the number of people identifying themselves as Native Americans reflects an Indian cultural and political renaissance during the past quarter century. During the 1960s and 1970s ethnic consciousness and political militancy, particularly among the younger and better educated, increased substantially. As a result, many people who once were ashamed of their Native American ancestry today acknowledge or assert it. In addition, some people may be motivated by special educational, medical, and economic benefits available to Indians through treaties with the federal government (Snipp 1997). Finally, the number of "wannabees"—whites for whom it is fashionable to proclaim Indian ancestry—may have increased (Nagel 1995, 1996).

As noted before, a substantial portion of American Indian lands were ceded to colonists and early settlers by treaties, first with the colonial British governments and later with the United States government. In signing these treaties, Indian peoples agreed to give up certain things (most frequently, land) in return for concessions and commitments to them by the United States government. Most treaties, which involved water, fishing, and territorial agreements, guaranteed that Indians would retain the treaty rights granted to them (including sovereignty over remaining lands) in perpetuity—"as long as the grass shall grow and the rivers shall run." Treaties therefore form the basis of the unique legal and political status of American Indians today. In contrast to other American racial and ethnic minorities, American Indian tribes "are due certain privileges, protections, and benefits of yielding some of their sovereignty to the United

States" (Dorris 1981:54). Among these commitments are the obligations of the federal government to protect Indian lands and to provide social, medical, and educational services. These legal responsibilities, however, are invariably affected by national, state, and local politics, in which Indian interests are usually of little concern. Recently efforts by the Congress and the President to balance the federal budget led to cutbacks in programs critical to many American Indians. For example, between 1995 and 1996, the Federal repair budget for Indian housing was cut by one-third, leaving many Indians ill-equipped to confront the harsh winters in northern states (Brooke 1996: A1).

Despite persistent and recurring efforts to undermine the reservation system, these treaties did permit Indians to preserve some of their dwindling lands. Although the lands held by American Indians today represent only a small portion of those originally guaranteed in treaties, they include vast and extremely valuable agricultural, water, timber, fishing, and energy resources. However, until recently Indians have seldom received significant income from these resources because they have been developed and exploited primarily by non-Indian interests. For example, Indian reservations have provided water for the extensive urban development of the Southwest and have received almost nothing in return. Similarly, mining and mineral development on Indian lands has often resulted in exploitative leases that provided only a small fraction of the value of the resources being used; for example, because of leases signed by the Bureau of Indian Affairs on their behalf, in 1981 the Navajo Nation received 15 to 38 cents a ton for coal that was sold by American suppliers to foreign buyers for $70 a ton (Snipp 1986). Development also had a devastating effect on the environment of many reservations, destroying habitat, polluting streams and rivers, and desecrating Indian spiritual sites (Robbins 1997:17).

Snipp contends that the increasing attempts to develop and exploit American Indian resources for external economic interests reflect a shift in policy toward Indian peoples from "captive nationhood" to *internal colonialism*. The former represented political domination but did not dramatically disrupt the economic lives of American Indian people. Internal colonialism, on the other hand, involves economic as well as political domination. As pressures for development of the scarce resources found on tribal lands continue, such internal colonialism is likely to become more pronounced.

As a result, Native Americans are today among the poorest and least educated groups in American society. In 1989 Indian median household income was less than two-thirds (64 percent) that of whites; nearly one-third (31 percent) of Native Americans lived below the poverty level. The problems of poverty are especially acute on Indian reservations—the lands to which native peoples have title and over which they exercise sovereignty. Among reservation Indians, from one-third to one-half of all families have incomes below the poverty level; on some reservations the unemployment rates exceed 80 percent. By 1990, two-thirds (66 percent) of all Indians twenty-five and older had completed high school, compared with four-fifths (80 percent) of whites. The percentage of Indians at that age category (9.3 percent) who had graduated from college was less than half the percentage of whites (21.5) (U.S. Bureau of the Census 1992b).

In response to the exploitation and depletion of their resources, Native Americans are increasingly challenging their political and economic domination by outsiders, and they are seeking to exert Indian control over reservation resources in order to address some of the severe economic problems confronting Indian peoples (Cornell 1988a). Indian activists have mounted legal challenges to ensure that the U.S. government honors the terms of treaties that it has made with Indian tribes. In one of the most celebrated legal cases involving Indian claims that the Federal Government had not fulfilled its treaty obligations, in 1975 a Federal District judge awarded half the annual salmon catch in Puget Sound to Indian tribes who had signed an 1855 treaty with the United States (Egan 1992). Similarly, in 1990 the Passamaquoddy Indians gained a $40 million settlement of their land claims against the state of Maine, and the Puyallup (Washington) tribe ceded 20,000 acres of land in Tacoma for a $162 million package (Associated Press: 1990). New York Seneca Indians threatened to reclaim the lands on the Allegheny reservation on which the town of Salamanca, New York, was built, under a ninety-nine year lease that expired in 1991. As part of the settlement, the annual lease payments of non-Indians living in Salamanca increased dramatically (*New York Times* June 11, 1990).

Indian activism has also been reflected in their efforts to develop organizations to advance Indian economic interests by resisting external exploitation of their resource base, including timber, water, and, especially, minerals. One of the most prominent of these has been the Council of Energy Resource Tribes (CERT), which was formed to promote Indian economic interests in the substantial coal, gas, oil, and uranium reserves that are found on Indian lands (Snipp 1986). Moreover, rather than lease their lands to drill for oil or gas or mine for coal, several tribes have formed their own high-technology mining ventures that enable them, rather than large energy companies, to retain the profits from these enterprises (Johnson 1994). As the powerful economic and political pressures intensify over increasingly scarce and valuable native resources, it seems inevitable that conflicts will increase in the future (Cornell 1988a; Erdrich and Dorris 1988).

In addition to exploiting their own energy resources, Indian peoples have embarked on a number of other forms of economic development, such as tourism among the White Mountain Apache and Havasupai tribes of Arizona and the Nez Percé in northeastern Oregon; the Wisconsin Oneida and the Mississippi Choctaw have invested in plants that manufacture products as diverse as auto parts and greeting cards (White 1990; Egan 1996).

Probably the most widely publicized enterprise that Indians have developed on reservations lands, however, is gambling. In 1987 the Supreme Court ruled that American Indian tribes had the authority to operate gambling enterprises on tribal lands and were exempt from most state gambling laws and regulations. The next year, Congress passed the Indian Gaming Regulatory Act (IGRA) of 1988, which established federal regulations for the overall conduct of Indian gaming. By 1997, 184 tribes had opened gambling facilities and another 32 had such facilities in the planning stages. A study by the U.S. General Accounting Office (1997) found that during the decade between 1985 and 1995, income from Indian gaming rose dramatically, increasing from $125 million to over $4.5 billion. By 1995 Indian gaming accounted for at least 10 percent of all revenues from legal gambling in the United States; revenues generated by Indian casinos throughout the country were comparable to those of Atlantic City casinos and were more than half the revenues of Nevada casinos.

However, whether gambling is the solution to the problems of Native American poverty is questionable. Many critics—Indian and non-Indian—have criticized the social and cultural consequences of gambling and its corrosive effects on traditional Indian values (Dao 1993). Moreover, reservations located in areas remote from major population centers encounter difficulties attracting patrons. The GAO study found that a few tribes (for example, the Pequot, a Connecticut tribe that operates Foxwoods, the nation's wealthiest casino) are doing very well; about half of all the Indian casino revenues were generated by just eight facilities that had incomes of over $100 million each. However, a majority of tribes had revenues of less than $15 million (U.S. General Accounting Office 1997), and their overall impact on tribal economic development was modest, at best. The Oglala Sioux of the Pine Ridge Reservation in South Dakota, for example, earned $1 million annually from their casinos—about $38 per capita (Kilborn 1997). Despite widely publicized examples of casino-generated wealth, the vast majority of American Indian people have yet to experience an economic renaissance.

European Americans

The migratory movement of European peoples from the seventeenth through the twentieth centuries has been the greatest in human history. Since the beginning of the seventeenth century, more than seventy million people have emigrated from Europe; about three-fourths of this number have come to the United States. The uprooting that millions of European immigrants experienced comprises one of the most dramatic sagas in American—indeed, world—history. This massive migration and its impact on American society, and the experience of European immigrants and their descendants have been widely described and debated among social historians and sociologists (Handlin 1951; Taylor 1971; Jones 1960, 1976; Seller 1977; Daniels, 1990; Dinnerstein, Nichols, and Reimers 1996; Dinnerstein and Reimers 1987; Bodnar 1985; Archdeacon 1983).

For nearly two centuries—from the beginning of the seventeenth to the beginning of the nineteenth century—the European population of America was overwhelmingly Protestant and British. The first European immigrants to settle permanently in what is now the United States were almost exclusively English. The first substantial English migration occurred between 1607 and 1660. The economic, legal, and political traditions that English settlers brought to America established an English foundation for American institutions, language, and culture. Although ethnic groups who later migrated contributed substantially to the distinctively American nature of political, economic, and social institutions, language and culture, they were also forced to adapt to the cultural and social systems that the English had established.

Although the English comprised the greatest proportion of the total colonial population, the middle colonies (New York, New Jersey, Pennsylvania, Delaware) contained substantial settlements of Germans, Dutch, Scotch-Irish, Scots, Swedes, and French Huguenots. Because the middle colonies contained the greatest variety of European cultures, they provided a context within which interethnic relations among European peoples in American society can first be observed. Here the ideal of America as a *melting pot,* in which diverse cultures come together to form a new people, was first formulated. In 1782 a Frenchman, Hector St. John de Crèvecoeur, wrote the following:

> *What then is the American, this new man. . . . Here in America individuals of all nations are melted into a new race of men, whose labours and posterity will one day cause great changes in the world. (Crèvecoeur 1782/1957:39)*

As we will consider more fully in Part 3, the idealistic notion of the melting pot has greatly influenced later conceptions of how the various cultures comprising the American people have adapted and interacted (for many people, how they *should* adapt and interact).

However, relations between ethnic groups in the middle colonies sometimes fell short of this ideal. Spurred by William Penn's promotional efforts during the late seventeenth and early eighteenth centuries, many Germans settled in Pennsylvania, where they formed prosperous farming communities. Because they insisted on maintaining their own language, churches, and culture, their presence generated some of the earliest recorded conflicts among European ethnic groups in America. In 1752 Benjamin Franklin expressed the widely held fears of the "Germanization" of Pennsylvania:

> *Why should the Palatine Boors [Germans] be suffered to swarm into our Settlements, and by herding together, establish their Language and Manners, to the Exclusion of ours? Why should Pennsylvania, founded by the English, become a Colony of Aliens, who will shortly be so numerous as to Germanize us instead of Anglifying them . . . ? (Cited in Dinnerstein and Reimers 1987:7)*

Thus, colonial attitudes toward immigrants were marked by considerable ambivalence. This same uncertainty still characterizes America's response to ethnic diversity. Throughout the American experience, immigrant groups have been regarded both positively and negatively. On the one hand, immigration has provided a steady source of labor that has fueled the country's economic development and expansion. Until the twentieth century, inducements in the form of land, jobs, and exemption from taxation were offered to encourage settlement and to assist American economic development. Americans have also celebrated the idea of America as a haven for the oppressed, as in Emma Lazarus's classic poem, "Give me your tired, your poor / your huddled masses yearning to breathe free . . . ," which is inscribed on the Statue of Liberty.

On the other hand, the concern expressed by Benjamin Franklin over the impact of ethnic diversity on the society's institutions has been a persistent one. Lazarus's poem further characterizes those "tired," "poor," "huddled masses" as "wretched refuse," and, in fact, many immigrant groups have been perceived as undesirable wretched refuse. In practice, Americans have been less charitable than their idealized accounts indicate. Americans have frequently rejected ethnic differences as alien and as a threat to American political, social, and cultural institutions. Some ethnic groups in particular have been rejected or excluded as un-American and incapable of assimilating. Thus, while the labor of immigrants was accepted, their cultural traditions usually were not.

In 1790 when the first United States census was taken, the population of the new American nation numbered nearly four million. It was overwhelmingly British in composition, with the English comprising 60 to 80 percent of the population, and with other people from the British Isles (Scots, Welsh, and Scotch-Irish) contributing substantially. Between 1830 and 1930, the United States population experienced dramatic growth and change. During this period, the nation changed from a small group of tenuously related state governments to the most politically and economically powerful nation on earth. The area of European settlement moved progressively westward at the same time that the country became the world's leading industrial nation.

Peoples of many lands contributed to this dramatic growth. During the century between 1830 and 1930, nearly 35 million immigrants entered the country, swelling its total population to more than 123 million (see Figure 2). In contrast to the relative ethnic homogeneity of colonial immigration, the immigrants who arrived in the nineteenth and early twentieth centuries represented many different countries and peoples, including German, Russian, Mexican, British, Polish, Japanese, Scandinavian, Irish, Italian, Slavic, Greek, Chinese, and Portuguese. European immigration since 1790 has been divided into two broad categories: *"old"* immigrants from northern and western Europe and *"new"* immigrants from southern and eastern Europe (see Figure 3).

The "Old" Immigration

Immigration to the United States increased dramatically throughout the nineteenth century. In the peak year of the 1830s, slightly more than 70,000 immigrants entered. By the 1850s, this annual figure had increased to 400,000; by the 1880s, to 650,000; and by the first decade of the twentieth century, there were several years in which more than one million immigrants were admitted.

Until the 1890s, immigration was drawn principally from countries of northern and western Europe: Germany, Ireland, Great Britain (England, Scotland, and Wales), and Scandinavia (Norway, Sweden, and Denmark). With the exception of the Roman Catholic Irish, the old immigration was substantially Protestant. These groups, again

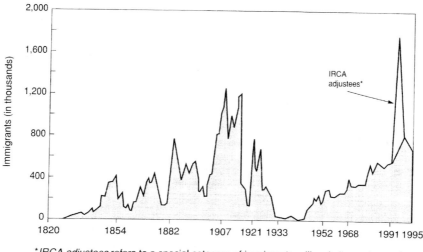

IRCA adjustees refers to a special category of immigrants—illegal aliens who, under the provisions of the Immigration and Control Act of 1986 (IRCA), were permitted to apply for regular permanent resident status in the United States. By 1994 virtually all those eligible for permanent residence had achieved that status.

FIGURE 2 *Immigration to the United States, 1821–1995*

Source: U.S. Immigration and Naturalization Service. *Statistical Yearbook of the Immigration and Naturalization Service, 1993.* Washington, D.C.: U.S. Government Printing Office, 1994. Data for 1994 and 1995 provided by Immigration and Naturalization Service internet home page, 1996.

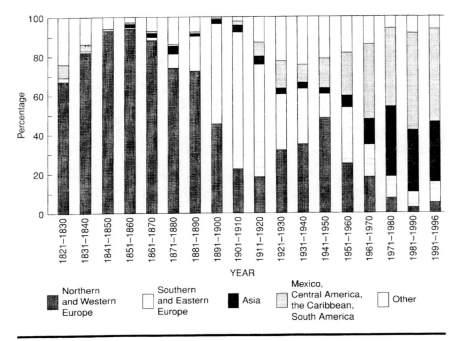

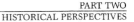

FIGURE 3 *Origins of U.S. Immigration by Region, 1821–1996*

Source: Statistical Yearbook of the Immigration and Naturalization Service, 1988, pp. 11–12; Statistical Yearbook of Immigration and Naturalization Service, 1996, p. 28.

with the exception of the Irish, the first immigrant group to settle primarily in cities, were attracted by the opportunities of free or relatively cheap land, and therefore often settled in the rural areas of the country. There were several common factors in their countries of origin that led people to emigrate: drastic population increases, displacement of traditional handicraft industries by the Industrial Revolution, an upheaval in agriculture that transformed traditional agrarian land patterns, and the migration of substantial numbers of people from rural to urban areas. Above all, the promise of economic opportunity lured people to the United States.

The "New" Immigration

European immigration to the United States reached its peak between 1890 and the outbreak of World War I in 1914. During this period, the United States received more than 14 million immigrants. As dramatic as the numerical increase was the shift in the sources of immigration. Prior to the 1880s, immigrants had come almost exclusively from northern and western Europe. By the first decade of the twentieth century, however, more than 70 percent of all immigrants came from southern and eastern Europe.

This shift brought large numbers of immigrants from a great variety of countries—Greeks, Croatians, Italians, Russians (primarily Jews), Poles, Hungarians, Czechs, and Lithuanians. These groups were culturally different from those who had previously migrated to this country. Unlike the old immigration, which was heavily Protestant and followed agricultural pursuits, the new immigrants were overwhelmingly Roman Catholic or Jewish, and, although they may have originated in rural areas or small towns, were drawn primarily to the economic opportunities in the rapidly expanding cities. The changes in the ethnic composition of this immigration caused "native" whites to fear the impact of non-English cultures on American institutions.

The shift in immigration patterns coincided with the flowering of the ideology of "scientific" racism, which reached its height about the turn of the twentieth century. As noted in the introduction to Part 1, at this time scientific and lay opinion concurred in the idea of the inherent mental and moral inferiority of all those who were not of Anglo-Saxon or Teutonic ancestry. To the already existing conceptions of black, American Indian, and Asian inferiority was added the notion of the racial inferiority and the unassimilability of immigrant groups from southern and eastern Europe. Never before or since have racist ideologies been so pervasive and so intellectually respectable in the United States as they were at this time. Moreover, these racist ideologies, which have had an enduring impact on policies and practices in American society throughout the twentieth century, were given intellectual legitimation by the nation's social and intellectual elites—the "best and brightest."

Such beliefs in the racial and cultural inferiority of new immigrants provided foundation for American immigration policy from 1917 to 1965. The first general restrictive legislation, passed in 1917, was a literacy test, which was used precisely because it was believed to discriminate against "new" immigrants, limiting their numbers while still permitting substantial numbers of "old" immigrants to enter. In the 1920s, even more stringent restrictive measures were enacted, each one assuming the desirability of restricting immigration in order to include those from the countries of the "old" immigration. In 1921 and 1924 further legislation designed to curtail new immigration was enacted. Finally, in 1929, the National Origins Quota Act, which was based on the rationale of ensuring the maintenance of Anglo-Saxon "racial" purity, went into effect. The law limited total immigration to 150,000 annually and established numerical quotas for each nation. Derived by a complicated calculation, each nation's quota was supposed to be "in proportion to its [the nation's] contribution to the American population." The measure assigned the highest quotas to those nations of northern and western Europe whose "racial" stock was believed to be closest to that of the original settlers of the country and who were therefore considered more assimilable and more desirable. More than four-fifths of the total quota was allocated to countries of the "old" immigration. For instance, Great Britain had an admission quota exceeding 65,000, but Italy was allocated fewer than 6,000, Hungary fewer than 1,000, and Greece a mere 310. Reflecting the racist assumptions on which it was based, the law excluded most Asians and Africans completely. These blatantly racist immigration policies were retained virtually intact until 1965, when the Immigration Act, which we will describe more fully in Part 4, was enacted.

Despite fears that they were undesirable and unassimilable and that they represented a threat to American society, the descendants of new immigrants, today referred to as *white ethnics*, have achieved socioeconomic attainments comparable to descendants of the old immigrants (see also Model 1988). In Article 23, "The New Immigration and Ethnicity in the United States," Douglas Massey contends that "the remarkable amalgamation of European immigrants into the society and culture of the United States is a historical fact." By almost any measure, descendants of southern and eastern European immigrants (Italians, Jews, Poles, Greeks, Hungarians) have become culturally and structurally assimilated into American life to a degree that few would have predicted even as late as the end of World War II. Indeed, Milton Gordon (Article 12), in his classic discussion of the process of assimilation in American life, which was published in 1961, contended that, although the descendants of the "new" immigrants had become culturally assimilated into the mainstream of American life, they remained structurally unassimilated—that is, they were living, working, and marrying within their own separate worlds. However, a scant decade later, Andrew Greeley was able to celebrate what he termed the "ethnic miracle." Greeley contended that, despite their lowly socioeconomic status three generations earlier, "the ethnics have made it." By the early 1970s Jews had attained the highest income levels of all European ethnic groups in American society, and they were followed by Irish, German, Italian, and Polish Catholics, not by white Anglo-Saxon Protestants. Moreover, when parental educational levels were held constant, Catholic ethnics showed higher educational achievement than any other European groups except Jews. Writing nearly twenty years later, Richard Alba ("Assimilation's Quiet Tide," Article 15) has confirmed that the trends toward greater structural assimilation that Greeley identified have become even more pronounced. "Assimilation was, and is, a reality for the majority of the descendants of earlier waves of immigration from Europe. . . . Long-term processes . . . have whittled away at the social foundations for ethnic distinctions . . . [and produced] a rough parity of opportunities to attain such socioeconomic goods as educational credentials and prestigious jobs. . . ."

Despite their economic and educational achievements, many white ethnics still retain a sense of cultural identity with their ethnic and national roots (Waters 1990). But, as we noted in the introduction to Part 1, increasingly people of European descent, no matter what their ethnic or national origins, are subsumed within the broad category of "white," and their ethnic identity (as, for instance, Irish, Italian, English, Norwegian) increasingly has become what Gans has characterized as "symbolic"— that is, primarily of ritual or symbolic significance but of little consequence on a daily basis.

In 1990, three-fourths of the American people were identified by the U.S. census as non-Hispanic whites. However, primarily because of their lower fertility and immigration rates, the white population is projected to decline to less than two-thirds of the total population in 2020 and to about only one-half of the American people by 2050 (Day 1993). In Part 3 we will examine in greater depth some of the competing explanations for differences in adaptation among ethnic groups in American society. Moreover, because the experience of European American ethnic groups often serves as an implicit and unspoken background to current discussions of multiculturalism and the future of ethnic integration in American society, in Part 4 we will explore some of the implications and consequences of the "quiet tide" of assimilation of European ethnic groups to which Alba refers.

African Americans

From the earliest settlement to the present, the principal racial division in American society has been between white and black, between those of European ancestry and those whose ancestral origins can be traced to the African continent. From the arrival of the first African at Jamestown in 1619 to the present, the meanings attributed to the physical traits of black people have been more important than all other racial divisions in American society; no other minority group has experienced discrimination so intense, pervasive, and enduring as have African Americans. African Americans were enslaved for more than two centuries, and although more than a century has passed since slavery was legally abolished, the rationale for slavery that emphasized the racial and cultural differences between blacks and whites persists to this day.

By 1998 numbering more than 34 million—nearly 13 percent of the total American population—African Americans have been the largest racial minority in American society since the eighteenth century. Today their numbers total more than the entire population of Canada or of the Scandinavian countries of Sweden, Denmark, Norway, Finland, and Iceland combined. Only Nigeria, Ethiopia, and Zaire have larger black populations than the United States has. Moreover, the black population of the United States is expected to double in the first half of the twenty-first century, reaching 62 million, or about one-sixth of the American population, by 2050 (Day 1993).

In Article 7, "The Declining Significance of Race," William Julius Wilson distinguishes among three major periods or stages of black-white relations in American history: preindustrial, industrial, and modern industrial. Let us review briefly here the African American experience during the first two of these three periods. (We will examine the racial dynamics of the most recent period, the modern industrial stage, in Part 4.)

Slavery: The "Peculiar Institution"

During the preindustrial period, a plantation economy dominated and defined the lives of black people, the most important aspect of which was the institution of slavery. Slavery is a system of social relations in which some persons are involuntarily placed in perpetual servitude, are defined as property, and are denied rights generally given to other members of the society. Throughout human history, many societies have limited the freedom and rights of particular classes of people. Other systems of servile status, such as serfdom, debt bondage, and indentureship, have involved some degree of unfreedom and rightlessness. What distinguishes these statuses from slavery is therefore not absolute. "Slaves are [simply] the most deprived and oppressed class of serviles" (Noel 1972:5). This definition of slavery is useful because it provides a standard against which social systems can be compared. In other words, if slavery is conceived as being located at the far end of a continuum ranging from absolute rightlessness, on the one hand, to absolute autonomy on the other, one may examine each case of oppression in terms of its location between the extremes on this continuum.

Slavery was not an American invention. It existed in ancient civilizations, was widespread throughout the Middle Ages, and was practiced legally until 1962 on the Arabian peninsula; and it remains today, unofficially, in countries such as the Sudan and Mauritania. For example, in 1996, in response to a United Nations report of "an alarming increase . . . in cases of slavery, slave trade, and forced labor" and to subsequent denials of these charges by Sudanese officials and by Reverend Louis Farrakhan, head of the Nation of Islam, two *Baltimore Sun* reporters journeyed illegally to the Sudan, where they bought two Dinka boys for $500 each from an Arab trader and returned them to their families, from whom they had been kidnapped (Lewthwaite and Kane 1996). Similarly, although slavery was formally abolished in Mauritania in 1961, it remained so widespread that in 1980 the country's president once again proclaimed it illegal. However, because the law freeing slaves specified that masters should be compensated for the loss of their property, the practice has persisted virtually unchanged to this day. As a woman whose ancestors had for generations been held in similar bondage recently reported to a *New York Times* reporter, "God created me to be a slave, just as he created a camel to be a camel" (Burkett 1997:56).

Even though there was a surge of historical interest in the institution of American slavery, especially during the 1970s and 1980s (Elkins 1959; Davis 1966, 1975; Genovese 1974; Gutman 1976; Yetman 1970, 1984; Blassingame 1972; Rawick 1972; Fogel and Engerman 1974; Levine 1977; Parish 1989), there has been a relative dearth of attention to comparisons of the wide range of forms of unfreedom that have existed throughout human history and that persist today. As we suggested earlier, examining the institution of slavery in the United States raises questions not only of its similarities to and differences from other slave systems, but also about what constitutes unfreedom itself and, thus, about the more general question of the nature and effects of institutional regimentation and exploitation. The implications of an analysis of slavery in America could be used to examine the dynamics of other total institutions (Goffman 1961) and other dominant-subordinate relationships (serfdom, caste systems, debt bondage, racial or ethnic ghettos, and various aboriginal reservation systems) that have not yet been considered in these terms.

Thus slavery and slave trading were well established among European and African peoples by the late–fifteenth century, when Columbus's encounter with the Americas triggered a dramatic expansion of European exploration, expansion, and colonization. However, the slave trade from Africa to the Western Hemisphere from the mid-1400s to the 1800s resulted in a system of exploitation that dwarfed the forms of slavery developed in Africa. The introduction of national monarchies and the growing industrial and commercial revolutions in the sixteenth through the nineteenth centuries acted as catalysts for the development of Western slave systems, in which slave labor became an indispensable component of European expansion and settlement of the New World. Between twelve to fifteen million people were uprooted in a forced migration unparalleled in human history. By the mid–nineteenth century, the United States had become the world's leading slave power, but slave systems had penetrated societies throughout South and Central America and the Caribbean.

Despite a history of slavery that preceded European settlement of the New World and some similarities to other slave systems in the Americas, the slave system that emerged in the United States was the outcome of a process that developed primarily in this country. Earlier we used Noel's (1972) model of the development of ethnic stratification to describe the process whereby Indian-European equality at their initial contacts was eventually transformed into a system of vast inequalities between them. We return to Noel's model, which emphasizes three conditions—ethnocentrism, competition, and differences in power—to examine the manner in which the system of racial stratification emerged in what is now the United States.

Anglo-American attitudes toward Africans had their origins in late sixteenth-century Elizabethan England, an era during which England had begun to expand its power and domination throughout the world. World exploration and colonial expansion brought the English into increasing contact with African peoples. From the beginning, these contacts were marked by extreme ethnocentrism on the part of the English. Because Africans had vastly different customs, languages, religious practices, and skin color, they were viewed negatively by the English.

In the English mainland colonies in America, some blacks initially held the same legal status—indentured servant—as certain whites and Indians. Upon completion of a stipulated period of service (usually seven years), indentured servants were entitled to the rights of free persons. Although blacks initially possessed a similar legal status with white indentured servants, by the 1660s the slave status, with its assumption of lifetime hereditary service, had evolved, and whatever ambiguity of status had previously existed for African peoples had now vanished. Thereafter the status of slave became reserved almost exclusively for blacks, and whites came to think of blacks primarily as slaves.

Ethnocentrism alone would not have resulted in blacks' being placed in a slave status. As Cornell points out in his analysis of the development of the minority statuses of Indians and African Americans (Article 8, "Land, Labour, and Group Formation"), the English need for land and for labor, respectively, undergirded their relationships with these two different categories of peoples. Whereas the desire for land led to competition with native peoples, cheap and abundant labor was essential if the English were to develop a dynamic plantation economy in the New World. The English turned to the vast labor supply that was to be found on the African continent and to the trade in enforced labor that was already flourishing by the time the English began to establish their mainland colonies in the seventeenth century.

Slavery was, above all, a power relationship. Had the English not possessed greater power in the form of superior weaponry, naval technology, and products with which to induce some Africans to assist them in enslaving other blacks, the system could not have developed. In other words, if one group had not possessed superior power, it would have been impossible to create a system of social inequality based on race alone. The Africans who were imported to the British colonies were doubly disadvantaged. Of all the groups (such as other English, Irish, and American Indians) whom the English had employed in the role of indentured servants, Africans were culturally and physically most alien and thus the object of greatest ethnocentrism. Equally critical, however, was that Africans were also the most defenseless and powerless. Africans had been forcibly uprooted from their own land, separated from family, kin, and tribe, and transported to a new and strange continent where they were thrown together with other Africans from a great diversity of ethnic backgrounds. This diversity undermined the unity or social solidarity upon which they might have collectively drawn to resist.

By contrast, because American Indians retained their tribal organizations and posed a substantial political and military threat to the colonies, they were less vulnerable to white domination as slaves. Indian slaves were also much more difficult to retain because, being familiar with the terrain, they could escape relatively easily and be reunited with their own peoples. Finally, because trade with Indian nations was important to local economies, Native Americans possessed power to discourage wholesale enslavement of their people to a far greater degree than did blacks. "Though [they were] exploited, excluded, and sometimes decimated in [their] contacts with European civilization, Indians always maneuvered from a position of strength which Africans, devoid of tribal unity, unaccustomed to the environment, and relatively defenseless, never enjoyed" (Noel 1972:148). Blacks were enslaved primarily because they provided a labor supply crucial to an emerging American economy, were culturally and physically distinct from the English, and, most important, possessed few resources with which to resist the imposition of the slave status by whites.

Slavery and Caste

However, if one closely examines the dynamics of black-white relations throughout the American experience, it is problematic whether slavery alone was the most critical feature in defining the enduring social inequalities that have characterized the status of African Americans. Crucial to an understanding of the dynamics of black-white relations in the United States is a racial distinction; slaves in the United States were subjected to racial discrimination as well as legal servitude. The most distinctive feature of black-white relations in the United States was not slavery, per se, but that blacks—slave or free—occupied a lower *caste* status as well. American slaves had to contend with the sanctions and effects of *two* inferior statuses—slave and lower-caste member—that were mutually reinforcing. Unlike the situation in many other slave societies, manumission (granting of freedom) of slaves in the United States was extremely difficult, and blacks who were free could not anticipate participation in the society on an equal basis.

Although slavery represented the most extreme form of institutionalized inequality between black and white in America, Leon Litwack (1961) has pointed out that during the slavery era, the rights and privileges of free blacks also were severely circumscribed throughout the entire society; critical to the understanding of the dynamics of race relations in the United States is that even those African Americans who were free during the slavery era (more than one-tenth of the black population) did not have the same rights and privileges as whites and were not accepted into society on an equal basis. Oppression of African Americans was by no means restricted to the South or to slaveholders; throughout the North, too, the freedom, rights, and privileges of free blacks were severely curtailed. At no time did the words *free person* or *freedom* mean the same thing to blacks as to whites. In many states, barriers to voting were initiated for blacks at the same time that restrictions for whites were being liberalized or eliminated. Court testimony and the formation of legal contracts and lawsuits by African Americans were also forbidden in many states. Several states prohibited immigration; others required that blacks carry identification passes (as in South Africa under apartheid). Excluded from public schools, African Americans were generally denied the benefits of formal education. In addition to these officially imposed disabilities, blacks in most areas were subjected to ridicule, harassment, and occasional mob violence (Litwack 1961).

Thus, in contrast to slaves in many other societies, slaves in the United States were subject to *racial* as well as legal servitude. For example, although Brazilian slavery was racially based, the inferior status of the slave did not persist into freedom in

Brazil with anything near the tenacity that it did in the United States. "In Brazil the slave may have been feared, but the black man was not, whereas in the United States both the slave and the black man were feared. . . . In the United States, slavery was always a means of organizing dangerous blacks as well as a way of organizing labor" (Degler 1971:89). Brazilians did not assume that a black person was a slave or that he or she would identify with slaves, an attitude that was in striking contrast to the perception in the United States. Brazilians used free blacks extensively as overseers, slave catchers, and slave dealers, a situation that would have been unthinkable in the United States. Brazilians also did not develop an elaborate racial justification for or defense of slavery. In sum, in Brazil, in contrast to the United States, a person's *legal* status (whether slave or free), not his or her *racial* identity, determined his or her standing in Brazilian society. In the United States, an individual's racial identity, not his or her legal status, was crucial.[2]

Therefore, the relegation of blacks to a lower caste status is of crucial importance, for it not only defined the experiences of both blacks and whites in the United States for the more than two-hundred years of slavery but also provided the basis for a system of social inequality that persisted long after the "peculiar institution" had been legally abolished in 1865. The most enduring feature of black-white relations in the United States has been that of caste.

The Aftermath of Slavery

Immediately after the Civil War, a period of fluid race relations occurred. Bolstered by passage of the 13th Amendment, which abolished slavery; the 14th Amendment, which extended to former slaves the equal protection of the law; and the 15th Amendment, which guaranteed to them the right to vote, African Americans actively sought to realize the opportunities and responsibilities of their new status (Litwak 1979).

Nevertheless, the reality of caste persisted. Patterns of black-white relations formed under slavery did not automatically change after emancipation; race relations continued to be based on a rigid caste system. The roles of African Americans after their emancipation became well defined and tightly circumscribed. The new legal status conferred by emancipation and the Reconstruction Amendments did little to alter the patterns of social relations in the plantation South, or to promote the acquisition of new values, habits, and attitudes by either black or white. Former slaves were formally given liberty but not the means (that is, economic, political, educational, and social equality) to realize it. Through intimidation, violence, lynching, and terrorism, African Americans were kept in a subordinate status and subjected to systematic racial discrimination long after slavery had been legally abolished. Blacks remained largely unskilled and illiterate, most of them living lives of enforced dependence on the still-dominant whites. The result was a black peasantry dominated by an agricultural system that ensured dependence on the land and isolation from the main currents of American society.

Northern troops, which had occupied the South during the period of Reconstruction, were removed in 1877, and Southern whites then resorted to a wide range of devices to ensure the maintenance of white dominance. Blacks, who during Reconstruction had voted and held public office, were systematically disenfranchised by a variety of mechanisms: white primary elections from which African Americans were excluded; poll taxes (which were cumulative); "grandfather clauses," which restricted voting to those (and their descendants) who had been eligible to vote before the Civil War; and literacy requirements, which, because they were selectively enforced, restricted even the most educated and literate African Americans from exercising the constitutionally mandated right to vote. The effects of these efforts to disfranchise blacks were dramatic. For example, in 1896 over 130,000 blacks were registered to vote in Louisiana; by 1904 this number had dropped to 1,342 (Norton et al. 1982:459). Moreover, although the 14th Amendment, which was adopted in 1868, includes explicit provisions that states restricting black access to the franchise would have their Congressional representation reduced, those provisions were never enforced.

Moreover, to ensure that white dominance would be perpetuated, a series of laws designed to maintain a strict caste system of black subordination and white dominance was enacted throughout the South during the last decade of the nineteenth and the first two decades of the twentieth century. Southern state legislatures enacted an extraordinary variety of state and municipal ordinances requiring racial separation and exclusion of African Americans from the legal, political, economic, and educational opportunities available to most other Americans. Virtually every aspect of contact between whites and blacks was legally regulated. The pervasiveness of the segregated system was signaled by a profusion of "Whites Only" and "Colored" signs that governed working conditions, public accommodations, state institutions, recreation, resorts, cemeteries, and housing.

It is important to emphasize that the racially segregated system of the South, which became known as "Jim Crow," was not simply a "natural" result of "traditional" relationships between black and white; rather, it was consciously *created* by whites to impose and maintain their political and economic power. During the 1950s and 1960s conservative resistance to the enactment of civil rights legislation to outlaw racial discrimination frequently invoked the argument that such legislation was unnecessary and inappropriate, and would be ineffective because "laws can't change the mores." Most who used this argument conveniently failed to recognize that the Jim Crow system itself had been constructed by the myriad number of discriminatory laws that had been enacted around the turn of the twentieth century.

In 1896 in the famous *Plessy v. Ferguson* decision, the United States Supreme Court provided judicial legitimation for the Jim Crow system, contending that

> the object of [Fourteenth Amendment's "equal protection clause"] was undoubtedly to enforce the absolute equality of the two races before the law, but in the nature of things it could not have been intended to abolish distinctions based upon color, or to enforce social, as distinguished from political equality, or a commingling of the two races upon terms unsatisfactory to either. (quoted in Kluger 1975:74)

Therefore, the Court reasoned, racially separate facilities required by the state do not imply the superiority of one group and the inferiority of another. If blacks perceive the restrictions placed on them as implying a "badge of inferiority," it is solely because they interpret the restrictions that way. The result was that, so long as the facilities were equal, legal segregation could not be construed as discrimination and was therefore constitutional. The *Plessy* "separate-but-equal" doctrine would stand for more than half a century as the law of the land, during which time the barriers of caste in virtually all arenas of American life—especially throughout the South—would be strengthened.

However, the Jim Crow system of racial segregation and the racial caste system on which it was based not only was supported by "legal" means but also was ultimately maintained through the use of force, violence, and intimidation, including lynching and terrorism. Between 1879 and 1909, more than 2,400 blacks were lynched throughout the South, often in response to white perceptions that they had violated "acceptable" patterns of deference expressed in terms of address, demeanor, and social relationships (the "etiquette of race relations") (Norton et al. 1994:524).

As a result of these legal and extralegal sanctions, the subordinate and subservient status of African Americans in the South persisted long after slavery had been abolished. Writing in 1929, Charles S. Johnson, a pioneer African American sociologist, noted the continuity between the slave plantation and rural Macon County, Alabama, during the 1920s:

> There have been retained only slightly modified most of the features of the plantation under the institution of slavery. . . . The Negro population of this section of Macon County has its own social heritage which, in a relatively complete isolation has had little chance for modification from without or within. Patterns of life, social codes, as well as social attitudes were set in the economy of slavery. The political and economic revolution through which they have passed has affected only slightly the social relationships of the community or the mores upon which these relations have been based. The strength and apparent permanence of this early cultural set have made it virtually impossible for new generations to escape the influence of the patterns of work and general social behavior transmitted by their elders. (Johnson 1934:16)

Similar reports noted the persistence of the slave plantation in many areas of the rural south well into the 1930s.

The Great Migration: From Plantation to Ghetto

In response to these oppressive conditions, after the turn of the twentieth century African Americans began to leave the South, a movement that has been called the Great Migration. For nearly a half century after Emancipation, the overwhelming majority of blacks lived in the South; in 1860, 92 percent lived there, and by 1910, this percentage had declined only slightly—to 89 percent. Although blacks migrated from east to west *within* the South during the late nineteenth century, the most noteworthy movement of African Americans out of the South was the "Exoduster Movement" of blacks to Kansas in the late 1870s. As Table 2 indicates, although there was a steady increase in black out-migration from the South after 1870, it was not until the 1910s that substantial numbers began to leave. Except for the 1930s, when the nation was locked in the throes of the Great Depression, these numbers increased in every decade until the 1960s, with the greatest numbers occurring during and after World War II.

Moving primarily to Northern urban areas, African Americans congregated in urban ghettos, geographically defined residential areas to which minority groups are restricted. This migration out of the rural South and the transformation of African Americans from an essentially rural to a predominantly urban people has been one of the most momentous events in the African-American experience and one of the most important demographic shifts in American history. As noted before, in 1900 almost

TABLE 2 *Black Out-Migration from the South, 1870–1970 (in thousands)*

1870–80	71
1880–90	80
1890–00	174
1900–10	197
1910–20	525
1920–30	877
1930–40	398
1940–50	1,468
1950–60	1,473
1960–70	1,380

Source: Farley and Allen 1987:113.

90 percent of the black population lived in the South; by 1990 the percentage in the South had declined to only 53 percent. In 1900 blacks were primarily rural residents, with only 23 percent living in urban areas. By 1996 nearly nine-tenths (86 percent) of the African American population lived in urban areas, indicating that blacks have become a more urbanized population than whites. Although a substantial portion of the increase in the number of urbanized African Americans was in the North, many lived in southern cities, such as Atlanta, Birmingham, New Orleans, Miami, and Houston as well. Between 1900 and 1996, the percentage of the Southern black population residing in metropolitan areas increased from 17 percent to 77 percent. Table 3 shows the percentage that blacks comprised in the major American cities for the years 1920, 1950, 1970, 1980, and 1990.

TABLE 3 *African American Population as Percent of the Total Population of the Ten Largest U.S. Cities,* * 1920, 1950, 1970, 1980, and 1990*

	1920[†]	1950[†]	1970	1980	1990
New York	2.7%	9.8%	21.1%	25.2%	28.7%
Los Angeles	2.7	10.7	17.9	17.0	14.0
Chicago	4.1	14.1	32.7	39.8	39.1
Houston	24.6	21.1	25.7	27.6	28.1
Philadelphia	7.4	18.3	33.6	37.8	39.9
San Diego	1.2	4.5	7.6	8.9	9.4
Detroit	4.1	16.4	43.7	63.1	75.7
Dallas	15.1	13.2	24.9	29.4	29.5
Phoenix	3.7	6.0	4.8	4.8	5.2
San Antonio	8.9	6.7	7.6	7.3	7.0

Source: U.S. Census of 1920; U.S. Census of 1950; U.S. Bureau of the Census. *Negroes in the United States, 1920–1932,* Washington, D.C.: U.S. Government Printing Office, 1935; "Characteristics of the Population," *Statistical Abstract of the United States,* 1972, pp. 21–23; *Statistical Abstract of the United States,* 1984, pp. 28–30; U.S. Department of Commerce, *Statistical Abstract of the United States, 1996,* Washington, D.C.: U.S. Government Printing Office, 1996, pp. 44–46.

*These were the ten largest cities in the United States in 1990.

[†]Figures pertain to "nonwhite" population, of which over 90 percent was black.

The massive migration of African Americans out of the South transformed race relations in the United States. As Waldo Martin has written, "urbanization has nationalized the locus of African American life and culture" (Martin 1992:354).

Wilson has characterized the period from the late nineteenth century to the post–World War II era as the *industrial* period of race relations. His description of the transition from preindustrial to industrial parallels van den Berghe's distinction between *paternalistic* race relations, which were characteristic of a plantation economy, and *competitive* race relations, which are found in an urban, industrial setting. In the industrial setting, competition for jobs generated considerable racial antagonism, tension, and conflict. (For a superb analysis of this conflict, see Tuttle 1972, especially Chapter 4.)

The Great Migration of African Americans out of the South ultimately proved to be one of the most important factors underlying the Black Protest Movement that swept the nation during the late 1950s and 1960s. Although discrimination against African Americans in education, employment, housing, and the administration of justice also prevailed in the North, a greater range of opportunities for blacks was available in northern urban areas than in the South. Especially after World War II, increasing numbers of African Americans obtained college educations and found employment in skilled and white-collar occupations. These changes expanded the African American middle class, which provided the primary source of leadership for the Black Protest Movement. The educated and articulate African American middle class played an especially important role in providing legal challenges to the southern Jim Crow system, which culminated in the Supreme Court's 1954 *Brown vs. Board of Education* decision that segregated schools were inherently unequal and therefore unconstitutional. The *Brown* decision, which overturned the 1896 separate-but-equal doctrine, symbolized the beginning of an era in which the legal basis for the caste system would crumble. In Part 4, we will examine the changing status of African Americans during the post–World War II era, the period that Wilson has characterized as the *modern industrial* stage of American race relations.

Hispanic Americans/Latinos

Hispanic Americans constitute one of the largest and most rapidly growing ethnic categories in contemporary American society. During the 1980s the *Hispanic* or *Latino* population grew nearly five times faster than the rest of the population, and their rate of growth has declined only slightly during the 1990s. By 1998 the U.S. Census Bureau estimated the Hispanic population at nearly 30 million, or 11.1 percent of the total population. Recent projections suggest that the Latino population will surpass the African American population by 2010, and total nearly 90 million, or 22 percent of the population, by 2050 (Day 1993). This dramatic increase in the Hispanic population in the United States is the result of both higher Hispanic fertility rates and substantially increased rates of immigration from Latin America, especially from Mexico.

The recent growth of the Latino population has produced some dramatic changes in the ethnic composition of many American cities. By 1994 Hispanics outnumbered blacks in four of the nation's ten largest cities—Los Angeles, Houston, Phoenix, and San Antonio, as well as such other major cities as Miami, El Paso, Pittsburgh, and San

Francisco. And, given their higher growth rates, Hispanics are projected to exceed blacks in New York City in the very near future.

As we will see in Part 4, vast social inequalities, poverty, and political repression all influence migration pressures in Latin America. A crucial dimension contributing to these problems is demographic: the recent rapid population growth in both Central and South America. During the 1950s, the total population for all of Latin America was approximately the same as that of the United States—about 150 million. However, by 2025 it is expected to be 845 million, or about three times the projections of the U.S. population (Fallows 1983:45; Davis, Haub, and Willette 1983:39).

The overall economic status of Latinos, which until the 1990s had been consistently higher than that of African Americans, began a steady decline in the early 1980s, which by 1995 resulted in a median family income below that of African Americans. In 1979 Hispanic median family income stood at $29,180 (in 1995 dollars) —71 percent of white median family income; it has never since achieved this level, standing at $24,569 (or 58 percent of white income) in 1995 (see Table 4). More than one-quarter (27 percent) of Hispanic families lived in poverty. Reflecting the interrelated impact of class, gender, and ethnicity, more than half (53 percent) of poor Hispanic families were headed by women (compared with 30 percent of non-Hispanic white families in poverty) (U.S. Bureau of the Census 1996a; 1996b). Forty percent of all Hispanic children lived in poverty, and during the 1980s, childhood poverty increased more rapidly among Hispanics than among any other racial or ethnic category (U.S. Bureau of the Census 1996b). Finally, by 1993 the median net worth of Hispanic households had declined to one-tenth that of white households, approximately the same as that of African Americans (U.S. Bureau of the Census 1997).

Since 1970 the educational attainments of Hispanic Americans have improved substantially. The proportion of adult Hispanics with less than a fifth-grade education declined. The proportion who were high school graduates increased from less than one-third (32 percent) in 1970 to more than half (53 percent) in 1993; similarly, the proportion who were college graduates doubled, increasing from less than one-twentieth (4.5 percent) in 1970 to nearly one-tenth (9.4 percent) of the adult Hispanic population in 1992 (U.S. Bureau of the Census 1993; 1994). Nevertheless, Hispanics still lag considerably behind the educational attainments of non-Hispanic whites, Asian Americans, and African Americans. In 1995 only slightly more than half of 18- to 24-year-old Hispanics had graduated from high school, compared with seven-eighths (87 percent) of both blacks and non-Hispanic whites. Moreover, only 21 percent of 18- to 24-year old Latinos were enrolled in college, compared with 35 percent of non-Hispanic whites and 25 percent of African Americans (Carter and Wilson 1994; 1995).

The Latino political presence in American society has changed substantially in the past quarter century. Between 1972 and 1992 the Latino electorate increased by 162 percent—from 5.6 million to 14.7 million. Reflecting the impact of the 1965 Voting Rights Act and the rapidly increasing Hispanic population, in the past two decades Latinos have gained political strength; by 1995, 5,459 Hispanics held public office in the United States. Nevertheless, Hispanics still accounted for only about 1 percent of all elected public officials, far below the nearly 11 percent of the population that they represent (Brimhall-Vargas 1994).

One reason for the relatively small number of Latino elected officials figures is that although Latinos have been numerically the fastest-growing ethnic category in the United States in the past quarter century, Latino political *participation*—both as voters and as candidates for public office—has not increased proportionately. On the one hand, a substantial portion of the Hispanic population is recent immigrants, who are ineligible for citizenship until they have lived in the country for at least five years. Moreover, Latinos (Mexican Americans, in particular) are characterized by extremely low rates of naturalization. For example, in 1989, only 13 percent of Mexican immigrants who had arrived in the U.S. during the 1970s had become citizens, whereas 55 percent of Asians had. Moreover, the Hispanic population is very young, with a median age of twenty-six, compared with thirty-four for whites, twenty-eight for blacks, and thirty for Asians. Thus a substantial proportion of the Hispanic population is either not yet old enough to vote or among the extremely young voters, whose rates of political participation are typically the lowest. However, as their population ages and increasing numbers of immigrants achieve citizenship, "Latinos remain poised to wield the political power that has remained elusive thus far" (Coleman 1995:28). The increasing impact of Latino political strength was apparent during the 1996 presidential and congressional elections, in which Hispanic voters went to the polls in record numbers, where they overwhelmingly supported President Clinton and contributed to upset victories by several Hispanic congressional candidates.

However, to refer to Spanish-speaking people as a single ethnic category is misleading. The terms *Hispanic* or *Latino*, which are of recent origin, obscure the great diversity of historical, cultural, and geographic backgrounds among them. Although Latinos are more likely than the rest of the U.S. population to be Spanish-speaking, Catholic, and poor, they do not constitute a single ethnic category. The category of "Hispanics" includes representatives from more than twenty Latin American and Caribbean nations, as well as from Spain and Portugal. More than three-fourths of Hispanic Americans are of Mexican, Puerto Rican, or Cuban descent, but there are also substantial communities of people from the Dominican Republic, Colombia, Ecuador, El Salvador, Guatemala, Nicaragua, and several other Caribbean, Central American, and South American nations (U.S. Bureau of the Census 1993). These groups also differ in their socioeconomic status and in their regional distribution in the United States. We focus here on the three largest Hispanic groups: Mexicans, Puerto Ricans, and Cubans, which together make up more than three-fourths of the Hispanic population.

Mexican Americans

Mexican Americans, or Chicanos (from the Spanish *Mexicanos*), are the largest Hispanic group and (after African Americans) the second largest ethnic minority in American society. Today nearly 18 million people of Mexican ancestry live in the United States, about 90 percent of them in the five southwestern states of Texas, New Mexico, Arizona, Colorado, and California. Next to the North American Indians, with whom they share a common ancestry, they represent the oldest ethnic category in American society. The Mexican American people are the biological and cultural descendants of the Spanish military and religious conquest of the native peoples of northern Central America. From the early 1600s to the mid-1800s, Spain, and, later, Mexico, colonized and exerted political, economic, and cultural dominance over the region. By the turn of the nineteenth century, Mexican culture, a mixture of Spanish and American Indian influences, was well established throughout what is today the southwestern United States.

The process of contact between Mexicans and the Anglo immigrants who settled in Texas in increasing numbers during the early nineteenth century provides another opportunity to test Noel's model of the emergence of ethnic stratification. Initially Anglos and Mexicans coexisted, although each viewed the other warily and with antipathy and distrust that had grown out of two centuries of English and Spanish competition for world dominance. Mutual ethnocentrism between the two peoples occurred from the start, with Anglos regarding the darker-skinned Mexicans as "racially" and culturally inferior, and with Mexicans seeing in the growing encroachment of the Americans confirmation of their stereotypes of Yankee aggressiveness and greed. Anglos and Mexicans also differed in religion and class structure. To ensure the loyalty of early–nineteenth-century Anglo colonists, most of whom were Protestants, the Mexican government required that they become Roman Catholics as well as Mexican citizens. Even more offensive to the sensibilities of Anglo settlers, many of whom had emigrated from the American South and were slaveholders, was the Mexican prohibition of slavery. Although slavery was illegal, Mexican society was highly stratified, with a small, wealthy upper class and a large class of the very poor. Anglo-Americans, literate and middle-class in outlook, developed a perception of the Mexican people as indolent and lazy (McLemore 1973).

Despite these differences, Anglo and Mexican Texans initially coexisted, cooperated, and in the Texas Revolt of 1835–36 together fought a common enemy, the Mexican central government controlled by Santa Ana. Both Anglos and Mexicans died fighting Santa Ana in the Alamo. After Santa Ana's defeat, however, competition between Anglo and Mexican for land in the newly independent Texas Republic became increasingly intense. In 1845 the United States granted statehood to Texas, and a year later the United States and Mexico were engaged in a war that would result in the loss of over half of Mexico's previous territory. The 1848 Treaty of Guadalupe-Hidalgo, in which Mexico ceded to the United States most of the land of the present-day Southwest, signaled the triumph of Anglo power. Although the treaty guaranteed legal and property rights to Mexican citizens in the newly acquired territories, Mexican Americans soon became the object of persistent discrimination. Anglos, especially in Texas, established a system of caste relations, which ensured Chicano political, social, and economic subordination. By the eve of the Civil War, the American military conquest of Mexican lands in the Southwest had been completed. In the ensuing years those Mexicans who chose to remain in the annexed territories were largely dispossessed of both their land and the prominence they had occupied in Mexican society. By the turn of the twentieth century, Mexicans had been "relegated to a lower-class status, [in which] they were overwhelmingly dispossessed landless laborers, politically and economically impotent," which was justified by notions of racial inferiority (Estrada et al. 1981:109). For this reason, Alvarez (1973) has argued that the subjugation of this "creation generation" after the Mexican War was formative, in much the same sense that Bryce-Laporte (1969) has characterized slavery as "the contextual baseline of Black American experience."

The vast territory incorporated into the United States as a result of the 1848 Treaty of Guadalupe-Hidalgo was at the time extremely sparsely settled, with those identifying themselves as Mexican (as opposed to various American Indian identities) numbering only about 60,000. However, as American settlement increased throughout the last half of the nineteenth century, the Mexican presence dwindled and their political and economic influence declined.

Whereas the earliest Mexican American population became an American minority through the annexation of Mexican lands by the United States, the primary source of the majority of the Chicano population in the United States has been immigration, both legal and undocumented.

Although a substantial proportion of the contemporary Chicano population is derived from the migrant generation that followed that surge of European immigration into the United States during the early twentieth century, the situation of Mexican immigrants differed substantially from that of European immigrant groups because Mexican immigrants entered a society that had already adopted a clearly defined lower-caste role for them as a result of the mid–nineteenth-century conquest patterns of subordination.

This immigration, most of which has occurred during the twentieth century, has been instrumental in the economic development of the American Southwest. Mexican immigrants provided a readily available and exploitable source of cheap labor, especially for the expansion of the railroad industry, mining, and above all, agriculture (Estrada et al. 1981). Indeed, Mexican labor played an integral role in the dramatic expansion of agribusiness interests in the Southwest. During the first two decades of the twentieth century, many Mexicans fled to the United States from the upheavals of the Mexican Revolution. As European immigration to the United States was curtailed by the outbreak of World War I and the passage of the restrictive legislation of the 1920s, Mexican labor filled the growing demand for agricultural workers to replace those who had left for jobs in the nation's industrial sector. The defense employment boom generated by World War II produced a shift of the Chicano population away from rural areas and agricultural pursuits, while at the same time the bracero program, which ran from 1942 to 1965, ensured a continuing source of cheap agricultural labor from Mexico. As Massey (1986b; Massey et al. 1987) and Rouse (Article 26) have pointed out, the general migration of Mexicans to work in the United States earlier in the twentieth century and in the bracero program, in particular, played a major role in establishing the circular migration networks that sustain Mexican migration to the United States today.

Several indicators reveal that Mexican Americans lag considerably behind the mainstream of American society in socioeconomic status. Despite some evidence of improvement among younger generations, Mexican American educational attainment is less than that of both whites and African Americans. However, they tend to be found primarily in low-paying blue-collar and semiskilled occupations that have been especially hard hit by the decline of manufacturing and by the downsizing of economic sectors, such as military-related jobs, that have contributed to rising Hispanic unemployment during a period of economic growth (1992—1998) in which overall unemployment declined. As Table 4 indicates, in 1995 median family income for Mexican Americans was only 58 percent of white median family income; more than one-fourth (28 percent) of Mexican American families had incomes below the poverty level (U.S. Bureau of the Census 1995).

Although Chicanos still comprise a substantial proportion of the nation's migratory farmworkers, today they are overwhelmingly—more than 80 percent—urban residents, especially in the major urban areas of the Southwest. Indeed, today more people of Mexican descent live in Los Angeles than in any other city except Mexico City and Guadalajara. As their numbers and their concentration in urban areas has increased, Mexican Americans, like other Hispanic groups, have also become an increasingly

TABLE 4 *Median Family Income, 1995*

	Income in Dollars	*Percent of White Income*
All races	40,612	
White	42,646	
Black	25,970	61%
Hispanic	24,569	58
Mexican	23,485	55
Puerto Rican	22,121	52
Cuban	32,471	76
Central & South American	26,915	63
Other Hispanic*	26,826	63

Sources: U.S Bureau of the Census, "Money Income in the United States, 1995," *Current Population Reports,* P60–193, Washington, D.C.: U.S. Government Printing Office, 1996. U.S. Bureau of the Census, "The Hispanic Population of the United States: Current Population Survey, March 1996." [online] Available: http://www.census.gov/population/socdemo/hispanic/cps96/sumtab-4.txt [1998, March 12].

*Includes those who identified themselves as from Spain or as Hispanic, Spanish, Spanish American, Hispanic, or Latino.

salient force in American politics, especially because of their substantial presence in the electorally significant states of Texas and California.

The other major groups of Spanish-speaking people are relatively recent immigrant groups who have settled primarily in urban areas on the East coast since the end of World War II. Although the number of immigrants from countries throughout the Caribbean and Central and South America has increased markedly during this period, the two Caribbean islands of Puerto Rico and Cuba have been the primary sources of this influx of Spanish-speaking peoples. These two groups provide an interesting contrast in backgrounds and adaptations to American society.

Puerto Ricans

Puerto Ricans, who, unlike other immigrants, are American citizens, began migrating to the mainland primarily after World War II. Today nearly two-thirds of the more than 2 million Puerto Ricans on the mainland live in New York City, which has been the principal magnet for these immigrants. This migration to the mainland has been prompted primarily by economic pressures among the impoverished lower strata of Puerto Rican society.

Among Hispanic groups, Puerto Ricans have a unique relationship with the United States. The island of Puerto Rico was ceded to the United States in 1898 after the United States defeat of Spain in the Spanish-American War. Despite changes in the twentieth century, the status of Puerto Rico has in many respects continued to resemble that of a colonial dependency. Although Puerto Ricans were granted American citizenship in 1917, they have retained their language and cultural traditions, which are different from the dominant language and culture of the United States. Puerto Ricans' determination to maintain their cultural distinctiveness has been an important element in the continuing debate over whether the island should become an independent nation, become the fifty-first American state, or retain its present commonwealth status.

Numbering 2.3 million people on the mainland, Puerto Ricans are today the largest Hispanic group outside the Southwest. Puerto Rican residents began migrating to the United States early in the twentieth century, but it was not until the advent of relatively cheap commercial air travel after World War II that they began to arrive in substantial numbers, settling primarily in New York City. Today about 40 percent of all Puerto Ricans live on the mainland, and because of the ease of travel to and from the island and the personal networks that it has facilitated, it has been estimated that half of all island Puerto Ricans have at some time shared the mainland experience (Levine 1987:95). Although Puerto Ricans continue to reside primarily on the East coast, especially in New York City, increasing numbers have recently begun to settle in midwestern and far western cities such as Chicago, Cleveland, and Los Angeles.

The Puerto Rican migration to the mainland must be seen in the context of the economic and political relationship between the United States and Puerto Rico, which Levine (1987) has characterized as "imperial development." The migration was prompted primarily by extremely high unemployment in Puerto Rico, and it has fluctuated in response to economic opportunities in the United States. Given the historic underdevelopment of the Puerto Rican economy, Puerto Rican immigrants to the United States have been overwhelmingly unskilled and have experienced difficulties in an increasingly technological society. Concentrated in blue-collar semiskilled and unskilled occupations and subjected to racial discrimination, Puerto Ricans are, as Bean and Tienda (Article 10) point out, "the most socially and economically disadvantaged of Hispanic origin groups with poverty, labor force participation and unemployment rates and average earnings comparable to those of Native Americans and blacks." As Table 4 indicates, Puerto Rican median family income (in 1995, 52 percent of white median family income) is the lowest, and their poverty rate (36 percent) is among the highest among American ethnic groups.

Cuban Americans

Although Cuban immigrants to the United States have been recorded as early as the 1870s, the Cuban American community today is composed primarily of relatively recent political refugees. Approximately 750,000 Cubans have entered the United States since Fidel Castro's rise to power in 1959, and today they number more than one million. In contrast to most previous immigrations to the United States (with the notable exception of the Huguenots during the colonial period and those fleeing from Nazi Germany during the 1930s), the initial Cuban émigrés tended to be drawn mainly from the upper social and economic strata of Cuban society. Drawn disproportionately from well-educated middle-class and upper-class professional and business backgrounds, they brought skills (educational, occupational, business, and managerial), entrepreneurial values, and substantial amounts of financial capital that enabled them to prosper and achieve relatively rapid socioeconomic success. Assisted by federal government programs that facilitated their adjustment to American society, in the thirty years since their initial migration, Cubans have become the most affluent of all Hispanic groups and are an integral part of the economies of a number of American cities, especially Miami, Florida, which they have transformed into a major international business and commercial center with ties throughout Latin America. Nevertheless, in 1995 Cuban family income was still only three-fourths (76 percent) of non-Hispanic white income, and the Cuban poverty rate was 16 percent compared with the overall white rate of 11 percent (U.S. Bureau of the Census 1995).

The most recent influx of Cubans—those who left Cuba during the so-called Freedom Flotilla or Mariel Boatlift of 1980—numbered about 125,000. A substantial proportion of this recent migration was people of working-class and lower-class origins (Davis, Haub, and Willette 1983:23).

Asian Americans

Asians are an extremely diverse category, differing in linguistic, cultural, historical, national, and class backgrounds. Historically the Chinese, the Japanese, and, later, the Filipinos, have been the most prominent Asian groups; most Koreans, Asian Indians, Vietnamese, Cambodians, and Laotians are more recent arrivals. Compared with the many millions of Europeans who have migrated to the United States, Asian immigration has, until recently, been modest. At no time until the past two decades did the numbers of Asian immigrants ever approximate those from Europe. For example, Chinese immigration reached its peak during the decade from 1873 to 1882, when 161,000 Chinese entered the country (a period during which nearly half a million Irish and nearly a million German immigrants were received). Peak Japanese immigration occurred during the decade between 1900 and 1909, when 139,000 entered (at the same time that nearly 2 million immigrants from Italy and more than 1.5 million from what later became the Soviet Union were admitted). In contrast, between 1840 and 1920 there were thirty-one different years when the number of immigrants from a *single* European country alone exceeded 150,000. As Figure 3 on page 98 reveals, the total number of immigrants from Asia, in general, and Japan and China, in particular, have been insubstantial when considered in the context of American immigration as a whole. What is significant, however, is the response that the presence of Asian immigrants generated, and the subsequent adaptation of Asian peoples to discrimination in the United States, which we will discuss later.

However, partly as a result of changes in American immigration laws, which before 1965 had virtually excluded them, Asians are today *proportionately* the nation's fastest-growing racial category. Since 1970, Asians have constituted more than one-third (35 percent) of all legal immigrants, and the Asian population of the United States has increased by 648 percent, compared with increases by Hispanics of 219 percent, by American Indians of 179 percent, by African Americans of 50 percent, and by European Americans of 24 percent. By 1998 Asians numbered 10.2 million, which represented 3.8 percent of the American people. The rapid growth of the Asian American population is expected to continue during the twenty-first century, reaching over 40 million (or 10 percent of the population) by 2050 (Day 1993). Although almost all states have experienced substantial increases in Asian residents during the last quarter of the twentieth century, almost 40 percent of Asian Americans live in California, where they make up 10 percent of the state's population (Barringer 1991; U.S. Immigration and Naturalization Service 1997; U.S. Bureau of the Census online 1997).

Early Immigrants: Chinese and Japanese

The earliest modern Asian immigrants were the Chinese, who migrated to North America beginning in the 1840s. During the next four decades more than 200,000 Chinese immigrants, primarily unskilled laborers, arrived. Filling a need for labor created by the economic development of the West in the mid–nineteenth century (especially in mining and in building the transcontinental railroad), the Chinese were initially welcomed. As their numbers increased, however, the Chinese became perceived as an economic threat to native labor, and racist opposition to them mounted. As a consequence the Chinese were subjected to various forms of harassment, mob violence, and discriminatory legislation, including laws designed specifically to harass them. Finally, in response to anti-Chinese agitation in California, Congress passed the Chinese Exclusion Act of 1882, which was the first federal law to restrict immigration of a specific nationality to the United States. In contrast, more than forty years were to pass before substantial restrictions were placed on European immigration (Hsu 1971; Lyman 1974; Nee and Nee 1973).

The anti-Asian sentiment that pervaded the hysteria over Chinese immigration was revived when the Japanese immigrated in the early twentieth century. Although the Japanese represented an extremely small proportion of the population of both California and the nation as a whole, their presence generated intense nativist hostility. Like the Chinese before them, the Japanese were the object of legislation designed to harass and intimidate them. In 1906 the San Francisco Board of Education precipitated an international incident when it attempted to place all Japanese children, native and foreign-born, in a segregated "Oriental" school in Chinatown. Immediate protests from the Japanese ambassador ultimately led the school board to rescind its order; but the Board of Education's segregation efforts in reality were stymied only because President Theodore Roosevelt was able in 1907 to negotiate the so-called Gentleman's Agreement with Japan. Under this agreement, the American government agreed to end discrimination against Japanese living in the United States, and Japan pledged to grant visas to the United States only to family members of Japanese citizens residing there.

Even this accommodation failed to satisfy exclusionists, and in 1913 the California legislature enacted an alien land law barring the Japanese, who had become successful farmers, from owning agricultural land. As sentiment for the general restriction of immigration increased during the first three decades of the twentieth century, further limitations were placed on Asian immigration; in 1924 the Johnson-Reed Act prohibited completely all Asian immigration, and the provisions of this legislation remained virtually intact (with some minor adjustments during the 1940s and 1950s) until the antidiscriminatory Immigration Act of 1965 went into effect in the late 1960s.

This anti-Asian agitation, to which the early Chinese and Japanese immigrants especially were subjected, drew support from the same "scientific" sources that provided the intellectual respectability for racist thought described earlier. Ultimately, this fear of the "yellow peril" contributed to the forcible evacuation and relocation of nearly 120,000 Japanese Americans—more than two-thirds of them American citizens—by the federal government during World War II (Thomas and Nishimoto 1969; Grodzins 1966; Bosworth 1967; Kitano 1969; Daniels 1972, 1993). In Article 11, "Asian Pacific Americans," Don Mar and Marlene Kim contextualize Asian migration and adaptation to the United States in terms of broad structural changes in American society and the global economy.

Despite early antipathy toward the Chinese and Japanese, and the particular hostility toward the Japanese during World War II, both groups have made substantial improvements in socioeconomic status. Their achievements have contributed substantially to the overall socioeconomic status of Asian Americans. By 1990, 37 percent of the Asian population over age twenty-five had completed at least four years of college, which was nearly double the figure (22 percent) for non-Hispanic whites (U.S. Bureau of the Census 1992). So extraordinary have Asian educational attainments been that charges have been raised that many of the nation's most prestigious universities have placed limits on the numbers of Asian students they would admit (Mathews 1987).

As a consequence of their relatively high educational attainments, a disproportionate percentage of Japanese and Chinese are found in professional occupational categories. By the 1980s the income levels of American-born and immigrant Asians were not significantly different from those of whites who had comparable skills, and by 1990 actually slightly exceeded those of whites; in 1990 more than one-third (35 percent) of Asian American households had incomes of $50,000 or more, compared with 26 percent of non-Hispanic white households. By 1995 Asian median family income was 109 percent of white family income (compared with 61 percent for black and 58 percent for Hispanic families) (U.S. Bureau of the Census 1992; U.S. Bureau of the Census 1997 online). As we will explore more fully in Parts 3 and 4, these educational and economic attainments have contributed to the stereotype of Asian Americans as "model minorities."

The public perception of Asian educational and economic success, however, masks continued discrimination against them (Kuo 1995). Asians generally earn less than do non-Hispanic whites of the same age and educational characteristics, and studies have demonstrated that Asians gain 21 percent less than do non-Hispanic whites from each year of schooling. Moreover, the relatively high levels of Asian household income may reflect a greater number of family household members who work (O'Hare and Felt 1991). Finally, focusing on overall income and educational attainments obscures substantial differences among Asian groups. Although Japanese, Chinese, and Koreans have incomes above those of whites, Filipinos, Asian Indians, and Vietnamese earn less. Reflecting this fact, during the 1980s the poverty rate for Asians actually increased, and by 1995 it was 12.4 percent, nearly double the rate (6.4 percent) for non-Hispanic whites (U.S. Commission on Civil Rights 1988; U.S. Bureau of the Census 1996, vii).

Later Immigrants: Filipinos, Koreans, Indochinese, and Indians

As the data in Figure 3 on page 98 indicate, the numbers of several Asian groups—especially Chinese, Filipinos, Koreans, Indochinese, and Asian Indians—have recently increased dramatically. With the exception of the Chinese, whose presence in the United States was firmly established in the nineteenth century, these groups have emerged primarily since passage of the 1965 Immigration Reform Act.

Like Puerto Rico, the Philippine Islands were acquired by the United States from Spain in 1898 after the Spanish-American War, and the country has been economically dependent on the United States throughout the twentieth century, even after it gained its political independence in 1946. Because the Philippines was considered a territory of the United States, Filipinos were not initially subject to the immigration restrictions placed on other Asian groups. As residents of a U.S. possession, Filipinos were not included in the provisions of the 1924 Johnson-Reed Act that excluded immigration from elsewhere in Asia. Thus, when other Asian immigration was halted, Filipino laborers replaced the Chinese and Japanese as agricultural workers in California and Hawaii, and they also worked in the Alaskan salmon fisheries. However, in 1935, in the midst of the Great Depression, Filipino immigration was restricted as well. An annual quota of 50 Filipinos was established, and it was "liberalized" to 100 in 1946, when the Philippines was granted full political independence. Thus Filipino immigration between 1935 and 1965, when the Immigration Act eliminated national quotas, was negligible.

In 1960 Filipinos numbered only 176,000, a substantial portion of whom lived in Hawaii. The great preponderance of Filipino immigration to the United States, therefore, has come since 1965. The 1970 census recorded 343,000 Filipinos. Their numbers more than doubled, to 775,000 during the 1970s and nearly doubled again during the 1980s, recording a total of 1.4 million in 1990 (see Table 1). However, because Filipinos, unlike other recent Asian immigrants, have not established identifiable ethnic communities, they have tended to be invisible, and their status as the second-largest Asian group in the United States today may therefore come as a surprise to many people. Like many other recent Asian immigrant groups, Filipino immigrants today have much higher educational levels than previous Filipino immigrants, and they have included high percentages of professional and technical workers, especially physicians and nurses. Despite these qualifications, Filipinos are much more likely than whites to work in occupations below their educational levels (Takaki 1989:434–436).

Koreans are also a relatively recent ethnic group in American society. Although a small number of Koreans, primarily agricultural laborers who migrated to Hawaii, were recorded in the census as early as 1910, as late as 1950 there were still fewer than 10,000 in the United States. A small portion of the increase since 1950 resulted from marriages of Koreans to members of the American armed forces stationed in Korea during and after the Korean War and from the adoption of Korean orphans.

However, most of the dramatic increase in Korean Americans—nearly 800,000 in 1990—has occurred since the 1965 Immigration Act went into effect in 1968. Reflecting their relatively recent arrival, in 1980 nearly seven in ten Koreans (69.3 percent) had arrived in the previous decade (Xenos et al. 1987:256). Reflecting the post–Korean War modernization of South Korea, Koreans, like most other recent Asian immigrants, have had high educational attainments—for example, in 1980 more than 93 percent of Koreans had completed high school (Xenos 1987:270). Moreover, Koreans are more likely than the white population to be found in the two most prestigious and best paid occupational categories: executive, administrative, and managerial positions and the professions (Xenos et al. 1987). In contrast to the invisibility of the Filipinos, Korean communities have recently become very visible in several American cities, most notably New York City and Los Angeles. One of the most distinctive features of these communities has been the prominence of Korean small business enterprises, a phenomenon that is discussed in Part 3. Utilizing ethnic resources such as the *kye,* or rotating credit association, and capital accumulated in Korea, they have been especially prominent as proprietors of greengroceries, fish retail businesses, and dry cleaning establishments (Kim 1981, 1988; Light and Bonacich 1988; Takaki 1989:436–445).

The migration of Asian Indians to the United States began as early as the 1880s, when Hawaii's sugar planters recruited Indian workers to supply their labor needs. During the last decade of the nineteenth and the first two decades of the twentieth century, small numbers of Indians—primarily male sojourners who worked in the railroad and lumber industries and in agriculture—immigrated to the U.S. mainland. Although these early immigrants were called "Hindus" by Americans, they included Muslims and Sikhs as well. Although Caucasian, they were included in the anti-Asian hysteria directed against the Chinese, Japanese, and Koreans and the subsequent legislation restricting Asian immigration. By the end of World War II, the Asian-Indian population numbered only 1,500 (Takaki 1989). Most Asian Indians in the United States today, therefore, are products of the second wave of Indian migration begun after 1968. The 1980 census found 362,000 Indians, and this number increased to 815,000 by 1990 (see Table 1). Unlike earlier Indian immigrants, who were unskilled, this second wave has overwhelmingly been comprised of highly educated professionals. For example, 1980 census data revealed that nearly 90 percent of all Asian Indians over the age of twenty-five had completed high school, and two-thirds had completed college, in contrast to two-thirds of the total U.S. population who had completed high school and only one-sixth who had completed college (Bouvier and Gardner 1986:22).

Peoples from Indochina, the country's most recent arrivals, represent a diversity of ethnic groups from Vietnam, Laos, and Cambodia. Most Indochinese have been refugees who have immigrated since the fall of Saigon in 1975. In 1990 they collectively totaled about 1 million, approximately two-thirds of whom are Vietnamese (Bouvier and Agresta 1987:292). It is anticipated that, because of the continuing social, political, and economic upheavals in southeast Asia, these numbers will continue to be reinforced in the near future. Many of the earliest Vietnamese immigrants were highly educated and possessed marketable technical skills. Later arrivals, including most Laotians, Cambodians, and Hmong have had fewer such resources and no established ethnic enclave to provide economic and social support. Consequently, their adjustment to American society has been much more difficult than that of many other recent Asian immigrants.

The recent increase of immigration from the Third World—especially from Latin America and Asia—has contributed substantially to some of the most dramatic changes in the ethnic composition of the United States in its history. Today more than one-quarter of all Americans are of Native American, African, Hispanic, or Asian descent. By the year 2020—approximately one generation from now—nearly one-third of the nation will be nonwhite (Quality Education for Minorities Project 1990). Any effort to comprehend both the short-term and long-term implications of these changes in the ethnic composition of American society must consider at least three basic factors: (1) recent changes in global political and economic structures; (2) structural changes in the American economy; and (3) the patterns of ethnic and racial relations that have previously been manifested in the American experience. In Parts 3 and 4 we will examine the nature of intergroup relations in, and ethnic adaptations to, American society. We will also speculate on how these recent trends may affect future patterns of race and ethnicity in the United States.

ENDNOTES

1. The total number of federally recognized Indian tribes and Alaska Native groups in 1997 was 554 (U.S. Department of the Interior, 1997).

2. Whether these historical differences have produced a racially more open society—a "racial democracy"—in contemporary Brazil, as much of the previous scholarship has assumed, has recently been questioned. See, for example, Skidmore 1993.

Patterns of Ethnic Integration in America

3

The dominant conceptual framework in the analysis of American ethnic and racial relations has been an assimilation model. One of the earliest and most influential statements of the assimilation model was embodied in the classic "race relations cycle" advanced by sociologist Robert E. Park in 1926:

> In the relations of races there is a cycle of events which tends everywhere to repeat itself. The race relations cycle, which takes the form . . . of contacts, competition, accommodation, and eventual assimilation, is apparently progressive and irreversible. Customs regulations, immigration restrictions, and racial barriers may slacken the tempo of the movement; may perhaps halt it altogether for a time, but cannot change its direction, cannot, at any rate, reverse it. (Park 1950:150)

According to the assimilation model of intergroup contact, interethnic relations inevitably go through successive stages of competition, conflict, accommodation, and assimilation. In Article 13 ("Revisiting Assimilation") Russell Kazal documents the widespread and enduring impact of the assimilation model.

In Part 2 we focused especially on the first phase of Park's race relations cycle: the *origins* of ethnic stratification that are characterized by contact and competition. However, the succeeding stages in Park's cycle are more problematic. For example, Lieberson (1961) contends that the Park race relations cycle is inadequate because it fails to recognize that differences in power relations in the original contact situations produce different stratification outcomes. Lieberson distinguishes between two different situations of ethnic stratification: one in which the migrating group is the dominant ethnic group (immigrant superordination) and one in which the group residing in the region at the time of contact is dominant (indigenous superordination). In migrant superordination, the economic, political, and cultural institutions of the subjugated indigenous population are undermined. However, because the subordinate indigenous group seeks to maintain its traditional institutions, conflict with the dominant group can persist over long periods of time. This situation, exemplified by Indian-white relations in the United States, is classic colonialism, in which the subordinate group strenuously resists assimilation. When the migrating group is subordinate, on the other hand, its decision to enter another society is more likely to be voluntary, and it is much more likely to accept assimilation into the dominant society, as exemplified by the experience of most European immigrants to America. In Article 18 ("Minority Status and Literacy in Comparative Perspective"), John Ogbu explores the implications of these differences in explaining varying ethnic responses to educational achievement.

Most discussions of assimilation in the United States have focused on the adaptation of immigrant groups that have voluntarily entered American society. The experience of African Americans, whose ancestors were involuntarily imported from Africa, does not fall into either contact situation—migrant or indigenous subordination. Wilson (1973) maintains that slave transfers constitute a third major contact situation, the one in which the power and coercion of the dominant group is greatest. In contrast to colonization, in which the indigenous group, although subordinate, is able to maintain elements of its own cultures, slave transfers involve the forcible and involuntary uprooting of people from families and traditional cultures, which places them in a much greater dependent relationship with the dominant group (Wilson 1973:19-20). The extent to which differences between migrant superordination, indigenous superordination, and slave transfers have affected the nature of intergroup relations has been the subject of considerable controversy among social scientists, especially as they have sought to compare the patterns of integration among different ethnic groups and to develop explanations for the differences that exist.

An important assumption of the assimilation model has been that, as American society became more modernized, ethnic and racial distinctions would become insignificant, diminish, or eventually disappear. According to this conception, the forces of modernity—democratic and egalitarian political norms and institutions, industrialization, urbanization, and bureaucratization—place increasing emphasis on rationality, impersonality, status by achievement, physical and social mobility, and equal opportunity. Traditional social systems, in which social position is based on ascriptive racial and ethnic origins rather than on individual merit, become increasingly burdensome (and even expensive) to maintain. Thus, the Southern caste system, in which selection was based on the irrational ascriptive criterion of race, was perceived by advocates of an assimilation model to be a vestige of a premodern, agrarian society that ultimately and inevitably would be undermined as the modernization process transformed the society by emphasizing a selection process based on merit, credentials, and skills.

This position was nowhere more clearly articulated than in Gunnar Murdal's *An American Dilemma*, probably the most important book ever written on the subject of American race relations. Published in 1944, *An American Dilemma* became an instant classic and exerted a profound influence on white America by drawing attention to the dynamics of race in American society in a way that had not been accomplished since the formal abolition of slavery. Myrdal's title reflected his basic thesis: the American creed of "liberty, equality, justice, and fair opportunity" was violated by the subordinate status to which African Americans had been relegated. Myrdal felt that the contradiction between white America's deeply felt professions of equality and brotherhood, on the one hand, and its treatment of African American people, on the other, presented an "embarrassing" dilemma that made for "moral uneasiness" in the hearts and minds of white Americans. He also optimistically thought that the primary thrust of American institutions was in a direction that would ultimately undermine the last vestiges of the racial caste system.

The assumption that the forces of modernization will progressively weaken the ties of race and ethnicity has been questioned, however (see, for example, Nagel's discussion in Article 2). In his classic essay, "Industrialization and Race Relations," Herbert Blumer (1965) noted that the projected effects of industrialization are not, in reality, inevitable. An emphasis on rationality may not make job opportunities available to the best qualified individuals irrespective of race; rather, the goal of efficiency and social harmony may impel managers *rationally* to discriminate because to hire minority applicants might disrupt the efficient and harmonious functioning of the enterprise. "*Rational* operation of industrial enterprises which are introduced into a racially ordered society may call for a deferential respect for the canons and sensitivities of that racial order" (Blumer 1965:233). In other words, modernization and industrialization do not necessarily change the order of majority-minority relations; rather, these processes adapt and conform to existing systems of racial etiquette. Blumer contended that changes in race relations in the workplace are brought about not by an inherent dynamic of the modernization process but by forces outside the world of work.

The Assimilation Model as Ideology

Assimilation involves efforts to integrate or incorporate a group into the mainstream of a society. The objective of assimilation is a homogeneous society. In general, the assimilation model of racial and ethnic contact assumes that the unique and distinctive characteristics of a minority will be erased and that the minority's culture, social institutions, and identity will be replaced by those of the dominant group.

Critics of the assimilation model have charged that it reflects a "liberal" view of the manner in which racial and ethnic diversity should be resolved. That is, an assimilationist perspective has frequently served an ideological function of specifying how racial and ethnic groups *should* relate to each other, instead of assessing the process whereby they *do* interact. In many circumstances, assimilationist analyses have served to legitimize the basic ideology of American society as a land of opportunity. Metzger (1971) has argued that, in general, the assimilationist perspective assumes that

> The incorporation of America's ethnic and racial groups into the mainstream culture is virtually inevitable. . . . Successful assimilation, moreover, has been viewed as synonymous with equality of opportunity and upward mobility for the members of minority groups. "Opportunity," in this system, is the opportunity to discard one's ethnicity and to partake fully in the "American Way of Life." In this sense, assimilation is viewed as the embodiment of the democratic ethos. (Metzger 1971:628–629)

Myrdal's monumental *An American Dilemma* reflected this general liberal notion of how racial and ethnic groups should come together in American society. The basic framework within which Myrdal conceptualized American race relations is perhaps most clearly reflected in his examination of the nature of African American culture and community life. To the extent to which African American culture diverged from dominant white culture patterns, Myrdal considered it a "distorted development, or a pathological condition, of the general American culture." Therefore, the primary thrust of black efforts toward institutional change in American society should be toward acquiring the characteristics of the dominant group. "It is to the advantage of American Negroes as individuals and as a group," wrote Myrdal, "to become assimilated into American culture, to acquire the traits held in esteem by the dominant white Americans."

One of the implications of such a model is that frequently the sources of ethnic conflict are perceived to reside not within the structure of society or within the dominant group but within the "pathological" or "maladjusted" behavior of the minority group. In such circumstances, resolution of ethnic conflict involves a minority group adapting to the standards of the majority. As we will note more fully in the introduction to Part 4, the Black Protest Movement of the late 1960s and early 1970s was in many respects a reaction against such an assimilationist stance.

Majority Policies Toward Racial and Ethnic Minorities

The nature of the assimilation process and the extent to which various racial and ethnic groups should be permitted or permit themselves to be integrated, incorporated, or absorbed into American society have been the source of considerable controversy. In his now classic analysis, *Assimilation in American Life* (1964), Milton Gordon (Article 12) distinguished among three ideologies—Anglo-conformity, the melting pot, and cultural pluralism—that have been used to explain the dynamics of intergroup relations in American life.

Anglo-Conformity/Transmuting Pot

The principal assimilationist model in the American experience has emphasized conformity by minority groups to dominant group standards—the desirability and necessity of maintaining English social institutions, language, and cultural patterns. Termed Anglo-conformity, this model assumes that ethnic minorities should give up their distinctive cultural characteristics and adopt those of the dominant group. It can be expressed by the formula $A + B + C = A$, in which A is the dominant group and B and C represent ethnic minority groups that must conform to the values and life styles of the dominant group; they must "disappear" if they wish to achieve positions of power and prestige in the society (Newman 1973:53).

Not only does a policy of Anglo-conformity seek a homogeneous society organized around the idealized cultural standards, social institutions, and language of the dominant group, but it also assumes the inferiority of the cultures of other ethnic groups. Many first- and second-generation Americans retain vivid and painful recollections of the ridicule of their cultural ways and the pressures for them to become "Americanized." Many tried to rid themselves of their traditional beliefs and practices. A daughter of Slovenian immigrant parents recalled her childhood:

In the 9th grade, a boy said to me, "You talk funny." I wondered what he meant. I listened to my friends, and I did not think they "talked funny." Then, that great American experiment, the public high school, opened my ears. I heard the English language spoken as I had never heard it spoken. . . . I began to hear that I did indeed pronounce my words differently, and so did my friends. I practiced [English] in secret, in the bathroom, of course, until I could pronounce properly the difficult "th" sound, which seemed the most distinctive and, therefore, the most necessary to conquer. How superior I felt when I had mastered this sound. . . . Alas, however, I refused to speak Slovenian. (Prosen 1976:2–3)

Such a conception of how a minority group should relate to the majority is not unique to the United States. Consider, for example, the statement of an Australian Minister for Immigration concerning the objective of his country's immigration policy:

It is cardinal with us that Australia, though attracting many different people, should remain a substantially homogeneous society, that there is no place in it for enclaves or minorities, that all whom we admit to reside permanently should be equal here and capable themselves of becoming substantially Australians after a few years of residence, with their children in the next generation wholly so. (Opperman 1966)

For this model to be applicable to majority-minority relations in societies other than the United States, the culture-specific term *Anglo-conformity* must be replaced by the more general term *transmuting pot* (Cole and Cole 1954).

The Melting Pot

Like Anglo-conformity, the objective of a *melting pot* policy is a society without ethnic differences. More tolerant than a policy of Anglo-conformity, the melting pot ideal sees ethnic differences as being lost in the creation of a new society and a new people —a synthesis unique and distinct from any of the different groups that formed it. Unlike Anglo-conformity, none of the contributing groups is considered to be superior; each is considered to have contributed the best of its cultural heritage to the creation of something new. The melting pot ideal can be expressed by the formula $A + B + C = D$, in which A, B, and C represent the different contributing groups and D is the product of their synthesis (Newman 1973:631). As Ralph Waldo Emerson expressed it in the mid–nineteenth century:

As in the old burning of the Temple at Corinth, by the melting and intermixture of silver and gold and other metals a new compound more precious than any, called Corinthian brass, was formed, so in this continent—asylum of all nations—the energy of Irish, Germans, Swedes, Poles, and Cossacks and all the European tribes—of the Africans and of the Polynesians—will construct a new race, a new religion, a new state, a new literature. (Quoted in Gordon 1964:117)

The melting pot conception has been perhaps the most widely idealized popular conception of how ethnic groups have been integrated into American society. As both Gordon and Kazal point out, the melting pot notion has pervaded American intellectual life and popular culture. It was a prominent feature of Frederick Jackson Turner's 1893 frontier thesis, which for generations provided the most definitive and compelling interpretation of what was most distinctive about American society. According to Turner, "in the crucible of the frontier the immigrants were Americanized, liberated, and fused into a mixed race" (Turner 1894/1966:12).

Pluralism

Pluralism, on the other hand, rejects the inevitability of cultural assimilation. As the term has been applied to American society, pluralism refers to a system in which groups with different cultural practices can coexist and be preserved but simultaneously embrace common values and beliefs and participate in common economic, political, and social institutions. According to this notion, which is embedded in assumptions of American multiculturalism, the strength and vitality of American society is derived from the many different ethnic groups that have made it a "nation of nations." Each group should be permitted to retain its unique qualities while affirming its allegiance to the larger society. It can be expressed by the equation $A + B + C = A + B + C$, in which A, B, and C are each ethnic groups that maintain their distinctiveness over time (Newman 1973).

Pluralism is more tolerant of diversity than either Anglo-conformity or the melting pot, for it implies recognition of cultural equality among ethnic groups, not the superiority of one group. It accepts and encourages—even celebrates—cultural differences but generally assumes that different ethnic groups will coexist within a common political and economic framework. For example, religion in American society has historically been characterized by denominational pluralism, so that today more than 1,200 different religious organizations coexist. Members of most religious groups retain their doctrinal and ritualistic distinctiveness while simultaneously participating in the political and economic life of the country.

However, the American conception of pluralism is a much narrower conception of ethnic coexistence than is implied in the use of the term in many other societies. In the American conception of pluralism, diverse ethnic groups maintain some elements of cultural distinctiveness but accept core elements of the dominant culture and seek participation in the mainstream economic and political institutions. However, in addition to possessing cultural heterogeneity, most genuinely "plural" societies are characterized by "mutually incompatible institutional systems—social structures, value and belief systems, and systems of action" (Horowitz 1985:136) akin to what we will define later as separatism.

The three types that Gordon delineated can be placed on a continuum ranging from lesser to greater minority-group integrity and autonomy. Each type merges imperceptibly with the adjacent type. For example, Anglo-conformity is much closer to the melting pot than it is to pluralism. Moreover, the range of possible alternatives can be logically extended. Examination of the history of racial and ethnic contact in the United States and throughout the world makes it apparent that Anglo-conformity (the transmuting pot), the melting pot, and pluralism do not exhaust the theoretical possibilities or the historical examples of the consequences of intergroup contact. A policy of genocide, at one extreme, permits less minority autonomy, obviously, than does a policy based on the transmuting pot model. At the other extreme, *separatism*, or complete autonomy for the minority group, comprises a more expansive ideology than pluralism. When all of these ideologies are placed on a continuum, the result looks like

Figure 1. Let us review the alternative possible dominant policies toward racial and ethnic minorities suggested by this continuum.

Genocide/Extermination

The most repressive and destructive dominant-group policy toward a minority group is *extermination* or *genocide,* which denies the minority's very right to live. The objective of a policy of extermination is to eliminate or substantially reduce the minority group. The post–World War II International Genocide Convention, which was convened in response to the atrocities committed by the Nazi regime between 1933 and 1945, developed the following definition of genocide:

> . . . *any of the following acts committed with intent to destroy, in whole or in part, a national, ethnic, racial, or religious group as such: (a) killing members of the group; (b) causing serious bodily or mental harm to members of the group; (c) deliberately inflicting on the group conditions of life calculated to bring about its physical destruction in whole or in part; (d) imposing measures intended to prevent births within the group; (e) forcibly transferring children of the group to another group. (O'Brien 1968:516)*

Although efforts to exterminate minorities are not confined to the modern era, some of the most notorious instances of genocide have occurred in the twentieth century. In 1915 1.5 million Armenians were massacred by the Turks. As noted in Part 1, in the small African country of Burundi, members of the Hutu minority have been periodically systematically murdered by the dominant Tutsi people; in 1972 more than 100,000 were killed, and the wholesale slaughter of the Hutu population was renewed in clashes that erupted with increasing frequency between 1988 and 1995. In 1994 the tables were turned in the neighboring country of Rwanda, where an estimated 750,000 Tutsi were systematically annihilated in just a few months and over 1 million refugees fled to neighboring countries (such as Zaire [now the Congo], where this ethnic strife still smolders).

During the 1970s approximately one million Cambodians—30 percent of the population—were killed or died from hunger, disease, and overwork as a result of conditions created by the American bombing that devastated the country and by atrocities committed by the Khmer Rouge. The country's ethnic and religious minorities, especially the Muslim Chams, were special targets for extermination by the Pol Pot regime (Kiljunen 1985; Kiernan 1988). During their 1975 invasion of East Timor, Indonesians indiscriminately wiped out entire villages, killing over a hundred thousand in a population of less than one million. Moreover, the Indonesian destruction of East Timorese

	Exclusion/ Expulsion		Transmuting Pot		Pluralism	
Genocide/ Extermination		Oppression		Melting Pot		Separatism

FIGURE 1   *Types of Dominant Group Policies Toward Racial and Ethnic Minorities*

farms and villages led to famine, starvation, and disease, as a consequence of which "half a generation of Timorese children has been rendered mentally retarded" (Sidell 1981:50).

A clearly articulated policy of genocide was most systematically implemented under the Nazi extermination program, in which Hitler's objective was the extinction of several million Jews and other "non-Aryan" groups (such as Gypsies). Between 1935 and 1945 more than six million people perished as a consequence of this policy.

In American society, a policy of genocide was one of the several policies pursued by dominant whites in their effort to wrest control of the country's vast lands from the American Indians. The slogan "the only good Indian is a dead Indian" was common among frontier whites, who consistently encountered Indian resistance to their continued encroachment on Indian lands. As noted in Part 2, by the turn of the twentieth century, the American Indian population of the United States had been brought to the point of virtual extinction by a combination of European diseases, disintegration of tribal cultures, and an aggressive military policy by the federal government.

Because genocide violates the sanctity of human life, an ideology of *racism* is often developed to justify it. Racism involves a belief in the inherent superiority of one racial group and the inherent inferiority of others. Its primary function is to provide a set of ideas and beliefs that can be used to explain, rationalize, and justify a system of racial domination. By denying that a racial minority has human qualities or by depicting it as subhuman or destructive of human values and life, the minority's extermination is made morally justifiable and acceptable. For example, in 1876 an Australian writer defended efforts to annihilate the native people of New Zealand (Maoris), Australia, and Tasmania: "When exterminating the inferior Australian and Maori races . . . the world is better for it. . . . [By] protecting the propagation of the imprudent, the diseased, the defective, the criminal . . . we tend to destroy the human race" (quoted in Hartwig 1972:16).

Expulsion and Exclusion

Extermination clearly represents the most extreme dominant-group method for dealing with the existence of minorities and the potential for interethnic conflict in a multicultural society. The objective of extermination is to reduce or eliminate contact between majority and minority and to create an ethnically (or racially) homogeneous society. A similar rationale underlies the process of *expulsion,* that is, the ejection of a minority group from areas controlled by the dominant group. Minorities are told, in essence, not "You have no right to live" (as in a policy of genocide), but rather "Because you differ from us so greatly, you have no right to live *among us."*

Expulsion can be of two types: *direct* and *indirect* (Simpson and Yinger 1985: 19–20), which are often interrelated. *Direct expulsion* occurs when minorities are forcibly ejected by the dominant group, often through military or other governmental force. A policy of direct expulsion was at no time more pronounced in American history than during the nineteenth century, when thousands of American Indians were removed from the East to areas beyond the Mississippi River. During World War II, 120,000 Japanese Americans, two-thirds of them United States citizens, were forcibly removed from their homes and placed in detention camps in remote areas of the country.

Indirect expulsion occurs when harassment, discrimination, and persecution of a minority become so intense that members "voluntarily" choose to emigrate. Harassment and persecution of minorities, particularly religious minorities, have led many groups to seek refuge in the United States. Persecuted Protestant sects were among the earliest European immigrants to the American colonies, and the tradition of America as an asylum for the oppressed has continued to be a prominent feature of American ideals. The most dramatic emigration in modern Jewish history occurred in the late nineteenth and early twentieth centuries when millions (more than one-third of all Eastern European Jews) fled czarist Russia. Recently the persecution of Jews has revived in Russia and other former Soviet-bloc countries in Eastern Europe, forcing Jews by the thousand to seek refuge in other countries.

Several noted instances of expulsion have occurred throughout the world in the past two decades. In 1989 more than 310,000 Bulgarians of Turkish descent (of a Bulgarian Turkish community estimated at between 900,000 and 1.5 million), whose ancestors had lived in Bulgaria for generations, fled to Turkey, forming one of Europe's largest refugee populations since World War II. Some Turks were forcibly expelled by Bulgarian authorities, while others were subjected to forced assimilation and repression of their Muslim faith, were forced to take Slavic names, and were beaten and abused for speaking Turkish in public (Haberman 1989:1). On two separate occasions —in 1983 and 1985—the government of Nigeria resorted to mass expulsion. In 1983 Nigeria expelled about 2 million immigrants from the neighboring countries of Ghana, Cameroon, Benin, Chad, and Niger. In 1985 another 700,000 people were forced to leave (*The Economist* 1985). In Israel, Meir Kahane, a U.S.-born rabbi, gained considerable political support for his proposal to resolve Arab-Jewish tensions in that country by forcibly removing all Arabs from Israel and its occupied territories and making Israel into an exclusively Jewish state (Friedman 1985:1).

However, the most dramatic recent example of expulsion has occurred in the former nation of Yugoslavia, which since its dissolution in 1991 has been the scene of brutal ethnic violence that has driven more than 2.3 million people from their homes and villages. Formerly one of the Yugoslav republics, Bosnia and Herzegovina was the home of three ethnic groups—Slavic Muslims (44 percent), Serbs (31 percent), and Croats (17 percent). After Bosnia declared its independence in 1992, Serbian militiamen embarked on a campaign to create ethnically homogeneous enclaves by forcibly removing and displacing non-Serbs, especially Muslims. The Serbian campaign took many forms: arson, rape, and terror against civilian populations; executions; imprisonment and torture in concentration camps and prisons; removal and confinement to ghetto areas for non-Serbs; and forcible deportation. Moreover, non-Serbs were intimidated by the Serbian reign of terror into signing "voluntary" letters giving up their property and possessions in return for being "permitted" to leave Bosnia alive (Human Rights Watch 1992). The terms that the Serbs used to describe their objectives—"ethnic cleansing" and "ethnic purification"—epitomize the quest for ethnic homogeneity and exclusivity that underlies a policy of expulsion.

Essential to an expulsionist policy is the desire to achieve or retain ethnic or racial homogeneity. This end may occur not only when an ethnic group is expelled from the society but also when a host society refuses to admit another group because that group is perceived as a threat to the society's basic social institutions. Policies that refuse to admit ethnically or racially different groups can be termed *exclusion*. As noted in

Part 2, between 1917 and 1965 American immigration policy was based on the assumption that immigrants from southern and eastern Europe and Asia represented a threat to the biological, social, and political fabric of American society and therefore should be substantially or completely restricted. This assumption was embodied in the 1924 immigration legislation, which established numerical quotas for each nation. More than four-fifths of the quotas were assigned to those nations of northern and western Europe whose ethnic characteristics were perceived to be most similar to those of the "original" European settlers of the country. Although Great Britain had an admissions quota exceeding 65,000, Italy was allocated less than 6,000, and Hungary less than 1,000. Asians were almost completely excluded. As we will note more fully in Part 4, this policy remained virtually intact until its repeal in 1965.

Oppression

Oppression involves exploitation of a minority group by excluding it from equal participation in a society (Turner, Singleton, and Musick 1984:1–2). Oppression "depends on exclusiveness rather than exclusion" (Bonacich 1972:555). Positions of higher prestige, power, and income are reserved exclusively for dominant group members. Unlike extermination, expulsion, or exclusion, a system of oppression accepts the existence of minorities but subjugates them and confines them to inferior social positions. The majority group uses its power to maintain its access to scarce and valued resources in a system of social inequality.

Slavery, in which the slave's labor was a valuable resource exploited by the slave owner, was an example of oppression in American society. As we noted in the introduction to Part 2, even after slavery was legally abolished, the Jim Crow system of racial segregation that ensued was organized to exploit blacks for the benefit of the dominant whites. After taking a tour of the South at the turn of the twentieth century, a prominent journalist remarked on the exploitative nature of black-white relations:

> *One of the most significant things I saw in the South—and I saw it everywhere—was the way in which the white people were torn between their feelings of race prejudice and their downright economic needs. Hating and fearing the Negro as a race (though often loving individual Negroes) they yet want him to work for them; they can't get along without him. In one impulse a community will rise to mob Negroes or to drive them out of the country because of Negro crime or Negro vagrancy or because the Negro is becoming educated, acquiring property, and "getting out of his place," and in the next impulse laws are passed or other remarkable measures taken to keep him at work—because this South can't get along without him. (Baker 1964:81)*

A classic contemporary example of oppression was the South African system of apartheid, or "separate development," which functioned to maintain the privileged position of whites, who enjoyed one of the highest standards of living in the world but who represent only 15 percent of the country's population. On the other hand, South African blacks, who comprise more than two-thirds (69 percent) of the population, were excluded from genuine participation in the nation's political system and were legally confined to rural reserves, or "homelands," that represented only 13 percent of the land. However, black labor provided a cheap labor supply for South African mines, farms, manufacturing, and domestic help that was—and is—essential to the South African economy and the system of white privilege that persists. Therefore, the entire system of state controls restricting black political power, residence, and education was designed to perpetuate the system of white privilege (Cohen 1986).

Separatism

At the other end of the continuum from genocide is *separatism,* which is the most tolerant and expansive of the several majority group policies or practices that we have considered. Like pluralism, *separatism* implies social and cultural equality among ethnic groups, not the superiority of one. Both pluralism and separatism accept and encourage—even celebrate—cultural diversity. Separatism differs from pluralism in that the former includes some form of geographic and social separation.

In the American experience, pluralism and separatism have seldom been advocated by the majority; the primary advocates of each stance have been minority spokespersons, whose desire to maintain their distinct ethnic identity and organizational structure has led such groups to proscribe contact with the broader society and culture. The basic difference between policies of separatism and exclusion is that under separatism, the minority chooses to place itself apart culturally, socially, and physically, whereas under exclusion, the separation is dictated by the majority group. Under separatism the majority does not require separation of ethnic and racial groups; it simply permits it.

Throughout the American experience many ethnic groups have tried to avoid pressures of forced assimilation with the dominant society by embracing a form of ethnic pluralism as the most appropriate means of adjusting to American society. The adjustment of the immigrant Irish typifies a pluralist response that is characteristic of many other ethnic groups. Although the objects of discrimination by Protestant Americans, the Irish avoided much of the hostility directed toward them by creating a society within a society, a separate institutional system centered around the Roman Catholic church. The institutional system that developed around the church—its schools, hospitals, orphanages, asylums, homes for the aged, charitable and athletic organizations, and informal groups—integrated the Irish community and served to maintain Irish American solidarity and identity (Yetman 1975).

Separatism, on the other hand, involves minimal interaction by a minority group with the majority. The impulse for separatism frequently has been created by considerable conflict with the majority group and a desire to avoid a recurrence of discrimination or subjugation. For example, this impulse was an important factor contributing to the creation of the state of Israel. A separate nation was also the objective of the pre–Civil War colonization movement that aimed to return American slaves to Africa and of the African American Back-to-Africa campaign of Marcus Garvey during the 1920s.

The idea of separate ethnic areas or states has been advocated by spokespersons of a number of different ethnic groups in the United States—by African Americans, American Indians, and German Americans, among others. Religious groups such as the Amish, the Hutterites, and the Doukhobors have sought to protect their identity from the influences of the larger society by remaining not only culturally but also socially—and, often, geographically—separate from the rest of the society. Thus, in addition to seeking to retain their cultural distinctiveness, such groups refrain from extensive participation in the economic, political, and social life of the broader society in order to maintain their own subsocieties. For example, having endured great persecution for their beliefs during the mid–nineteenth century, members of the Church of Jesus Christ of Latter Day Saints (the Mormons) sought to isolate themselves from the corrupting influences of the larger society, an impulse reflected in a favorite Mormon hymn,

We'll find a place which God for us prepared
Far away in the West
Where none shall come to hurt or make afraid
There the Saints will be blessed.

The transmuting pot, the melting pot, and pluralism are all assimilation ideologies that imply the integration of majority and minority groups in some manner, whereas expulsion, exclusion, oppression, and separatism imply some form of minority group separation. The crucial distinction between separation ideologies is whether the separation of the minority group is achieved voluntarily or involuntarily, and whether the minority is relatively autonomous or relatively powerless. Thus, *exclusion* refers to separation by the decision of the majority group, whereas *separatism* means that the minority group has decided to place itself apart and is not prevented from doing so by the dominant group.

The case of American Indians demonstrates that these policies are not mutually exclusive; one or more of them may be embraced simultaneously or in different historical periods. In the early years of the republic, United States policy moved from genocide to expulsion and exclusion (the reservation system). Since the late nineteenth century, the ideology of Anglo-conformity has been predominant, with exclusion an acceptable alternative. For example, the purpose of governmental actions such as the Indian Allotment Act of 1887 was to force Indians to assimilate culturally. Even though many Indians would have welcomed separatism, their confinement to reservations has more closely resembled exclusion, because the reservations have been substantially controlled by the federal government and other extensions of white society (for example, missionaries, traders, and external economic interests).

Neither Anglo-conformity nor exclusion permits American Indians to exercise free choice. To assimilate or adopt the European-derived norms, values, and cultural standards of the larger society means to cease being an American Indian culturally. On the other hand, to be restricted to the reservation is to have life choices and chances severely circumscribed by powerful external forces. In spite of these exigencies, there seems little likelihood that the stubbornly purposeful maintenance of Indian traditions, values, and aloofness from the rest of the society will be surrendered. As Snipp points out in Article 5, even in urban areas, where increasing numbers have migrated since World War II, American Indians are resisting assimilation, forming their own ongoing communities, and increasingly asserting their rights to sovereignty and self-determination.

Dimensions of Assimilation

In his classic article, "Assimilation in America" (Article 12), which was published in 1961, Milton M. Gordon recognizes that each of the three theories—Anglo-conformity, melting pot, and cultural pluralism—on which his analysis focuses are primarily ideologies: that is, prescriptive models of how the process of intergroup relations in American society *should* proceed. He contends, therefore, that such idealized conceptions are of limited utility in analyzing precisely how diverse ethnic groups in American society have interacted.

Gordon argues that in order to assess accurately how extensively different ethnic groups have intermingled, it is essential to recognize that assimilation is not a single phenomenon but involves several related but analytically distinct processes. The three most important of these processes are cultural assimilation, structural assimilation, and marital assimilation, each of which may take place in varying degrees (Gordon 1964:71).

Popular discussions of assimilation usually are concerned with *cultural assimilation,* or what Gordon terms *behavioral assimilation* or *acculturation*—that is, the acquisition of the *cultural* characteristics of the dominant group, including its values, beliefs, language, and behaviors. However, Gordon contends that cultural assimilation is not sufficient to ensure *structural*—or social—assimilation. Writing during the early 1960s, he perceived that, although many ethnic groups—primarily the "white ethnic" descendants of European "new" immigrants—had become fully acculturated to the dominant American culture and had lost most traces of their ancestral cultures, they still had not been able to achieve full *social* participation in American society. Therefore, he concludes that sharing the same language, norms, behaviors, and cultural characteristics does not ensure access to informal social organizations, clubs, cliques, and friendship groups. Even sharing membership in secondary groups such as schools, jobs, and community and political organizations does not necessarily provide access to primary-group associations for those who have been culturally assimilated.

Because it is possible for a group to become culturally assimilated but to remain socially excluded, isolated, or segregated, it is important to distinguish cultural assimilation from *structural assimilation,* which involves social interaction among individuals of different ethnic and racial backgrounds. Two types of structural assimilation can be distinguished: secondary and primary. *Secondary structural assimilation* is the ethnic or racial integration of settings characterized by impersonal secondary relationships: jobs, schools, political organizations, neighborhoods, and public recreation. However, even sharing participation in such secondary groups does not necessarily involve primary-group associations—relationships that are warm, intimate, and personal. *Primary structural assimilation* is the ethnic integration of primary relationships, such as those found in religious communities, social clubs, informal social organizations, close friendships, and family relationships. Finally, the third subprocess, which is closely related to and, Gordon maintains, follows from primary structural assimilation, is *marital assimilation* —amalgamation or intermarriage among different ethnic or racial groups.

These distinctions enable us to compare and contrast the relative degree of integration or separation of different ethnic groups in American society in a relatively systematic fashion. Considerable research has been directed toward developing empirical indicators with which to measure assimilation: among the indicators are years of schooling, income levels, occupational characteristics, segregation indices, and rates of intermarriage.

One of the important issues in assessing Park's original model of the assimilation process, however, is whether rates of assimilation are changing over time. In other words, are there differences between the first generation (the immigrants themselves), the second generation (the American-born offspring of immigrants), the third generation (the grandchildren of immigrants), and subsequent generations?

There have been two basic interpretations of the effect of generational differences on ethnicity. *Straight-line theory,* most closely identified with Herbert Gans (see Article 22, "Symbolic Ethnicity"), predicts increasing assimilation with each succeeding generation. According to this model, English would be more likely to be spoken in the home, occupational characteristics would be higher, and there would be higher rates of intermarriage among the second generation than among the first, and, moreover, these trends toward assimilation would increase with each succeeding generation.

A contrasting model of the assimilation process was proposed by the historian Marcus Lee Hansen. Hansen contended that whereas children of immigrants seek to shed evidence of their foreignness as fully as possible and to "become American," the immigrants' grandchildren—the third generation—seek to rediscover their roots and retain their ethnic distinctiveness. He formulated the notion of the *third generation return:* "What the son wishes to forget, the grandson wishes to remember" (Hansen 1938:9). This model, which has become known as *Hansen's Law,* suggests that increasing assimilation with each succeeding generation is not inevitable. Instead, there can be variations among generations in rates of assimilation; the third generation, in particular, may identify more closely with their grandparents' ethnic backgrounds than did their parents, producing a cultural or ethnic revival.

In one of the most celebrated interpretations of American religious life, Will Herberg (1955) employed a variant of Hansen's Law to account for changing patterns of religiosity in America. Herberg argued that because American religious communities have been so strongly linked to ethnicity, Hansen's model could be extended to explain patterns of religious practice among American ethnic groups. According to Herberg, religiosity was high among the first generation, but because it was perceived as something "foreign" and thus something to escape, it declined among the second generation. For the third generation, however, affiliation with and participation in one of the three broad American religious traditions—Protestantism, Catholicism, and Judaism—provided a socially acceptable way in which to maintain ethnic identity in modern society. Therefore, Herberg argued, members of the third generation would tend to have higher rates of religious participation than their second-generation parents.

Herberg's bold and imaginative interpretation stimulated considerable controversy. In one important study, Abramson (1975) showed that empirical data did not support the three-generations hypothesis as a general interpretation of the process of immigrant adjustment. Analyzing data on the religious beliefs and behavior of ten religioethnic groups, Abramson found great variation in generational patterns of religiosity. In general there was little support for the hypothesized decline-and-rise pattern; only one of the ten religioethnic groups in his study (Eastern European Catholics) conformed to the pattern. Although more groups manifested a consistent decline in religiosity over three generations, there was a sufficient number of alternative patterns (for example, an increase in religiosity in the second generation) to preclude unequivocal support for a straight-line interpretation. Abramson's study reveals that although ethnicity is still a salient factor affecting religious behavior, the diversity of experiences among American ethnic groups (such as the differences among Irish, Polish, and Italian Catholics) has been substantial.

Scholars have challenged the assimilation model on a variety of grounds, especially Park's view that assimilation is a linear process leading ultimately from cultural to marital assimilation and to the disappearance of ethnic identity. However, as Nagel argued in "Constructing Ethnicity" (Article 2), ethnicity remains a viable and vital force in modern societies precisely because it is functional and provides a source of emotional support and social solidarity in an increasingly fragmented and anonymous society. Thus Portes and Bach (1985), in their study comparing the adaptations of Cuban and Mexican immigrants to the United States, conclude that these immigrants' cultural and socioeconomic adaptation to American society, rather than being impeded, is facilitated by the maintenance of ethnic identity and close ethnic ties:

> *Those immigrants more able to relate effectively to various aspects of life in America are often those who most strongly adhere to personal relationships within their own communities. Awareness of barriers and, at times, outright hostility confronting them on the outside has its counterpart in the reaffirmation of primary relations within protected ethnic circles. . . . Rather than abandoning personal relationships within their own groups, immigrants who have moved farthest into the outside world seem to rely more heavily on such bonds. Ethnic resilience, not assimilation, is the theoretical perspective more congruent with this interpretation. This resilience is not, however, a force leading to collective withdrawal, but rather a moral resource, an integral part of the process of establishing and defining a place in a new society. (Portes and Bach 1985:333)*

In other words, maintaining ethnic primary group supports may actually enhance cultural and secondary structural assimilation.

Assimilation, therefore, is not a unidimensional or unilinear phenomenon, leading ultimately to an ethnically homogeneous society. Recognizing the multidimensional nature of assimilation, Gordon deplored the tendency to use the term in an inclusive way, and he argued that it was essential to identify its several forms. As we noted before, he argued that although extensive cultural assimilation had taken place in American life through the 1950s, there was only limited evidence of structural assimilation. For Gordon, a more accurate description of the realities of ethnic relations in American life at that time was *structural pluralism,* in which racial, ethnic, and, in particular, religious categories "retained their separate sociological structures."

To what extent has assimilation proceeded nearly forty years after Gordon published his classic essay? It is impossible to review in its entirety all of the voluminous research on the several dimensions of assimilation here, but we will examine several salient issues suggested by this literature. We will focus especially on the three key areas of socioeconomic status—income levels, occupational status, and educational attainment—as well as spatial assimilation and patterns of intermarriage.

Socioeconomic Assimilation

By almost any measure, descendants of southern and eastern European immigrants (Italians, Jews, Poles, Greeks, Hungarians) have become structurally assimilated into American life to a degree that few would have predicted at the end of World War II. During the 1950s one of the most striking findings in the social science literature dealing with assimilation was the rapid socioeconomic mobility of Jews, who, like most other "new" immigrant groups entering the United States between 1890 and 1915, had arrived virtually penniless (Strodtbeck 1958). By the 1960s, despite the relatively brief time in which they had resided in the United States, Jews had come to exceed all other ethnic groups (including the once-dominant white Anglo-Saxon Protestants) on the most common measures of socioeconomic status: median family income, educational attainment, and occupational prestige. The extremely rapid rise in the socioeconomic status of Jews historically contrasted sharply with that of other "new" immigrant groups (primarily southern and eastern European Catholics) who, with Jews, had entered American society in the massive wave of immigration near the turn of the twentieth century.

By the early 1970s, however, Andrew Greeley, the prolific sociologist and novelist, was able to celebrate what he characterized as the "ethnic miracle." Using extensive national social-survey data compiled between 1945 and 1970, Greeley contended that despite their lowly socioeconomic status three generations earlier, "the ethnics have made it." By 1970 the income levels of Irish, German, Italian, and Polish Catholics were exceeded only by that of Jews, not by white Anglo-Saxon Protestants, who in many accounts were still defined as the "establishment," or the "core" group to which all other ethnic groups compared themselves. In overall educational achievement, Polish, Italian, and Slavic Catholics still lagged somewhat behind the national white average, but when parental educational levels were held constant, Catholic ethnics showed higher educational levels than any other ethnic group except Jews. Indeed, Irish Catholics, once among the most despised and unfavorably stereotyped of all European ethnic groups, had by 1970 become "the richest, best educated, and most prestigious occupationally of any gentile religioethnic group." Thus, Greeley concluded, "In a very short space of time, the length of one generation, more or less, the American dream has come true" for European Catholic ethnic groups (Greeley 1976).

Neidert and Farley (1985) reported similar, although not identical, findings in their analysis of differences in socioeconomic status in a 1979 national survey of American ethnic groups. Their data showed that occupational returns for educational attainment tend generally to increase with each succeeding generation, thus providing strong support for a straight-line theory of assimilation. They also found that although ethnic differences exist in educational attainment, occupational prestige, and per capita income among non-English European ethnic groups, they were not at a disadvantage compared with those of English ancestry.

Several subsequent studies have reinforced these general findings. Generalizing from a comprehensive review of the voluminous literature on the economic attainments of American ethnic and racial groups, Model concluded that "members of most pre-1924 immigrant backgrounds fare at least as well as do other white Americans" (Model 1988:366). Similarly, Alba (Article 15) contends that "assimilation was, and is, a reality for the majority of the descendants of earlier waves of immigration from Europe." Basing his analysis on 1990 census data, Alba concluded that "long-term processes . . . have whittled away at the social foundations for ethnic distinctions [among European ancestry groups and] have brought about a rough parity of opportunities to attain such socioeconomic goods as educational credentials and prestigious jobs. . . . [T]he disadvantages that once were quite evident [among European ethnic] groups have largely faded and their socioeconomic attainments increasingly resemble, if not even surpass, those of the average white American."

However, as we have noted in the introduction to Part 2 and as Waters and Eschbach point out in Article 14, these patterns of educational and economic attainment are not repeated among all of the other categories in the American ethno-racial pentagon. Asian Americans, especially Chinese and Japanese, have been the object of considerable discrimination throughout their history in the United States. Indeed, so unfavorable were the perceptions of Asians by whites that, unlike any European ethnic groups, they were virtually excluded from immigrating to the United States for more than half a century. Moreover, in one of the most notorious instances of racism in American history, American citizens of Japanese descent were subjected to the humiliation of incarceration in detention camps during World War II.

As Waters and Eschbach point out in Article 14, numerous researchers have reported striking patterns of educational and economic social mobility among Asian Americans. As a result, during the past quarter century, there has been a notable change in perceptions of Asian Americans; the unfavorable stereotypes that were widely embraced by white Americans before, during, and immediately after World War II have metamorphosed into the controversial characterization of them as "model minorities," who, despite discrimination, have demonstrated remarkable patterns of educational, occupational, and financial success (Mazumdar 1996). Today the educational levels of Japanese, Chinese, Asian Indians, and Filipinos—immigrant as well as native-born—equal or exceed those of whites. These high levels of educational attainment are particularly pronounced among the younger segments of the population. Moreover, Asians are overrepresented in higher-status occupations, especially the professions. Although income levels among those of comparable occupational backgrounds tend to be lower than those of whites overall, income levels for native-born Japanese, Chinese, and Filipino males are about the same as for white males. Nevertheless, Hirschman and Wong (1986) caution against generalizing from these selected indices of secondary structural assimilation to other dimensions of assimilation. They conclude that Asian Americans tend to remain greatly underrepresented in many sectors of the dominant economy, society, and polity. Moreover, Hurh and Kim (1989) have shown that Asians with comparable educational attainments, occupational prestige, and hours worked per week earn less than their white counterparts. Thus, images of Asian American "success" obscure both the relatively heavier investments required for Asians to achieve such income levels and the discrimination to which they are still subject. It is because of images of Asian success that they encounter discrimination as a consequence of their minority status: Asians tend to be excluded from governmental programs designed to address such discrimination.

Hurh and Kim suggest that the widespread perception of the success image of Asian Americans has an additional consequence. If the situation of Asian Americans appears favorable, it is only in reference to the greater disadvantages of other minorities—African Americans, Hispanics, and American Indians. Indeed, the "model minority" stereotype of Asians serves to reinforce negative stereotypes of these other minorities and to blame them for the social, economic, and political conditions under which they find themselves.

However, as we noted in Part 2 and will discuss more fully in Part 4, the patterns of educational, occupational, and financial achievement found among European and Asian ethnic groups are not duplicated among Hispanics and African Americans. Bean and Tienda (1987) and Davis, Haub, and Willette (1983) have demonstrated that substantial gaps separate Hispanics from the Anglo population on these dimensions. Davis, Haub, and Willette anticipate that because there is evidence of increasing Hispanic educational attainments with each succeeding generation, the gap between Hispanics and Anglos in levels of educational achievement should narrow in the future. On the other hand, the historic concentration of Hispanics in lower-paid, less-skilled occupations has persisted, and the overall economic status of Hispanics, which until the 1990s had been consistently higher than for African Americans, began a steady decline in the early 1980s that by 1995 resulted in a median family income below that of African Americans. In 1979 Hispanic median family income stood at $29,180 (in 1995 dollars)—71 percent of white median family income; it has never since achieved this level, declining to $24,569 (or 58 percent of white income) in 1995. Today more than one-quarter of Hispanic families lives in poverty. Reflecting the interrelated impact of class, gender, and ethnicity, as well as their relatively recent arrival in American society, more than half (53 percent) of poor Hispanic families were headed by women (compared with 30 percent of non-Hispanic families in poverty) (U.S. Bureau of the Census 1996a; 1996b). Forty percent of all Hispanic children lived in poverty, and during the 1980s childhood poverty increased more rapidly among Hispanics than among any other racial or ethnic category (U.S. Bureau of the Census 1996b). Finally, the median net worth of Hispanic households was approximately one-eighth the net worth of white households (U.S. Bureau of the Census 1997). However, among Hispanic groups there are obvious disparities, most prominently those between Cubans, whose early migration, especially, was comprised substantially of middle-class and professional people, and Puerto Ricans, who were much more likely to have had lower levels of educational attainment and fewer occupational skills than Cubans.

As we will note more fully in Part 4, similar patterns have characterized African American socioeconomic status. During the 1970s, the African American community in general experienced gains in educational attainment and political participation. Paralleling the decline in income among Hispanics, though, the overall financial condition of black families deteriorated. However, Wilson (Article 7; 1987) contends that such generalizations obscure the increasing economic divergence within the African American community. Wilson contends that in the past two decades, blacks have had occupational opportunities unprecedented in the African American experience in America. On the other hand, the economic distress of the African American underclass, in particular, of female-headed families, has grown increasingly acute.

Spatial Assimilation

Each of the dimensions previously mentioned—years of schooling, occupational distribution, and income levels—in itself reveals little about the extent of social assimilation, integration, or incorporation of different ethnic groups in a society. In a genuinely plural society with unranked parallel social structures, for example, it is hypothetically possible for two or more ethnic groups to manifest high educational attainment, occupational status, and income levels without substantial physical interaction.

Patterns of residential integration have been one of the most frequently examined indices of assimilation. Massey and Mullan (1984) have referred to it as *spatial assim-*

ilation and defined it as the process whereby a group attains residential propinquity with members of a host society. Numerous scholars (such as Hershberg et al. 1979; Lieberson 1963, 1980; Marson and Van Valey 1979; Pettigrew 1979; Roof 1979; Taeuber 1990; Massey and Denton 1993; Farley and Frey 1994) have shown that there is a close interrelationship between housing and jobs, educational opportunities, and income. Indeed, Pettigrew (1979:122) has characterized racial residential segregation as the "structural linchpin" of American race relations, and Massey and Denton (Article 9) have underscored the critical role that it has played in the concentration of black poverty. Therefore, an ethnic group's spatial location is a crucial variable affecting its overall socioeconomic position. Residential location affects life chances in a wide variety of ways, including "cost and quality of housing, health and sanitary conditions, exposure to crime and violence, quality of services (the most important of which is education), and access to economic opportunity, as well as a host of less tangible factors ranging from the character of one's children's playmates to the kinds of role models they emulate" (Massey and Mullan 1984:838).

In *A Piece of the Pie: Black and White Immigrants since 1880* (1980), Stanley Lieberson undertook an exhaustive comparative analysis of the experiences of African Americans and "new" European immigrants in twentieth-century America. His examination of the patterns of residential segregation of African Americans and various "new" immigrant groups revealed several important features. First, at the beginning of the period of massive immigration from southern and eastern Europe (the last decade of the nineteenth century), blacks living in northern cities were less spatially segregated than the new southern and eastern European groups (e.g., Jews, Poles, Italians) who were beginning to arrive in substantial numbers. Second, the residential segregation of African Americans increased during the twentieth century, a process that correspondingly cut them off and isolated them from participation in most of the activities of the larger community. The position of blacks in northern cities deteriorated from the turn of the twentieth century onward. Moreover, the patterns of residential segregation of African Americans and southern European immigrant groups moved in opposite directions: at the same time that the rates of spatial assimilation for African Americans were declining, rates were increasing for southern and eastern European immigrants. Thus the deterioration of African Americans' position in northern urban areas occurred at precisely the time that the position of immigrant whites was beginning to improve.

As we noted in Part 2, the massive migration of African Americans out of the South to the North and from rural areas to the nation's cities has been one of the most important demographic shifts in American history. Today, African Americans are much more likely to live in metropolitan areas than are whites. Moreover, the percentage of metropolitan blacks who reside in central cities is more than double that of whites, creating the urban racial polarization that is one of the basic racial demographic facts of American life today (Pettigrew 1979:122; see Massey and Denton, Article 9, for a superb analysis of the historical development of American racial residential patterns).

The patterns of residential segregation experienced by African Americans in the twentieth century are not comparable to the immigrant neighborhoods or enclaves in which "new" immigrant groups congregated around the turn of the century. First, as Massey and Denton point out, although they were spatially isolated, at no time were immigrant neighborhoods as homogeneous or their spatial isolation as pronounced as in black neighborhoods today. In other words, the spatial isolation of white ethnics was never so extreme as that of African Americans during the last half century. From their examination of the experience of African Americans and ethnic groups in Philadelphia, Hershberg and his colleagues (1979) report that

> *The typical Irish immigrant in 1880 and the typical Italian immigrant in 1930 . . . shared a similar aspect of their residential experience. When the hypothetical immigrant in each era walked through his neighborhood, what kind of people might he have met? The Irishman in 1880 lived with 15 percent other Irish immigrants, 34 percent Irish stock, 26 percent all foreign-born persons and 68 percent all foreign stock. The typical Italian immigrant in 1930 had an almost identical experience. He lived with 14 percent other Italian immigrants, 38 percent Italian stock, 23 percent all foreign born persons and 57 percent all foreign stock. In striking contrast, the typical black in 1970 lived in a census tract in which 73 percent of the population was black. (Hershberg et al. 1979: 74–75)*

Thus the residential enclaves or neighborhoods of European immigrants were never so homogeneous as those of African Americans. The residential experience of European immigrants also differed from that of African Americans in that most European ethnics were not concentrated primarily in immigrant ghettos. Finally, as previously noted, patterns of European ethnic residential segregation were not enduring or permanent, but began to break down relatively quickly, whereas the characteristic feature of racial residential segregation since 1940 has been its persistence (Sorensen, Taeuber, and Hollingsworth 1975; Tauber 1983, 1990). As Massey and Denton (Article 9) point out, "for European immigrants, enclaves were places of absorption, adaptation, and adjustment to American society. They served as springboards for broader mobility in society, whereas blacks were trapped behind an increasingly impermeable color line."

One prominent measure that sociologists have developed to determine the extent of residential segregation or spatial isolation is the segregation index or *index of dissimilarity*. With this measure a score of 100 represents complete racial segregation, in which every city block is exclusively black or exclusively white; conversely, a score of zero represents a housing pattern in which members of different racial and ethnic groups are evenly distributed and each city block has the same percentage of blacks and whites as the city's overall population.

Taeuber (1990) analyzed trends in the index of dissimilarity between whites and nonwhites from 1940 to 1988 for 109 large cities. The average segregation index was 85 in 1940, 87 in 1950, 86 in 1960, 82 in 1970, 75 in 1980, and 76 in 1988 (Taeuber 1990:144–145). However, the segregation index was even higher for the twenty-eight cities that had an African American population of more than 100,000 in 1980. Already highly segregated by 1940, the patterns of racial residential isolation remained relatively stationary during the 1950s and 1960s. By 1970 the average segregation index for the twenty-eight American cities with African American populations of more than 100,000 was 87; by 1980 the index for these cities had declined to 81, although in some (such as Chicago and Cleveland) the index remained above 90 (Taeuber 1983). During the 1970s and 1980s, racial residential segregation declined modestly for the country as a whole. It persisted most dramatically in large industrial cities of the Northeast and Midwest (for example, Detroit, Chicago, Cleveland, Milwaukee, Newark, and Philadelphia still had segregation indices of over 80 in 1990). Indeed, Denton (1994) contends that those cities that were "hypersegregated" (that is, highly segregated on at least four of five different statistical measures) in 1980 remained equally—and in some instances more—hypersegrated in 1990. However, Farley and Frey (1994) point out that for most metropolitan areas—especially those in the South and West with substantial new housing construction and those centered around university communities or military bases—segregation indices declined during the 1990s (Farley and Frey 1994; Farley 1997).

These data document the highly segregated residential patterns that have characterized American cities during the modern industrial period. Despite declines in the previous two decades, by 1990 the general pattern of spatial isolation for African Americans was still more pronounced than for any other racial or ethnic group in American history. Moreover, the declines in residential segregation that did occur were so modest as to make problematic whether substantial increases in spatial assimilation for African Americans are likely in the near future.

As Massey and Denton point out in Article 9 ("The Construction of the Ghetto"), the black ghetto did not simply occur "naturally" but developed primarily in response to deliberate actions rooted in white prejudices throughout the twentieth century. Many different discriminatory mechanisms have been used to create the pattern of residential "apartheid" that today characterizes the housing patterns of black and white in American society: laws excluding blacks from "white" neighborhoods; violence, terrorism, and intimidation; the creation of neighborhood "improvement" associations designed principally to keep out black residents; *restrictive covenants* on real estate deeds specifying that properties would not be sold, leased, or rented to "undesirable" racial or ethnic groups; real estate "codes of ethics" and federal government (FHA and VA) policies specifying that "if a neighborhood is to retain stability, it is necessary that properties shall continue to be occupied by the same social and racial classes"; *racial steering*—the practice by realtors of showing white and black clients homes or apartments primarily in neighborhoods with residents similar to the client; and *redlining*—the deliberate decision by banks, other home lending institutions, and insurance companies to refuse loans or insurance to people trying to buy homes or insurance in lower-income minority neighborhoods.

A major source of housing discrimination involves home loans. A study that analyzed over 10 million applications for home loans from every savings and loan association in the country between 1983 and 1988 showed that applications from blacks were rejected more than twice as often as were applications from whites. Moreover, the applications of high-income blacks were rejected more often than were those of low-income whites. In 1991 a comprehensive Federal Reserve Board study of mortgage lending showed that even within the same income groups, whites were nearly twice as likely as blacks (and one-and-a-half times as likely as Hispanics) to get loans. Similarly, a 1993 study of five Midwestern cities found that insurance agents were five times more likely to refuse to sell insurance to inner-city homeowners than they were to residents of high-income areas. Studies such as these have led to increasing scrutiny of banking and insurance industry practices and, in some cases, legal settlements in which mortgage-lending and insurance companies have agreed to extend their activities more fully to lower-income neighborhoods (Dedman 1989; *Federal Reserve Bulletin* 1991; *USA Today* 1991; Kerr 1993; Passell 1996; Lewis 1997).

Although some of the mechanisms (e.g., restrictive covenants) through which residential racial segregation is perpetuated are no longer used as widely as in the past, the existence of racial housing discrimination has been extensively documented in what are called "fair housing audit studies." Like the bias studies described in Part 1, fair housing audits involve sending equally qualified individuals (auditors) who differ only in their racial or ethnic identity to investigate the availability of sale or rental housing. During the 1970s and 1980s more than 70 such studies were undertaken throughout the country and overwhelmingly documented widespread discrimination in virtually all phases of the process of seeking housing—from initial contacts with realtors to financing. The most comprehensive study, involving over 3,800 audits in 25 different metropolitan areas, found that

> between 5 and 10 percent of the time, all information about available housing units was with-held from black and Hispanic customers; that black and Hispanic home buyers and black renters were informed about 25 percent fewer housing units than comparable whites; and that whites were significantly more likely than blacks or Hispanics to receive follow-up calls from the housing agent or to hear positive comments about an available house, apartment, or apartment complex. (Yinger 1995)

The barriers that minority applicants encounter from real estate brokers in locating housing are repeated as minority auditors seek to obtain financing and insurance. "The evidence for discrimination against blacks and Hispanics [provided by the fair housing audits] in the loan approval process is strong, recent, and compelling. . . . After accounting for the applicant, property, and loan characteristics that lenders say they consider, minority applicants are turned down at a rate that is over 50 percent higher than the rate for comparable whites" (Yinger 1995:85).

Even if these practices had not been employed, federal government policies would have ensured that the suburban population that expanded dramatically after World War II would be overwhelmingly white and that African Americans would be relegated primarily to the inner cities. Most important was the decision—perfectly consistent with a capitalist economy—to permit private enterprise to meet the great demand for housing that had developed during the Depression and World War II. As a result, suburban housing was built almost exclusively for those who could afford to pay, while people unable to meet financing requirements were forced to accept housing vacated by those moving to the suburbs. On the other hand, low-cost, government-subsidized housing, which attracted a primarily black clientele, was constructed mostly in center cities rather than in the suburbs (Grier and Grier 1965). Therefore, organized neighborhood resistance to proposals for low-income and moderate-income housing is often a veiled form of attitudinal discrimination that serves to reinforce the patterns of residential segregation.

In their historical analysis of the development of residential racial segregation and economic opportunity in Philadelphia, Hershberg and his associates (1979) note the crucial importance of residential proximity to jobs in American history. For many whites, occupational opportunities have been the primary factor in determining where to live. Blacks, on the other hand, have been circumscribed by racial exclusion. In the nineteenth century, when they resided in close proximity to occupational opportunities, African Americans were arbitrarily excluded from jobs. Today, when employment discrimination has declined, they are excluded by physical distance. Pettigrew assesses the implications of the continuing spatial isolation of African Americans:

> This massive metropolitan pattern of housing segregation has now become the principal barrier to progress in other realms. Indeed, the residential segregation of blacks and whites has emerged as a functional equivalent for the explicit state segregation laws of the past in that it effectively acts to limit the life chances and choices of black people generally. (Pettigrew 1979:124)

Today, despite federal fair-housing legislation, a Supreme Court decision that declared housing discrimination illegal, generally more favorable racial attitudes by whites toward African Americans, and a substantial growth of the black middle class, residential segregation still persists on a massive scale in the United States.

Is the residential segregation of African Americans a result of racial discrimination, or is it a reflection of the generally lower overall class position of blacks? Taeuber and Taeuber (1965) have shown that the residential segregation of African Americans is not primarily a result of black income levels, which, they maintain, can account for only a small portion of residential segregation. High-income whites and high-income blacks do not live in the same neighborhoods, nor do low-income whites and low-income blacks; Massey and Denton conclude that in the debate over race versus class, when residence is considered, "race clearly predominates" (Massey and Denton 1993). Nevertheless, if, as Wilson argues, class factors have increasingly come to affect the life chances of American racial and ethnic minorities—not merely African Americans, but Hispanics and American Indians, as well—then these other minorities should experience comparable forms of residential segregation.

However, critics dispute the arguments that the effects of structural economic changes are equally devastating to other contemporary racial and ethnic minorities such as Hispanics and American Indians. Rather, they argue, because race remains an important determinant of opportunity in American life, other minorities, even those from comparable class locations, have been and will be able to experience spatial assimilation more easily than African Americans.

Massey and Mullan (1984) found substantial differences in the changes that occurred during the 1960s in the residential patterns of Hispanics and African Americans: "A barrio-centered residential pattern simply does not typify the experience of Hispanics in the same way that a ghetto-centered pattern typifies that of blacks" (Massey and Mullan 1984:870). African Americans who moved into previously white neighborhoods found that their presence led to white flight, but Hispanics did not:

> Residential succession (an exodus of current residents) is likely to follow the entry of Hispanics into an Anglo area when the incoming Hispanics are poorly educated and foreign, with low occupational statuses and incomes, and when the tract is near an established black or Hispanic area. In contrast, residential succession follows black entry into an Anglo area no matter what the objective social characteristics of the incoming blacks. . . . Because the Anglo response to Hispanic invasion is not universally one of avoidance and flight, Hispanics are much better able than blacks to translate social into residential mobility. . . .
>
> [Moreover,] the social status required of blacks before they are not threatening to Anglos appears to be significantly higher than that required of Hispanics. In other words, a black lawyer or doctor may be able to move into a mixed neighborhood with other professionals, but a black

plumber or bricklayer cannot buy into a working-class Anglo neighborhood. What is required for black spatial assimilation is a quantum leap in social status. (Massey and Mullan 1984: 851–852, 854, 856)

Massey and Mullan conclude that "Anglos avoid blacks on the basis of race, not class," whereas the converse was more likely to be true for Hispanics.

As previously noted, the processes of suburbanization and residential segregation have been intimately interwoven. As Americans—including racial and ethnic minorities—experience upward socioeconomic mobility, they try to move to better neighborhoods, which in the post–World War II era has frequently meant the suburbs. However, the range of residential opportunities available to African Americans has been much more limited than those for whites—or even for Hispanics or Asians. Although affluent Hispanics and Asians have been able to translate improved socioeconomic status into suburban spatial assimilation, blacks have largely been restricted to equally segregated black suburbs immediately adjacent to central cities. Massey and Mullan (1984) and Massey and Denton (1987) found that throughout the 1960s and 1970s, Asians and Hispanics (except for Puerto Ricans, who are more likely than other Hispanics to be identified as black) were not confronted with the same residential barriers encountered by blacks. As a consequence, "middle-class blacks live[d] in much poorer neighborhoods than [did] middle-class whites, Hispanics, or Asians" (Massey and Denton 1993:144).

During the 1980s, however, the residential patterns of African Americans, Latinos, and Asians converged somewhat. As we have seen, black segregation indices in many American cities and for the country as a whole declined between 1980 and 1990—from a mean segregation for 232 metropolitan areas of 69 in 1980 to 64 in 1990. On the other hand, while Latinos and Asians were significantly less segregated than blacks in 1980 (with overall indices of 42 and 41, respectively), each experienced slight overall increases in segregation by 1990. Frey and Farley (1996) found that during the 1980s "segregation between Latinos and non-Latinos increased in more than half (52%) [of the metropolitan areas] and between Asians and non-Asians in almost three-quarters (74%). In contrast, segregation between blacks and nonblacks rose in only 12% of the areas. In 1990, Latinos and Asians were far less segregated than blacks (with average segregation scores of 43, 43, and 64, respectively). Yet these averages for the former two groups increased over the 1980s while the score for blacks fell" (Frey and Farley 1996:36–37).

Unlike Wilson, who contends that economic class factors will in the future affect similar life chances for African Americans and Hispanics, Massey and Mullan (1984) contend that because blacks are unable to translate economic mobility into spatial assimilation in the same manner as Hispanics, "the discrepant patterns of black and Hispanic spatial assimilation portend very different futures for these groups." Because residential integration has strong effects on other patterns of social interaction such as friendships, marriage, and schooling, African Americans are likely to remain socially and spatially isolated in the United States. They therefore dispute the notion that Hispanics can be seen as an underclass in the same way as blacks: "Unlike blacks, [Hispanics] are able to translate social mobility into residential mobility. Hispanics are simply not trapped in the barrio in the same way that blacks are trapped in the ghetto" (Massey and Mullan 1984:870).

However, the growing concentration of Hispanic and Asian communities in proximity to black neighborhoods in many metropolitan areas suggests an increased "potential for greater mixed-race neighborhood living" (Frey and Farley 1996:49) and that in the future segregation *within* metropolitan areas may be less dramatic than what Frey (1996) has termed the "demographic balkanization" of the United States—the concentration of African Americans, Latinos, and Asians in certain metropolitan areas and regions and the white population in others.

Marital Assimilation

Gordon maintains that once structural assimilation has occurred, other dimensions of assimilation—most importantly, intermarriage, or what he terms marital *assimilation* or *amalgamation*—will follow. Marital assimilation, he claims, represents the final outcome of the assimilation process, in which "the minority group ultimately loses its ethnic identity in the larger host or core society" (Gordon 1964:80).

The extent to which marital assimilation has occurred among different ethnic groups has been the subject of considerable research. One of the most celebrated interpretations of intermarriage patterns among white Americans was the "triple melting pot" thesis, which saw intermarriage increasing across ethnic lines but remaining within the three religious communities of Protestants, Catholics, and Jews (Kennedy 1944, 1952). Although this interpretation was integral to Herberg's discussion (1955) of general patterns of ethnic identity discussed before, subsequent analyses have raised many questions concerning its validity (Peach 1981; Hirschman 1983). Richard Alba's analysis of ethnic marriage patterns among American Catholics (1981) demonstrated increasing rates of religious intermarriage, which in turn "point to a decline in the salience of religious boundaries for a good part of the Catholic group." This general inference about the waning significance of religious boundaries could be extended to Protestants, with whom Catholics most frequently intermarry, as well. In other words, religious affiliation is declining in salience as a factor influencing mate selection.

Moreover, recent analyses suggest that white ethnic groups generally have experienced substantial marital assimilation, especially among third and fourth generations and those from higher occupational categories. In national studies of assimilation among American Catholics, Alba (1976, 1981) and Alba and Kessler (1979) found that as early as 1963, marriage outside ethnic groups was extensive. Rates of intermarriage were most pronounced among the third generation and among the youngest adult members of each ethnic group. Similarly, in a study of ethnic consciousness in Providence, Rhode Island, Goering found that among the Irish and Italians, only 15 percent of the first generation had married outside their own ethnic group, whereas 63 percent of the third generation had done so (Goering 1971:382n). Later, utilizing the 1979 population survey on ancestry, Alba and Golden (1986) found high rates of intermarriage among Europeans but, except for Native Americans, relatively low rates between Europeans and non-Europeans, especially blacks. Intermarriage rates were higher for "old" immigrant European ancestry groups (British, Irish, German, and Scandinavian) than for "new" immigrant ancestry groups (Italian, Polish, Russian, and Slavic). However, in "Assimilation's Quiet Tide" (Article 15), Alba contends that 1990 census data point to dramatic increases in intermarriage among "new" immigrant ancestry groups as well. These data show that "more than half . . . of whites have spouses whose ethnic backgrounds do not overlap their own at all . . . [and] only one-fifth have spouses with similar ethnic backgrounds" and that these trends are especially pronounced among Italians and Poles.

Further dramatic evidence of this trend toward increased marital assimilation is shown in the rates of intermarriage for American Jews. Jewish rates of intermarriage vary by city. For example, in New York City less than one-sixth (14 percent of men and 12 percent of women) of Jews married non-Jewish spouses whereas in Denver more than half of spouses married were born as gentiles (Cohen 1988:27). The national rate of Jewish intermarriage with non-Jews has been most pronounced in the last generation. Basing their conclusions on a 1990 survey of American Jews—the most comprehensive ever undertaken—a study by the Council of Jewish Federations reported that 91 percent of Jews who married before 1965 had married non-Jews, but that this percentage had declined substantially in each succeeding decade. Of those Jews who married after 1985, less than half (48 percent) married other Jews. Moreover, the authors found that of those Jews who had married non-Jews, only slightly more than one-fourth (28 percent) of their children were being raised as Jews (Council of Jewish Federations 1991:13–16). This trend toward increasing rates of religious intermarriage has raised concerns among many Jews that the future of the American Jewish community may be threatened (Glazer 1987; Cohen 1988; Goldberg 1997).

Although interethnic and interfaith marriages among whites have been increasingly common through the twentieth century, interracial marriages have been—and continue to be—relatively rare in American society. As Table 1 indicates, in 1970 less than one percent (0.7%) of all marriages were across racial lines, while in 1995 that figure had increased substantially—more than doubling between 1980 and 1995—but still represented only 2.5 percent of all marriages.

Among racial categories, marital assimilation has been most pronounced among Asians. As early as 1973, Tinker (1973) found that more than half of the marriages by Japanese were to non-Japanese. Montero (1981), basing his analysis on 1970 census data, found that, except for American Indians, the rates of intermarriage for Asians were higher than for any other racial category. Levine (1989) has reported that 60 percent of the Sansei (third-generation Japanese Americans) have Caucasian spouses. Similarly, Wong (1989) documented a major increase in intermarriage among Chinese Americans during the past half century. Whereas Chinese American marriages were basically endogamous up to the 1930s, by 1980 over 30 percent of Chinese marriages were to non-Chinese, primarily whites. Extending this analysis to 1990, Qian (1997) examined data and found that only 39 percent of Asian men and 34 percent of Asian women between the ages of 20 and 29 had married other Asians.

However, the patterns of extensive intermarriage for European ethnic groups, Asians, and American Indians are not duplicated among Hispanics and especially African Americans, although recent data indicate substantial increases in intermarriages for these two categories (Qian 1997). The percentages of Hispanics marrying other Hispanics declined between 1980 and 1990; by 1990 the marriages of nearly identical proportions of 20- to 29-year-old Hispanic men and women (64% and 63%, respectively) were endogamous. Although the number of African American intermarriages also increased between 1980 and 1990, African Americans were the racial minority most likely to be endogamous; in 1990 better than 90 percent of 20- to 29-year-old African American men and women were married to other African Americans.

TABLE 1 *Married Couples of Same or Mixed Races and Origins, 1970 to 1995*

Race and Origin of Spouses	1970*	1980	1990	1995
Married Couples, total	44,598	49,714	53,256	54,937
RACE				
Same-race couples	43,922	48,264	50,889	51,733
White/white	40,578	44,910	47,202	48,030
Black/black	3,344	3,354	3,687	3,703
Interracial couples	310	651	964	1,392
Black/white	65	167	211	328
Black husband/white wife	41	122	150	206
White husband/black wife	24	45	61	122
White/other race[†]	233	450	720	988
Black/other race[†]	12	34	33	76
All other couples[†]	366	799	1,401	1,811
HISPANIC ORIGIN				
Hispanic/Hispanic	1,368	1,906	3,085	3,857
Hispanic/other origin (not Hispanic)	584	891	1,193	1,434
All other couples (not of Hispanic origin)	42,645	46,917	48,979	49,646

Source: U.S. Bureau of the Census. *Statistical Abstract of the United States: 1995.* (Washington, D.C.: Government Printing Office, 1996), p. 57.

*As of April and based on Census of Population

[†]Excluding white and black

In thousands. As of March, except as noted. Persons 15 years old and over. Persons of Hispanic origin may be of any race. Except as noted, based on Current Population Survey.

Thus, black-white marriages are the least frequent of all interracial marriage patterns. Although there was a five-fold increase in the number of black-white marriages between 1970 and 1995, such unions still represented only 0.59 percent of all marriages in the United States. In general, intermarriage rates among different racial and ethnic categories are influenced by such factors as cultural similarities, generational status, residential dispersion, and socioeconomic status.

Why Assimilation Rates Vary

Analyses of race and ethnicity in American life have frequently reflected social and political controversies within the broader society. As we noted in Part 1, the research agenda in the field of racial and ethnic relations—the issues considered and the questions posed—frequently has been drawn from social policy concerns, not from sociological theory alone.

One of the most striking changes in the research agenda in the field of racial and ethnic relations over the past two decades has been a shift to a broadly comparative perspective. Some scholars have taken a cross-cultural perspective, examining the dynamics of race and ethnicity throughout the world (for example, Burgess 1978; Francis 1976; Glazer and Moynihan 1975; Gordon 1978; Hechter 1975; Henry 1976; Horowitz 1985; Olzak and Nagel 1986; Rose 1976).

However, the black protest activity of the 1950s and 1960s, which sought to eliminate the chasm historically separating African Americans from the American mainstream, contributed substantially to a resurgence of interest in ethnicity that focused on other ethnic groups in American society as well. Since the late 1970s, research dealing with ethnicity in American society has proliferated (for example, Dinnerstein and Reimers 1983, 1987; Greeley 1976; Kinton 1977; Lieberson 1980; Mindel and Habenstein 1976; Patterson 1977; Seller 1977; Sowell 1978, 1980, 1981; Steinberg 1981). This shift from a focus almost exclusively on black-white relations to an examination of the role of ethnicity in American life was stimulated in part by the conflicts that emerged from African Americans' claims for equal participation and opportunity. As Steinberg has pointed out, "That the ethnic resurgence involved more than nostalgia became clear as racial minorities and white ethnics became polarized on a series of issues relating to schools, housing, local government and control over federal programs" (Steinberg 1981:50).

The resentment fueled by these conflicts with African Americans was reflected in the question frequently posed by white ethnics: "If we made it, why can't they?" If Greeley's characterization of the "ethnic miracle" is correct—if Jews, Poles, Italians, and the Irish today have "made it," how have they been able to do so while other groups have not? How do we account for the "extraordinary success story" of Catholics and Jews, who had to overcome poverty, discrimination, illiteracy, and chronic overcrowding in America's urban ghettos?

Explanations for differences in socioeconomic status—levels of income, educational attainment, and occupational prestige—among American ethnic groups that formerly were debated informally and privately in bull sessions, dinner parties, and cocktail parties, have increasingly become the focus of formal inquiry by social scientists, whose interpretations have become part of that public discourse. During the past decade, especially, there have been numerous comparative studies of American ethnic groups: advancing explanations for the differences in achievement levels among American ethnic groups has become a major preoccupation of specialists in the field.

Several explanations for the differences among American ethnic groups have been advanced. Although there are considerable differences among them, they can be divided into two broad categories: those that emphasize qualities and characteristics internal to an ethnic group, and those that emphasize the influence of factors external to an ethnic group—forces over which members of the group have little or no control.

Internal Explanations

Internal explanations of social inequality attribute racial and ethnic inequalities to each group's perceived abilities, attributes, and characteristics. An internal model explains an ethnic group's adaptation, adjustment, achievement, or assimilation as the result primarily of the traits, qualities, or characteristics that the group brings with it—the group's own "personality," if you will. The emphasis in this argument is on the "inheritance" or transmission of behavioral traits and characteristics and on their continuity across generations. Dominant groups have achieved their status because they possess desirable qualities; on the other hand, the economic, political, and social status of subordinate groups is attributed to their own deficiencies. Therefore, in this view, racial and ethnic groups are responsible for their own fate—for their own success or lack of it.

Biology

The most simplistic of the internal explanations is a biological or genetic argument. One of the oldest internal explanations is that American ethnic or racial groups have different *biological* endowments—innately different mental, emotional, and moral characteristics—that are genetically transmitted from generation to generation. Such biological explanations flourished during the late nineteenth and early twentieth centuries, when differences between the political, social, and economic institutions of Anglo-Saxon and non–Anglo-Saxon peoples were attributed to biologically transmitted—that is, "racial"—traits. Thus Senator Henry Cabot Lodge, in an 1896 Senate speech condemning continued unrestricted immigration by peoples from southern and eastern Europe, argued that the Anglo-Saxon capacity for democracy was instinctual:

> The men of each race possess an indestructible stock of ideas, traditions, sentiments, modes of thought, an unconscious inheritance from their ancestors, upon which argument has no effect. What makes a race are their mental and, above all, their moral characteristics, the slow growth and accumulation of centuries of toil and conflict. These are the qualities which determine the social efficiency as a people, which make one race rise and another fall. (Lodge 1896:2819)

Lodge, and most other intellectuals of the day, believed that the "old" immigrants from northern and western Europe (the British, Germans, and Scandinavians) were descended from common ancestors who were "historically free, energetic, and progressive," whereas Slavic, Latin, and Asiatic races were historically downtrodden, atavistic, and stagnant" (Quoted in Solomon 1956:111).

Given these assumptions, which were supposed to be scientifically valid, unrestricted immigration meant the introduction of millions of unassimilable people who lacked the "superior" instincts of northern and western Europeans. The absence of these instincts, Lodge believed, would ultimately bring about the "decline of human civilization." Much of the "scientific" research concerning racial inequality in the last half of the nineteenth and first half of the twentieth centuries involved examination of physical differences and differences in intelligence test performances among American racial and ethnic groups. Frequently, inferences from such studies were cited as evidence of the biological inferiority of non–Anglo-Saxon groups and then used to justify their subordinate status. As a consequence, during this period the ideology of racism gained respectability. As we noted in Part 1, *racism* refers to the belief that the members of one group are biologically superior, whereas other groups are inherently inferior and "incapable of ever achieving intellectual and moral equality" with them (Noel 1972:157).

For more than a century, the ideology of racism has been shaped and justified by "science." Early in the twentieth century, studies of cranial capacity—brain sizes and structures—became fashionable. Assuming that brain size and intelligence are related, scientists established a racial hierarchy of intelligence, with northern Europeans highest and Africans lowest. Recalculation of the data in many of these studies has shown that the procedures that were used to establish this hierarchy were not accurate and simply reflected the scientists' prejudices; these procedures amounted to "advocacy masquerading as objectivity" (Gould 1981). Although the studies were far from scientific, they were used to "prove" the biological superiority of northern and western Europeans and to justify social policies of racial domination.

Early in the twentieth century, intelligence testing replaced anatomic studies as a way of "scientifically" measuring and validating the "natural superiority" of socially dominant groups. Since then, intelligence tests have been widely administered, have played a crucial role in reinforcing the belief that racial, ethnic, and class inequalities result from innate qualities, and have had a widespread impact on public policy. For example, the poor performances of southern and eastern European immigrants (in which 80 percent of Hungarians, 79 percent of Italians, and 87 percent of Russians scored in the "feeble-minded" category) were frequently cited in the congressional debates that resulted in the discriminatory immigration quotas established during the 1920s. Moreover, racial differences in intelligence test results for years provided the justification for racial segregation, the vastly unequal school systems for blacks and whites, and the near-exclusion of blacks from higher education (Gould 1981; Weinberg 1983).

By the mid–twentieth century, as criticisms of these tests and their uses mounted, the notion of racial differences in intelligence found little support in the scientific community. After the Supreme Court's 1954 *Brown* decision, however, the issue of racial differences in intelligence was revived and became a prominent argument in the Southern campaign of "massive resistance" to school desegregation.

The alleged genetic component in racial differences in intelligence test performance became the subject of international debate in 1969 with the publication of an article by Arthur R. Jensen in the *Harvard Educational Review*. Jensen distinguished between two types of learning: *associative* (involving memory and rote learning) and *conceptual* (involving problem solving and the use of abstractions). He contended that although all children possess associative learning abilities, poor and minority children are deficient in conceptual learning abilities, and that these differences are "genetically conditioned" (Jensen 1969). Jensen's article was greeted by an avalanche of criticism from psychologists, sociologists, and geneticists who attacked his methods, logic, evidence, and, above all, the implication that differences in intelligence test scores should influence social and educational policy (Richardson and Spears 1972).

A quarter century later, *The Bell Curve,* a book by Richard Herrnstein and Charles Murray (1994), once again raised the claim that certain groups in American society—especially African Americans—are intellectually inferior because they generally have lower scores on standardized intelligence tests. Equally important, Herrnstein and Murray claim that the stratification system of the United States directly reflects the differential intelligence of individuals and groups and that intelligence is primarily inherited or genetic. The authors argue that intelligence ("a person's capacity for complex mental work") describes a real attribute of humans that is "substantially" (60 percent) inherited and remains stable over a person's lifetime. Moreover, they assert that intelligence "can be measured with accuracy and fairness by any number of standardized mental tests, [which] . . . are not biased against socioeconomic, ethnic, and racial groups." Numerical intelligence test (IQ) scores thus accurately reflect individual and group intelligence levels.

Examining a voluminous amount of data, Herrnstein and Murray maintain that in American society today, measured intelligence (IQ) is positively correlated with success as measured by educational and occupational attainment and overall socio-economic status, and that IQ is negatively correlated with poverty, unemployment, single-parent families, and criminality. They conclude that the class structure of contemporary American society reflects the distribution of intelligence; the upper classes comprise members of the "cognitive elite," whereas the less intelligent are overrepresented in the lower classes. Moreover, they contend that races differ in intelligence and that the lower IQ test performance of blacks and Latinos indicate that they are less intelligent than whites and Asians. Finally, they find that many modern social problems—poverty, unemployment, poor parenting, single-parent families, welfare dependency, and crime—result from low intelligence and, that, as a consequence, social and educational programs (e.g., Head Start) designed to improve and remedy such conditions are ineffective (Herrnstein and Murray 1994).

The response to Herrnstein and Murray's book was similar to that to Jensen's argument: critics vigorously challenged their basic assumptions, procedures and methods, evidence, interpretations, and conclusions. They argue that, despite the wealth of data Hernnstein and Murray cite in their massive (845-page) book, the authors ignore, omit, misrepresent, or use selectively evidence that contradicts their basic argument. *The Bell Curve*, according to one reviewer, is "clearly the most incendiary piece of social science to appear in the last decade or more" (Fraser 1995:1).

First, critics challenge Herrnstein and Murray's assumption that intelligence is a single, primarily inherited, trait that can be accurately measured by IQ tests; rather, they argue that intelligence involves multiple and distinctly different attributes —language skills, mathematical skills, musical ability, interpersonal skills, artistic ability, and spatial relations abilities, for example—that cannot be reduced to a single overall measure. Moreover, they reject the magnitude of Herrnstein and Murray's estimates of the genetic heritability of intelligence, which are based on inferences drawn from studies of pairs of biological relatives (i.e., different IQ correlations between identical twins, fraternal twins, siblings, and first cousins). Such studies measure not only inheritance but also the effects of environmental factors, which Herrnstein and Murray minimize. "The more similar a pair is biologically, then the more similar they are as well in their environments"—even among twins separated early in life and raised in different environments (Taylor 1995:156). Thus, performance on IQ tests depends not simply on an individual's innate "intelligence," but on what a person has previously learned (Hanson 1995:24).

Critics also contest Herrnstein and Murray's contention that because intelligence is substantially genetic, it changes little in the lives of individuals or the histories of racial and ethnic groups. Contrary to Herrnstein and Murray's objections that programs such as Head Start have failed to enhance educational performance, the American Psychological Association asserted that "there is a wealth of research evidence showing that early educational interventions are effective in raising performance and achievement levels for disadvantaged groups." Similarly, after recalculating data used by Hernnstein and Murray, Hauser and Nisbitt independently showed that improvements in black test scores between 1969 and 1990 undermine notions of the immutability of intelligence over time. Similarly, conservative economist Thomas Sowell has noted that the test performances of numerous American ethnic groups (Jews, Italians, Poles) have improved dramatically over the course of the twentieth century (Hauser 1995; Nisbitt 1995; Sowell 1995).

The reliability of IQ tests themselves has been questioned. Taylor rejects Herrnstein and Murray's assertion that such tests are free of cultural bias and argues that the authors selectively ignored evidence of such cultural bias in some of the studies that they themselves cite (Taylor 1995). Moreover, studies by psychologist Claude Steele suggest that, given the pervasiveness of stereotypes of black intellectual inferiority, black and white students respond differently to testing situations. When confronted with situations—including standardized tests, such as the SAT or ACT—in which they perceive that their academic performance will reflect upon or be interpreted in racial terms, African Americans are subject to what Steele terms "stereotype vulnerability." He contends that situations in which blacks risk conforming to negative stereotypes of their intellectual abilities introduce subtle psychological stresses that can undermine performance; when black students are presented with identical tests under conditions not defined as measuring their intellectual abilities, they perform as well as white students (Steele and Aronson 1995; Watters 1995; Steele 1997).

Wolfe (1995) challenges the notion that IQ predicts later career success, contending that there is no evidence that IQ test performance is related to job performance or to income attainments. Finally, assertions of intelligence differences between racial groups ignores the arbitrary, socially constructed nature of such categories. In American society the categories of "white," "black," and "Asian" are not real "biological" entities but rather consist of people with a wide range of biological characteristics. In order for inferences to be drawn about racial characteristics, it would necessary to have distinct, "pure" biological pools, which, given the extraordinary ethnic diversity of the American people, obviously is not the case in the United States.

Herrnstein and Murray conclude *The Bell Curve* with a discussion of the public policy implications of their findings. Critics charge that their social policy discussion reveals the real objective of *The Bell Curve:* to advance and provide justification for the authors' conservative political agenda; although Herrnstein and Murray cloak their argument in the mantle of "science," their real objective is to attack a number of public policies, including welfare, affirmative action, and immigration. Recognizing that the controversy over race and intelligence is primarily political, the Genetics Society of America addressed the issue with the following statement: "In our views, there is no convincing evidence as to whether there is or is not an appreciable genetic difference in intelligence between races. . . . Whether or not there are significant genetic inequalities in no way alters our ideal of political equality, nor justifies racism or discrimination in any form" (Quoted in Weinberg 1983:74).

As we pointed out in Part 1, the conceptions of "race" entertained by Henry Cabot Lodge, which, in one form or another, were shared by virtually all American social scientists at the turn of the twentieth century, are radically different from prevailing scientific notions today. As the intense critique of Jensen's and of Herrnstein and Murray's work indicates, biological explanations for racial and ethnic inequalities enjoy little legitimacy among contemporary social scientists. The important conceptual distinction between biological explanations and those embraced today resides in the understanding of the *process* by which behavioral traits and characteristics are transmitted. Traits that once were considered to be "instinctual," innate, and biologically inherited are today conceived to be learned—a product not of the genes but of socialization. Ethnic group traits and characteristics are considered by most social scientists to be derived not from biological but from cultural and social factors.

Culture

The most prominent contemporary internal explanation attributes an ethnic group's position in a society's stratification system to its *cultural* characteristics: the values, attitudes, beliefs, store of knowledge, customs, and habits learned in the family and the community. Almost by definition, ethnic groups are perceived to differ in their distinctive cultural inventory. Those groups that have succeeded have done so because they possess the values and cultural traits that make for success in American society—such as high achievement motivation, industriousness, perseverance, future orientation, ability to postpone immediate gratification for later rewards, and so forth. Groups that have internalized such values succeed, whereas those lacking them are doomed to failure. Those who have succeeded have done so because of the traits that their cultural tradition bequeathed them. On the other hand, a group's low socioeconomic status can be attributed to the fact that its cultural inventory did not include the requisite values, attitudes, and personal qualities. An underlying assumption of a cultural interpretation, therefore, is that "American society provides ample opportunity for class mobility and it is [the minority's] cultural institutions—'home and family and community'—that are problematic" (Steinberg 1981:119). Whether an ethnic group succeeds or fails, it is perceived as being responsible for its own fate—what William Ryan (1971) has called a "blaming the victim" ideology. By implication, those who have been less successful than others can ensure their entrance into the mainstream of American society by becoming more fully culturally assimilated, by adopting the cultural values of the dominant group.

Hershberg and his associates (1979) have identified two variants of the cultural argument: the "bootstraps" and the "last of the immigrants" explanations. The *bootstraps* explanation for the socioeconomic success of white ethnics and Asians is that they were able to overcome the disabilities with which they were confronted because through hard work, industriousness, perseverance, self-reliance, and thrift, they exploited as fully as possible the economic opportunity that America afforded. They pulled themselves up by their own bootstraps without governmental assistance. Andrew Greeley, whose empirical research on the socioeconomic attainments of European ancestry groups established that by the early 1970s, the "white ethnic" descendants of "new immigrants" had reached parity with and, indeed, in some instances had surpassed "old" immigrants, subscribes to a cultural explanation in his analysis of the post–World War II socioeconomic achievements of Catholic and Jewish Americans. Their achievements, he writes, were the consequence of "something in the culture of the immigrants themselves." Greeley contends that when "new" immigrants began their struggle for upward mobility in the first two decades of the twentieth century,

> There were no quotas, no affirmative action, no elaborate system of social services and, heaven knows, no ethnic militancy. There was no talk of reparations, no sense of guilt, no feeling of compassion for these immigrants. . . . Hard work, saving, sacrifice—such is a tentative explanation of the "ethnic miracle." (Greeley 1976:21, 31)

However, a cultural argument has been nowhere more clearly and effectively articulated than by Thomas Sowell, an economist who has written widely concerning American ethnic groups (Sowell 1978, 1980, 1981). Sowell contends that the variations in rates of socioeconomic status and achievement among American ethnic groups can best be explained by examining a group's cultural inheritance. "Whether in an ethnic context or among peoples and nations in general, much depends on the whole constellation of values, attitudes, skills, and contacts that many call a culture and that economists call 'human capital.'" That is, different rates of achievement among American ethnic groups are a result of differences in the cultural inventories that have been transmitted to them from previous generations. The different values, attitudes and moral disciplines that comprise each group's cultural inheritance, which "can be more important than biological inheritance," therefore provide the crucial ingredients that account for success or failure in American society. On the one hand, ethnic groups "that arrived in America financially destitute have rapidly risen to affluence, when their cultures stressed the values and behavior required in an industrial and commercial economy." On the other hand, "groups today plagued by absenteeism, tardiness, and a need for constant supervision at work or in school are typically descendants of people with the same habits a century or more ago" (Sowell 1981:282, 284).

An emphasis on education has often been cited as an explanation for the extremely high levels of achievement among Jews. For example, in a widely noted cultural explanation of differences in ethnic group achievement levels, Fred Strodtbeck (1958) argued that Jewish goals, values, and cultural norms were more compatible with the dominant values of American society than were those of other ethnic groups. In particular, the value of education, learning, and scholarly inquiry was long expressed in the intellectual tradition of orthodox Jewish culture. Jewish immigrants placed high prestige on education and educational attainments: the scholar was venerated and accorded respect. As Abraham Cahan wrote in his classic novel of Jewish immigrant life, *The Rise of David Levinsky,* "The ghetto rang with a clamor for knowledge. . . . To save up some money and prepare for college seemed to be the most natural thing to do" (Cahan 1966:156). By contrast, most Catholic "new" immigrants came from peasant backgrounds where formal education and learning were alien and remote. Southern Italian immigrants, who in many respects were typical of Catholic "new" immigrants, came from a society in which formal education clashed with traditional values. For them, education and learning were regarded as a threat to the integrity and strength of the family. Unlike Jews, Italian parents saw little value in education and did not encourage their children toward educational attainments (Strodtbeck 1958; Vecoli 1964).

A cultural explanation is frequently invoked to explain the economic and educational attainments of Asian Americans, who have frequently been characterized as "model minorities." As *Time* magazine recently proclaimed, "Asians have become exemplary immigrants . . . [who] have produced a veritable galaxy of stellar performers in the U.S., from the arts and sciences to business and finance. Like immigrating Jews of earlier generations, they have parlayed cultural emphases on education and hard work into brilliant attainments. . . . There is something in the Asian family that promotes success" (Walsh 1993:55). By contrast, the disadvantaged socioeconomic positions of African Americans, Latino Americans, and American Indians today are portrayed simply as a consequence of *their* cultural characteristics, which are perceived to be incompatible with a modern industrial society. By implication, groups that have been less successful can enter the American mainstream by changing their value system—by getting rid of the values that have kept them back and becoming more fully culturally assimilated, by simply adopting the cultural values of the dominant group.

The other, sometimes complementary, explanation is the *last-of-the-immigrants* argument. Whereas a bootstraps argument emphasizes the cultural characteristics of minorities who have attained socioeconomic mobility, a last-of-the-immigrants model focuses on the social system, or opportunity structure, within which they achieved their successes. According to this argument, ethnic socioeconomic success is only a matter of time, and those ethnic groups who have most recently migrated to the nation's cities (Chicanos, Puerto Ricans, American Indians, and, in particular, African Americans) must not be impatient with their present position at the bottom of the economic ladder. In several generations they will inevitably repeat the experience of European ethnic groups and climb into the American economic, educational, and political mainstream. Thomas Sowell, for example, contends that today's patterns of white flight from the central cities to the haven of suburbia are merely repeating the process of ethnic succession that has long been a characteristic feature of America's ethnically diverse cities; ethnic groups who arrive first move when their territory is invaded by a new and "inferior" ethnic group (Sowell 1981:277–278). Similarly, a recent *Time* magazine feature on the ethnic diversity of Lowell, Massachusetts, stressed the progression of immigrant groups—rural Yankees, Irish, French Canadian, Greek, Cambodian, and Lebanese—who have inhabited an area of the city known as the Acre. The city's Greek mayor, who grew up in the neighborhood, described the process of social mobility: "The Acre is the bottom of the social ladder. . . . The last group that comes in is always on the bottom rung. But you can climb that ladder. You just have to prove your worth to the group ahead of you to be accepted" (Blackman 1993:54).

Social Class

The traditional cultural explanation for the rapid mobility of Jewish immigrants (as contrasted to Catholic "new" immigrants) stressed the high value placed on education, learning, and scholarly achievement among immigrant Jews. However, Stephen Steinberg rejects the interpretation that Jewish *values* are the explanation for their success. Instead, he focuses on the impact of the different social-class backgrounds of entering immigrants. In *The Ethnic Myth* (1981/1989), he points out that although Jewish and Catholic "new" immigrants entered the United States with about the same meager amounts of money, their occupational backgrounds were not identical. Immigrant Jews came overwhelmingly from towns and cities of eastern Europe, where they had had extensive experience with manufacturing and commerce. More than two-thirds of Jewish immigrants were skilled workers, professionals, or merchants, as opposed to only one-sixth of southern Italians and one-sixteenth of Polish immigrants. More than two-thirds of Italian and three-fourths of Polish immigrants were unskilled laborers or farmers, in contrast to about one-seventh of entering Jews. The skills the Jews brought with them to the United States were needed by an expanding American economy and enabled them to enter at a higher-status level than most unskilled immigrants. These occupational backgrounds and experiences of immigrant Jews enabled their children—the second generation—to acquire relatively easily the middle-class skills that were a prerequisite for entrance into the professions—in particular, academic pursuits.

Jewish and Catholic "new" immigrants differed on another important characteristic: literacy. About one-fourth of all Jews entering the United States between 1899 and 1910 were unable to read and write, whereas more than half (54 percent) of southern Italians and one-third (35 percent) of Poles were illiterate. Similarly, because many Italians and Poles immigrated to the United States as temporary workers and did not intend to settle permanently in this country, they were much less likely to learn to speak English than were Jews, most of whom were fleeing religious persecution in eastern Europe and did not intend to return there. This stronger commitment to settlement in the United States increased the process of cultural assimilation for Jews. Italians and Poles, whose frames of reference remained in the old country, were much more likely to resist assimilation to American culture, a factor that greatly limited the occupational mobility of the second generation.

Steinberg shows how these background factors affected the occupational mobility of Jews and Catholics within the academic profession. Because professionals, especially academics, tend to be drawn from professional, managerial, and small-business backgrounds, individuals whose parents had such characteristics were favored in their access to such pursuits. Hence, the social class characteristics of Jewish and Catholic "new" immigrants were important influences on their patterns of occupational mobility. It was not simply that Jews embraced cultural values that extolled education and revered learning. It was rather "that cultural factors have little independent effect on educational outcomes, but are influential only as they interact with class factors. Thus, to whatever extent a reverence for learning was part of the religious and cultural heritage of Asians and Jews, it was activated and given existential significance by their social class circumstances" (Steinberg 1981:132).

The implication of Steinberg's analysis is that the social class characteristics of different American ethnic groups have played a crucial role in influencing the socioeconomic status of their descendants. As Portes and Bach have argued in their comparison of Mexican and Cuban immigrants to the United States, "the class composition of the different immigrant flows . . . played a decisive role in determining their modes of incorporation and subsequent economic destiny in the United States" (Portes and Bach 1985:48).

Culture and Social Class: A Synthesis

The prominence of small business enterprises among immigrants is one of the most widely documented and debated phenomena in recent ethnic group literature (Cheng and Bonacich 1984; Bonacich and Light 1988; Kim 1981; Waldinger 1987). In Article 16, "Immigrant and Ethnic Enterprise in North America," Ivan Light notes that since 1880, the foreign-born have been overrepresented in commercial small businesses, and he asks why immigrants should have higher rates of self-employment than native-born minorities. Light has sought to develop a synthesis of the role of cultural and class factors that more adequately explains this disproportion and, by implication, variations in ethnic socioeconomic status as well.

Light argues that immigrants may utilize either *ethnic resources* or *class resources* in developing business enterprises. The traditional "ethnic only," or what Light terms the "orthodox" cultural, argument of Greeley and Sowell is that a "tradition of enterprise" is part of the cultural inventory that certain immigrant groups (such as Jews or Japanese) bring with them from their countries of origin. In this "orthodox" cultural explanation of entrepreneurship, a version of Weber's Protestant Ethic, immigrant cultural endowments are transferred relatively intact and unmodified from the old country to the new. On the other hand, a "class only" argument, represented here by Steinberg, explains immigrant socioeconomic success as a function of immigrants' class position—most importantly, the human capital (educational and technical skills) that immigrants bring with them as a result of their class position.

Light suggests a more complex and dynamic model. He contends that it is not merely the cultural baggage or endowments that are crucial in determining the mode of economic incorporation into a new society; instead, cultural attributes are but *one* aspect of ethnic resources that can be drawn upon to promote entrepreneurship. The experience or process of migration and alien status themselves elicit certain distinctive responses from immigrants that contribute to the establishment of entrepreneurship; alien status releases "latent facilitators" that provide entrepreneurial resources independent of immigrants' cultural endowments. Among these factors are relative satisfaction—that many immigrants from low-wage countries are frequently willing to accept economic conditions that Americans are not; reactive solidarity—that ethnic minority status promotes ethnic solidarity, networks, and mutual aid organizations such as rotating credit associations; and that many immigrants come as sojourners, who, wishing to amass money as quickly as possible, consume little and save much. Through each of these mechanisms, the resources with which to establish small businesses are created.

Class resources, on the other hand, may be either cultural or material. The former include bourgeois values and attitudes that are, as Steinberg stressed, a function of class position, not of an entire culture. Material resources include property and money to invest. Light contends that, whereas ethnic resources were most important in establishing immigrant entrepreneurship in the past as the class backgrounds of contemporary immigrants (Koreans, Hong Kong Chinese, Cubans, Iranians) have shifted, class resources in the form of money, human capital, and bourgeois cultural values have increasingly played a prominent role. Therefore, Light argues, traditional cultural and class explanations are inadequate; entrepreneurial activity will be most pronounced when class resources are combined with ethnic resources; comprehending the dynamics of immigrant entrepreneurship today must take account of both factors.

The Enclave Economy Model

The emphasis on ethnic solidarity that is a crucial dimension of Light's ethnic enterprise model is also central to the immigrant enclave model, which emphasizes the social mobility opportunities that an immigrant enclave affords. As previously mentioned, in a dual or segmented labor market model, minorities and women are likely to be relegated to low-wage, dead-end jobs in the "peripheral" or "secondary" labor market, which provides few opportunities for promotion. Because immigrant workers are likely to be incorporated into the secondary sector of the economy, their prospects for mobility and, hence, assimilation into the receiving society are likely to be limited. Given the preference for skills in recent American immigration policy, a substantial portion of immigrants to the United States in the past three decades has been highly skilled and educated professionals and managers. For example, the 1980 census revealed that nearly half (45.6 percent) of all African immigrants and more than two-thirds (69.9 percent) of all Asian Indian immigrants had completed college (Bouvier and Gardner 1986:22). These highly skilled workers are much more likely to be incorporated into the "core" or "primary" sector of the economy than those who are less skilled. Thus, as Waters and Eschbach (Article 14) and Light (Article 16) point out, differences in the levels of class and ethnic resources with which immigrant groups enter American society can have a substantial impact on their incorporation into it.

On the other hand, Waters and Eschbach, summarizing the work of Portes and his associates (Wilson and Portes 1980; Portes and Bach 1985; Portes and Rumbaut 1996), emphasize that the social and economic contexts that immigrants encounter when they arrive are also critical to their incorporation into American society. Immigrant socioeconomic mobility is not simply a function of the immigrants' skill levels or of whether they enter the primary or secondary sector of the economy. Rather, they emphasize that the immigrant community is itself a major factor influencing the range of opportunities available to individual immigrants and, as a consequence, their adaptation to a new society. They have developed the concept of an *enclave economy,* which focuses on the manner in which several immigrant groups have been incorporated into the American economy. A critical element of the enclave model is the presence of coethnics with sufficient capital to provide employment opportunities for newly arrived immigrants. In an enclave economy, immigrant workers are not trapped in the secondary sector of a segmented labor market. Although immigrants are forced to work hard for low wages, their opportunities for upward mobility are not blocked, as is the case for most workers in the secondary labor market. Workers in an immigrant enclave "can be empirically distinguished from workers in both the primary and secondary labor market. Enclave workers will share with those in the primary sector a significant economic return to past human capital investments. Such a return will be absent among those in the 'open' secondary labor market" (Wilson and Portes 1980:302). In other words, the human capital resources (education and skills) brought from the home country will result in greater economic returns for individuals located in an ethnic enclave economy than for those in the outside labor market; an individual entering an enclave economy will ultimately fare better economically than someone with exactly the same level of skills who does not have the advantages of incorporation into an enclave.

The enclave model has been subjected to considerable criticism. For example, Sanders and Nee (1987) found that an enclave economy did not provide overall economic benefits to its participants. Immigrants living outside the enclave had higher socioeconomic status than those living in it. Moreover, they found that immigrant workers in the enclave economy received lower wages than workers in the outside economy. They questioned how truly effective employment in an enclave economy is in facilitating a worker's movement into self-employment. Responding to recent criticisms of the enclave model, Portes and Leif Jensen (1989) refined the notion to refer to a situation in which individuals both live in a community composed predominantly of coethnics and work in enterprises owned by coethnics. In an analysis of the Cuban enclave economy in Miami, they found that self-employed entrepreneurs earned significantly higher incomes if they were located within the enclave. In other words, Cuban entrepreneurship had a positive effect on earnings when it occurred within the enclave economy. Self-employment produced significantly higher increases in earnings among Cubans employed in the enclave when compared with those employed outside the enclave. Moreover, employment in Cuban firms did not reduce the earnings of fellow Cubans. Indeed, for women it actually increased them. Thus Portes and Jensen reject the thesis that small ethnic businesses are economically successful because they exploit their coethnics—the pattern in which entrepreneurship is economically advantageous for employers but comes at the expense of their coethnic employees. They found "no indication of a pattern of overall disadvantage or lower human capital returns among employees in enclave firms" (Portes and Jensen 1989:943).

External Explanations

Most American ethnic groups that have achieved prominence in American life have had to overcome obstacles, hardships, and barriers of some sort, and from an internal perspective their success is a result of their own efforts—they relied on their own resources and are therefore responsible for, and are the architects of, their own fate. Many people will point to the substantial obstacles that they and their ancestors overcame, the barriers that they confronted, and will argue, "We made it, why can't they?" Most internal explanations of social inequality tend to ignore or minimize the impact of external factors that may, on the one hand, limit group opportunities or, on the other, enhance them. An internal explanation therefore assumes that American society provides a relatively constant and level playing field for all racial and ethnic groups—that the structure of opportunity is basically the same for all.

On the other hand, throughout the American experience, different racial and ethnic groups have encountered dramatically different opportunity structures. In contrast to internal explanations of social inequality, *external explanations* emphasize the impact of factors external to the group over which they have no control—both the available opportunities and the constraints, disabilities, limitations, obstacles, and barriers to which a group is subjected. For example, in Article 23, Massey emphasizes two critical conditions that facilitated the dramatic socioeconomic attainments of "white ethnics": the period of unparalleled prosperity and economic opportunity following World War II and the hiatus that characterized immigration from Europe between 1930 and the post–World War II era, both of which contributed to opportunities for structural mobility that will not necessarily be available in the future for immigrant groups that have recently entered American society.

By contrast, some groups (for example, African Americans) have been confronted with substantial barriers that have circumscribed the resources and opportunities available to them and have precluded their full and equal participation in society. As noted in Part 2, there is a range of possible dominant-group policies that, to a greater or lesser degree, limit the options available to a minority group. These range from extermination to discrimination in many different forms.

A cultural explanation tends to minimize or dismiss the role of external factors, especially in contemporary American society. Sowell, for example, contends that the intergroup animosities and discrimination that existed in American society in the past have lessened in intensity and "in some respects disappeared" (Sowell 1981:7). Such a perspective presupposes that social structure is blind to group differences and does not play a significant role in affecting patterns of ethnic group achievement. Put another way, it assumes that the social structure is neutral when it comes to racial and ethnic factors, and that individuals from all ethnic backgrounds have relatively equal opportunities to succeed.

Moreover, a cultural interpretation assumes that external barriers are insignificant in affecting group outcomes because the opportunities of all American ethnic groups have at one time or another been circumscribed in some way. In a variant of the last-of-the-immigrants model, Sowell has contended that all American ethnic groups "have been discriminated against to one degree or another. Yet some of the most successful —such as the Orientals—have experienced worse discrimination than most, and the extraordinary success of Jews has been achieved in the face of centuries of anti-Semitism" (Sowell 1981:6).

Finally, a cultural model assumes that the distinctive traits and capacities that characterize a group will manifest themselves in spite of harsh and restrictive treatment by other groups. Thus, Sowell argues that the characteristics of "working harder and more relentlessly" will overcome even the most pronounced adversity (Sowell 1981:283).

Each of these assumptions has been vigorously challenged by critics who contend that the structural barriers confronting Chicanos, Puerto Ricans, American Indians, and, in particular, African Americans have been more severe and repressive than those encountered by "new" immigrants or even by Asians.

The most apparent external barrier distinguishing the experience of African Americans has been the disability of race, which has subjected blacks, in both the South and the North, to discrimination far more severe than that experienced by any European ethnic groups. For example, Lieberson's analysis (1980) demonstrates that prejudice and discrimination against African Americans in Northern cities intensified rather than diminished during the first few decades of the twentieth century. At the same time that spatial isolation declined for "new" immigrants, it increased markedly for African Americans. Moreover, the discrimination that African Americans encountered in education and employment was never so consistently a feature of the experience of "new" immigrant groups. Hershberg's analysis of Philadelphia (1979), showed that historically the occupational opportunity structure for African Americans had never been as open as that for *white* immigrants and that, because of levels of residential segregation never encountered by any European ancestry groups, blacks have been excluded from recent occupational opportunities.

The experience of Asians, in particular the Japanese and the Chinese, frequently is cited to support the claim that being nonwhite is not an insurmountable barrier to achievement in American society. In other words, Asian success casts considerable doubt on the notion that nonwhite racial status is inherently a liability to achievement. Indeed, as Waters and Eschbach (Article 14) point out, Asians are frequently cited as "model minorities" because they have been able to succeed despite extremely virulent forms of discrimination. They have been able to do so, Sowell writes, because of their cultural traits of "effort, thrift, dependability and foresight, [which] built businesses out of 'menial tasks' and turned sweat into capital" (Sowell 1981:7).

However, Asians were not forced to endure the historical experience of slavery and the discriminatory barriers that persisted on a pervasive scale after its legal elimination. Moreover, unlike the African American circumstance, the number of Asians in the United States was never so large as to represent a real threat to the existing white population. Even in California, the state in which Asians have been most highly concentrated, the highest-ever proportion of Japanese in the state's population was 2.1 percent, and the Chinese proportion was even smaller (Peterson 1971:30). When these extremely small numbers of Asians appeared to increase even slightly, the perceived threat they represented was reduced by changes in American immigration laws that effectively limited the Asian population to a tiny proportion of the total (Lieberson 1980:368). Moreover, Nee and Wong (1985:20) suggest that the number of African Americans who migrated to the West during and after World War II exceeded the small Asian population. Their increased presence, and the greater prejudice toward them on the part of white Americans, lessened the impact of anti-Asian discrimination and thus facilitated Asian American socioeconomic mobility.

Anthropologist John Ogbu (1978, 1988, 1990) contends that to focus solely on the cultural characteristics of various minority groups ignores the extent to which their different cultures have themselves been "shaped by the initial terms of their incorporation into American society and their subsequent treatment by white Americans" (Ogbu 1990:149). In Article 18, "Minority Status and Literacy in Comparative Perspective," Ogbu distinguishes between what he broadly terms *immigrant* or *voluntary* minorities, on the one hand, and *castelike* or *involuntary* minorities, on the other, and he argues that there have been qualitative differences in the experiences of these two categories. However much their immigration was compelled by conditions in their homelands over which they had no control, voluntary minorities have chosen to live in the United States, and they generally enter optimistically, with expectations that their lives will be improved. Consequently, they are much more likely to interpret the prejudice and discrimination they encounter in the host society as temporary, a consequence of their foreign origins, and something that they can overcome. In general, they are much more likely to accept the institutional structure (including the school system) uncritically and to encourage their children to work within it.

Most Asian Americans would be included in the category of voluntary minorities, and the academic achievements of Asian Americans generally could be cited as evidence of the manner in which Asian groups generally have accepted the existing culture and social institutions. For example, recently Caplan et al. (1992) have argued that the academic achievement of Vietnamese boat people has occurred because they perceive the language and cultural conflicts that they encounter in school and the wider society as hurdles that *can* be overcome, and they trust school officials and accept school rules and the formally prescribed practices for achieving academic success.

The historical and contemporary experiences of involuntary minorities, on the other hand, provide no such optimism that their minority status is likely to be temporary or that striving within existing institutions will, in fact, have the promised payoff. In contrast to voluntary minorities, involuntary minorities have been subjected to systematic, long-range economic subordination that has affected their perceptions of the nation's social, economic, political, and educational opportunity structures. Thus Ogbu contends that black academic performance is greatly affected by African American perceptions that academic achievement will not be rewarded because of the discriminatory job ceiling that African Americans historically have encountered. In other words, Ogbu argues that the absence of high educational aspirations, high achievement motivation, and a future orientation on the part of some minority-group members is a response to external circumstances, to their realistic perception that their opportunities in the work world are extremely restricted and circumscribed. Lower school performance is merely a symptom of the broader and more central societal problem of caste. Minority educational achievement will be improved only when there is a dramatic societal commitment to end discrimination in jobs and housing, and more fully to include American minorities in the decision-making process in institutions throughout

116

the whole of American society. "The only lasting solution to the problem of academic retardation," he writes, "is the elimination of caste barriers" (Ogbu 1978:357).

However, their exclusion from societal opportunity structures not only has affected the aspirations of involuntary minorities but also has had an impact on the group's cultural characteristics and the ways in which they perceive and respond to members of the dominant group and the social institutions (such as schools) that they control. A prominent response among involuntary minorities is *cultural inversion,* or the development of an oppositional culture—the tendency to reject certain forms of behavior, events, symbols, and meanings as inappropriate because they are characteristics of the dominant group and, conversely, to accept other forms of behavior, symbols, norms, and values, precisely because they are not (Ogbu 1990:148). Thus, because in the United States the school and its representatives symbolize the dominant culture, the cultures of involuntary minorities tend to disparage academic achievement, and those who are academically successful are subject to ridicule and ostracism from their peers. "Those minority students who adopt the attitudes and behaviors conducive to school success, who use standard English and behave according to standard school practices, are accused by their peers of 'acting white' or, in the case of black students, of being Uncle Toms." (Ogbu 1990:160–161)

Ogbu's interpretation of the disparities in levels of academic attainment among American ethnic and racial groups does not deny the importance of the cultural predispositions with which each group encounters the nation's social institutions; Ogbu's model clearly involves *both* cultural and structural dimensions. Cultural differences *are* important in accounting for these differences—certain voluntary minorities possess values that strongly support, encourage, and reward academic achievement, whereas among involuntary minorities, the behaviors necessary for success within the dominant educational institutions are disparaged. However, for Ogbu what is important are the sources of these differences in cultural perspectives toward formal education. He distinguishes between *primary* and *secondary* cultural differences. The former refer to cultural characteristics of groups before contact, while the latter occur in response to contact with other groups. This distinction is especially important because it recognizes that the cultural inventory of involuntary minorities is not simply inherited from the past or is inherent in a group's "essence." Rather, the cultural values with which groups perceive and respond to social institutions, including schools, are adaptive mechanisms that are shaped and molded by a group's historical experiences.

An external perspective places primary emphasis on a society's opportunity structure and interprets a minority's cultural characteristics as dependent variables. Although Ogbu's model involves a synthesis of cultural and structural variables in accounting for the different socioeconomic positions occupied by different ethnic groups, it emphasizes the structural constraints within which the cultural inventory of involuntary minorities was developed. From an external perspective, therefore, it is the opportunity structure, not biological or cultural characteristics, that accounts for racial and ethnic inequalities. Consequently, it is the opportunity structure, not minority cultures, that must first be changed to reduce inequalities in American life.

As noted in Part 1, the structure of opportunity may be circumscribed by what we have termed attitudinal discrimination, which is motivated by prejudices against racial or ethnic minorities. For example, as noted there, although there is evidence of a decline in attitudinal discrimination in the past quarter century, as Feagin points out in Article 20, it still remains a potent force in a wide range of settings in American life. However, an external model of racial and ethnic inequality also focuses on the impersonal, objective economic circumstances that confront caste minorities today, and compares them with those that ethnic groups—in particular "new" immigrants—encountered in the past.

Therefore, the assumptions of an internal explanation of inequality have been challenged by people who contend that the barriers confronting Chicanos, Puerto Ricans, American Indians, and, in particular, African Americans, have been qualitatively different from those encountered by European immigrants or even by Asians. External explanations focus on the broad social, economic, and political contexts confronting different ethnic groups and especially on the role of prejudice and discrimination in creating and maintaining racial and ethnic inequality.

Institutional Discrimination

As we noted in the Introduction to Part 1, the structure of opportunity may be limited by attitudinal discrimination, which is motivated by prejudices against racial and ethnic minorities. *Institutional discrimination*, by contrast, refers to rules, policies, practices, and laws that appear to be race-neutral (or gender-neutral) but still have a discriminatory effect on minorities. In its origins, unlike attitudinal discrimination, institutional discrimination may not have been intentional or a consequence of prejudice, but it still has an adverse impact on a minority group. In other words, even if all racial prejudice were suddenly and miraculously eliminated from the hearts and minds of Americans, it is unlikely that racial inequalities would disappear, primarily because racial discrimination and inequalities are perpetuated by the way in which economic and political institutions are structured and organized in American society.

William Julius Wilson has been among the foremost critics of a cultural perspective. As noted in Part 2, in *The Declining Significance of Race* (1978), Wilson divided the history of American race relations into three periods or stages—the preindustrial, industrial, and modern industrial, each reflecting changes in the nation's economic structure. Wilson acknowledged that in contemporary American society—the modern industrial period—attitudinal discrimination is still pervasive in many areas, such as housing, education, and municipal politics, and serves as a barrier to black participation in society's mainstream. However, he contended that in the economic sphere, institutional, not attitudinal, discrimination has become the primary source of continuing black inequalities. In the economic life of African Americans, "class has become more important than race in determining black access to privilege and power." (See Article 7, "The Declining Significance of Race," in Part 2.)

Wilson's thesis is based on the contention that during the modern industrial era, African American economic status has been influenced by substantial structural economic changes "such as the shift from goods-producing to service-producing industries, the increasing segmentation of the labor market, the growing use of industrial technology, and the relocation of industries out of the central city" that, in themselves, have little to do with race (Wilson 1981a:38).

As a result of changes in the economic structure and political culture of American life, the structure of the African American community has been altered. On the one hand, "educated blacks are experiencing unprecedented job opportunities in the growing government and corporate sectors, opportunities that are at least comparable to those of whites with equivalent qualifications." This advance has come about as a result of the expansion of salaried, white-collar positions and of changes in the role of government. Before the modern industrial era, the state merely reinforced patterns of race relations established in the economic sector. Recently, in response to the civil rights movement, the government has stood in formal opposition to discriminatory barriers. Indeed, with the enactment of affirmative action programs in the 1960s, government undertook the initiative in combating discrimination.

On the other hand, the social conditions of the African American underclass have deteriorated in the last quarter of a century. In *The Truly Disadvantaged* (1987) and his most recent book, *When Work Disappears* (1996), Wilson focuses on the crisis of the underclass in the inner city, where the broad economic changes mentioned before have caused extremely high levels of unemployment. Earlier in the twentieth century, relatively uneducated and unskilled native and immigrant workers were able to find stable employment and income in manufacturing. Today, however, the process of deindustrialization has created an economic "mismatch" between the kinds of jobs available and the qualifications of inner-city residents lacking highly sophisticated educational and technical skills. On the one hand, manufacturing jobs that do not require advanced skills have moved from inner cities to the suburbs, to the Sun Belt, or overseas. On the other hand, the jobs created in the cities demand highly technical credentials for which most inner-city residents are unqualified. Thus many inner-city residents find themselves without prospects for work. Moreover, as many stable working-class and middle-class residents with job qualifications have moved from the inner cities into better residential neighborhoods, the stability of neighborhood social institutions (such as churches, schools, newspapers, and recreational facilities) has been undermined, and the social fabric of community life has deteriorated. The underclass has become increasingly isolated, socially and economically. "Today's ghetto residents face a closed opportunity structure." In Article 19, "Work," Wilson describes the impact of institutional and structural changes in triggering a process of "hyperghettoization" or concentration of the very poor.

Wilson's argument has been subjected to considerable—often intense—criticism. One of the most frequent is that, in stressing the nonracial structural sources of the urban underclass, he ignores or underestimates the role of race. One of the most prominent examples of this perspective is Joe R. Feagin's "The Continuing Significance of Race" (Article 20), which represents a direct response to Wilson's contention that middle-class blacks—those whose education and skills provide them access to middle-class occupational opportunities—are no longer vulnerable to discrimination in employment and public accommodations. Drawing from in-depth interviews with a wide range of middle-class blacks, Feagin concludes that even African Americans who have achieved success and status continue to experience discrimination on a regular basis. Indeed, racial discrimination continues to be a pervasive and enduring feature of their lives, and, most important, its effects are cumulative: "Blacks confront not just isolated incidents [of discrimination] . . . but a lifelong series of such incidents."

Massey and Denton (Article 9; 1993) differ with Wilson's emphasis on the impersonal effects of deindustrialization on concentrating urban poverty in the ghettos of America's major cities. Race, they contend, has been and continues to be a fundamental cleavage in American society. The pervasive racial segregation of African Americans in most American metropolitan areas—what they refer to as "American apartheid"—is a consequence of both historic and contemporary patterns of racial discrimination in the sale and rental of housing, and it has led almost inevitably to the concentrated poverty and associated social dislocations that characterize many African American urban neighborhoods. While industrial restructuring and an exodus of middle-class blacks have contributed to the increasing concentration of urban poverty, the residential segregation of Africans Americans was *the* critical factor. Especially since the onset of the Great Migration out of the South early in the twentieth century, African Americans have been more highly residentially segregated regardless of their socioeconomic characteristics than any other racial or ethnic group in American history, so they have been more vulnerable to the cumulative impact of economic dislocations. As a consequence, as David R. James (Article 21) puts it, "Racial segregation in general and the racial ghetto in particular are race-making situations that perpetuate the color line in America."

Other critics have argued that Wilson's analysis tends to obscure continuing attitudinal discrimination in the economic sphere; not only is the contemporary underclass a consequence of historical patterns of racial discrimination, but also such discrimination continues today to affect black economic opportunities and life chances. For example, Steinberg has challenged Wilson's use of the "mismatch" explanation for black exclusion from the expanding service sector of the economy. The "mismatch" hypothesis, he contends, "seriously underestimates the color line in the world of work" (Steinberg 1989:289). It overlooks the large number of jobs that do not require extensive education, training, and skills, and it ignores the virtual exclusion of African Americans from certain segments of the labor market.

On the other hand, the mismatch hypothesis ignores the extent to which recent immigrants have taken many relatively unskilled jobs. Newcomers to America's major cities today are increasingly likely to be immigrants, not native-born whites or blacks. Waldinger (Article 27) contends that, far from declining, lower-level jobs in the postindustrial city have increased but have been filled by recent imimgrants from abroad rather than by African Americans. Waldinger argues that the shift to a postindustrial economy has resulted in a new ethnic division of labor; however, recent ethnic occupational restructuring cannot be reduced to a question simply of whether immigrants take jobs away from native-born workers (especially from the most prominent previous migrants to the nation's major cities—African Americans). Rather, Waldinger contends that it is necessary to focus on the complex and subtle processes through which different ethnic groups have come to fill and sustain the specific occupational niches that provide mobility ladders in this new ethnic division of labor.

Waldinger's critique of the mismatch hypothesis raises a critical question: If economic restructuring has left economic opportunities in the inner cities so bleak, why have immigrant groups flocked to them—contributing to an "urban renaissance"—in the past two decades? In Part 4 we will consider more fully the increasingly multiracial (not simply biracial) nature of American cities in the global, postindustrial economy, as well as the implications of these changes in ethnic composition for the future of racial and ethnic relations in American life.

Race and Ethnicity in the United States at Century's End

4

In a grandiloquent essay published in February 1941—ten months before the Japanese attack on Pearl Harbor—Henry Luce, head of the Time-Life publishing empire, provided one of the most provocative, enduring, and widely quoted characterizations of American society in the twentieth century: "The twentieth century is the American Century." Luce celebrated the rise of the United States to a position of economic, political, cultural, and military dominance in world affairs, but he also idealistically perceived America as the "sanctuary of the ideals of civilization" and called upon Americans to "spread throughout the world . . . the ideals of Freedom and Justice . . . [with] joy and gladness and vigor and enthusiasm" (Luce 1941:65).

However, as we near the end of the "American Century," the prescient words of W. E. B. DuBois, uttered at the beginning of the century, provide a different, but equally appropriate, epitaph: "The problem of the twentieth century is the problem of the color line—the relation of the darker to the lighter races of men in Asia and Africa, in America, and the islands of the sea" (DuBois 1903/1986:372). In the materials considered throughout this book, we have noted the changes that have occurred in the dynamics of race and ethnicity in American life throughout its history. Although the dynamics of the "problem of the color line" have changed dramatically throughout the course of the twentieth century, it remains perhaps the critical issue in defining the American people during that century. As Thomas and Mary Edsall have written, "When the official subject is presidential politics, taxes, welfare, crime, rights, or values . . . , the real subject is race" (Edsall and Edsall 1991:53).

In the last quarter century especially, the racial and ethnic composition of the United States has been altered significantly. Today the United States is characterized by a greater diversity of peoples and cultures than ever before. In 1960 African Americans, Asians, Hispanics, and American Indians represented less than one-sixth (15.2 percent) of the American population; by 1998 that figure had increased to more than one-fourth (28.5 percent), the highest proportion of non-Europeans in the country since it became an independent nation in the late eighteenth century. The increases were especially pronounced among the Asian and Hispanic populations, which grew by 825 percent and 325 percent, respectively, between 1960 and 1990. Census Bureau projections estimate that, if current trends in birth and immigration rates continue, by the middle of the twenty-first century, Hispanics and Asians together will comprise one-third (32 percent) of the total population and non-Hispanic whites will represent only a slight majority (53 percent) (Day 1993). As a consequence of these trends, *Time* magazine (1993) recently pronounced the United States "the world's first multicultural society," and Edward Luttwak has derisively talked of the "third-worldization of America" (Luttwak 1992).

Therefore, it is probable that issues of race and ethnicity, rather than diminishing in intensity, will assume even greater significance in American society in the twenty-first century. By the year 2000, one-third of all school-age children will be either African American, Hispanic, Asian, or American Indian (American Council on Education 1988). Furthermore, in some states (such as California), the majority of working-age adults will be members of these minorities (California Assembly Office of Research 1986). Therefore, in the very near future, "minority" peoples will affect the nation's prosperity more substantially than ever before in American history. All Americans, especially those who will be economically dependent on the productivity of the working-age population, will be directly affected by the manner in which racial and ethnic inequalities in American life are addressed.

This section will focus on several recent trends in American majority-minority relations: the impact of recent demographic changes, including the changing nature of immigration to the United States; the implications of the surge of interest in ethnicity and ethnic pluralism among European Americans; and the changing status of African Americans.

Demographic Changes in the Last Quarter of the Twentieth Century

In order to comprehend the dynamics of racial and ethnic relations during the past quarter century (and to anticipate the future), it is useful to examine briefly some of the demographic changes that have occurred during that time. See Table 1 in Part 2 (p. 88) for the basic data for several broad racial and ethnic categories.

As indicated in Part 2, African Americans, the nation's largest racial minority, today total more than 34 million, or more than the entire population of Canada or of Sweden, Denmark, Norway, Finland, and Iceland combined. As in 1990, African Americans continue to live overwhelmingly in urban areas, especially in the nation's largest cities. Today New York City has a black population of more than two million, more than any other city in the world (except Kinshasa, Democratic Republic of the Congo [formerly Zaire]) and more than any state (besides New York state) in the country. Chicago has more African Americans than Mississippi or South Carolina; and Philadelphia has about the same number as Arkansas and Kentucky combined. Throughout the 1980s and 1990s, blacks continued to be more likely than whites to live in urban areas, especially in central cities. However, during this period, for the first time in this century, the proportion of blacks living in the South increased, growing from 52 percent in 1980 to 55 percent in 1994 (Bennett 1995:35).

Since 1970, the Hispanic population has more than tripled, increasing from 9 million in 1970 to nearly 30 million in 1998. This increase is greater both proportionately and numerically than that of the African American population, which grew by 13 percent. In 1996 California had the greatest number of Hispanics—about ten million, or about 37 percent of the nation's total. Texas and New York together accounted for a nearly comparable number, thus bringing the Hispanic populations in these three states alone to nearly two-thirds (65 percent) of the Hispanics in the country overall. The Los Angeles metropolitan area contained the largest number of Hispanics (6.3 million), more than double the number in the metropolitan area with the next largest number—New York, with slightly over 3 million (National Association of Hispanic Publications 1995). Nevertheless, reflecting New York's historic role as the nation's—indeed the world's—most ethnically diverse city, in 1990 over 60 percent of its population was either Hispanic, African American, Asian American, or American Indian, and more than one-quarter (27 percent) of households of European ancestry were headed by immigrants (Halbfinger 1997).

Among the most striking demographic changes in the composition of the American people since 1970 has been the growth of the Asian population, which increased more than sixfold between 1970 and 1998. Like the dramatic growth among Hispanics, the increase in the Asian population has resulted primarily from substantial increases in immigration from Asian nations since the late 1960s. We will consider these increases more fully below. During the 1980s, the overall Asian population increased by 70 percent, with the most dramatic increases occurring among Koreans, Filipinos, Chinese, and Indochinese. By 1980 Chinese and Filipinos had both surpassed in number the Japanese, who until 1980 had been the largest Asian national group. Regionally, Asians were concentrated in the West, especially in California, which had more Chinese, Japanese, Filipinos, Koreans, and Vietnamese than any other state.

Contemporary Immigration and the Changing Face of America

When Henry Luce annointed the twentieth century as "The American Century" in 1941, he certainly was not thinking about the racial and ethnic diversity of the American people—indeed, he appears to have been oblivious to it. Thus, it is more than a little ironic that the two largest and most ethnically diverse waves of immigration in American history—or in the history of *any* nation, for that matter—took place at the beginning and at the end of The American Century, thus reflecting how crucial the notion of multiculturalism is to the very definition of what it means to be American.

In "The New Immigration and Ethnicity in the United States" (Article 23) Douglas Massey has divided The American Century into three distinct, albeit arbitrary, periods that roughly coincide with significant changes in American immigration policy. In Part 2 we considered the impact of the first of these periods—the era of massive European immigration that ended with restrictionist legislation enacted in the

1920s. During that era, Massey points out, the United States "became less black, more white, and more firmly European in culture and outlook." In this section we will examine the impact on American society and culture of the other two periods—the hiatus in immigration between 1930 and 1970, and the resumption of large-scale, primarily non-European immigration since 1970, both of which, in different ways, have affected patterns of racial and ethnic relations in contemporary American life.

The impact of the recent period has been most immediately visible; patterns of immigration into the United States have been radically transformed. This new immigrant wave promises to produce even more dramatic and far-reaching changes in the ethnic composition of the United States than the massive influx of southern and eastern European immigrants in the late nineteenth and early twentieth centuries. First, since the late 1960s, the number of immigrants to the United States has increased substantially. During the 1990s the number of immigrants admitted has averaged over one million annually, compared with 282,000 in the decade before 1965. In 1991 alone, more than 1.8 million immigrants were admitted, the greatest annual number in American history. Moreover, experts estimate that there is an annual net increase of about 275,000 illegal immigrants (Espenshade 1995; Martin and Midgley 1994).

The changes in the national origins of today's immigrants are as dramatic as their increasing numbers. Until the late 1960s immigration to the United States was overwhelmingly European, ranging from a high of 96 percent of all immigrants for the decade 1891–1900 to 53 percent for the decade 1950–1960. Today, as a result of changes in U.S. immigration laws, only a small percentage of immigrants come from Europe (see Table 1).

Today the predominant sources of immigration are Third World nations in Central and South America, the Caribbean, and Asia. As Table 2 indicates, in 1995 only *one* of the ten leading countries—Ukraine—from which the United States received immigrants was European; there were more immigrants from Ghana than from France, more from Bangladesh than from Ireland, more from Guatemala than from Italy, more from Bolivia than from Sweden, more from Ethiopia than from Germany, and more from Korea than from the United Kingdom (U.S. Immigration and Naturalization Service 1997:23, 52–53). The impact of these trends has been to create a genuinely multiracial, multicultural society—what Wattenberg has characterized as the "first universal nation" (Wattenberg 1991).

TABLE 1   *Immigrants from Europe as Percent of Total*

Years	Percentage
1941–1950	60%
1951–1960	53
1961–1970	34
1971–1980	18
1981–1990	10
1991–1996	14

Source: U.S. Immigration and Naturalization Service. *Statistical Yearbook of the Immigration and Naturalization Service 1995.* Washington, D.C.: U.S. Government Printing Service, 1997.

TABLE 2 *Immigrants Admitted to the United States from Top Ten Countries of Birth, 1995*

Country	Number
Mexico	89,932
Philippines	50,984
Vietnam	42,752
Dominican Republic	38,512
China	35,463
India	34,748
Cuba	17,937
Ukraine	17,432
Jamaica	16,398
Korea	16,047

Source: U.S. Immigration and Naturalization Service. *Statistical Yearbook of the Immigration and Naturalization Service, 1995.* U.S. Government Printing Office: Washington, D.C., 1997, p. 23.

When Americans think of immigrants, they often have an image of "huddled masses" who are poor, unskilled, and uneducated. Such a perception does not accurately characterize the recent wave of immigration, which is extremely complex in its composition. Changes in U.S. immigration laws since 1965 have affected the occupational and educational composition of the present immigrant population. Today the range of immigrants' occupations much more closely resembles that of the native population at the turn of the twentieth century.

On the one hand, whereas a substantial proportion of immigrants to the United States during the first two decades of the twentieth century were unskilled blue-collar workers, post–1965 immigration laws have established preferences for immigrants with skills needed in the United States. Physicians, nurses, scientists, architects, artists, entertainers, engineers, and others with highly technical skills have contributed to a "brain drain," first from Europe and later from Third World nations, and to the profile of contemporary immigrants as relatively highly educated and technically skilled. For example, the overall educational level of the foreign-born in the United States is similar to that of the native-born. The proportions of foreign-born and native who have completed college are virtually identical: in 1996, 23.6 percent of native-born U.S. adults aged twenty-five and over were college graduates, compared with 23.5 percent of foreign-born persons (Hansen and Faber 1997:4). Immigrants from Africa and Asia are especially well educated; in 1990, almost half (47 percent) of African and more than one-third (38) percent of Asian immigrants had completed college (Portes and Rumbaut 1996:61).

On the other hand, because the overwhelming majority of recent immigrants entered the United States under preferences for family reunification, a substantial proportion are also unskilled, poor, and relatively uneducated. Indeed, although immigrants are disproportionately represented among the nation's most highly educated people, they are also more likely than native-born Americans to be among the most poorly educated: in 1996 the proportion of the foreign-born who had not graduated from high school was double the proportion of natives (36 percent compared with 18 percent) (Hansen and Faber 1997). Immigrants are also more likely than natives to be poor and to be recipients of public assistance (Hansen and Faber 1997; Portes and Rumbaut 1996:78). Moreover, Borjas has argued that over the past two decades, overall immigrant skill levels have actually declined (Borjas 1994).

The preferences for immigrants with skills has meant that, unlike the situation for most of American history prior to 1965, it has become almost impossible for unskilled workers to enter the United States legally unless they can claim a close family relationship or a refugee status. As a consequence, less skilled workers, as well as skilled immigrants, such as students and tourists who overstay their visas, have increasingly resorted to entering the country illegally. In each year during the 1990s, more than a million illegal immigrants apprehended—from over one hundred countries—were apprehended, the vast majority from Latin America, especially Mexico (U.S. Immigration and Naturalization Service 1997:161–167). Although, as noted earlier, the annual net increase of illegal immigrants permanently living in the United States is lower than that from legal immigration, estimates of the total number of undocumented aliens range around 5 million (U.S. Immigration and Naturalization Service 1997:183; Espenshade 1995:201).

In a recent book, *Alien Nation,* Peter Brimelow, himself an immigrant to the United States, characterized American immigration policy—primarily the historic changes wrought by the 1965 Immigration Act—as a "disaster." Recent immigration, he wrote, has been "so huge and so systematically different from anything that had gone on before as to transform—and ultimately, perhaps even to destroy—the . . . American nation" (Brimelow 1995). Fears of an immigrant invasion that will destroy America have been voiced frequently throughout American history, especially during periods of heavy immigration and economic stagnation, often by previous immigrants or their immediate descendants.

Such sentiments have emerged again during the past quarter century. Until 1964, with the end of the Bracero Program, which enabled Mexican agricultural workers to enter the United States as temporary workers under legal contracts that provided a source of cheap labor for agricultural interests in the Southwest, illegal immigration was relatively low and was confined primarily to the rural Southwest. However, beginning in the late 1960s, the number of illegal immigrants apprehended increased dramatically, from 110,000 in 1965 to 250,000 in 1970 to 1.8 million in 1986 (U.S. Bureau of the Census 1997:164). Although Mexicans comprised the largest category of undocumented aliens, beginning in the 1960s, these illegal aliens were drawn increasingly from nations throughout the Caribbean, Latin America, and Asia as well. The growth of a large, urban illegal population dominated immigration politics during the 1970s and early 1980s. This rise in the apprehensions of illegal aliens, reinforced by sensational media coverage, contributed to growing fears that the United States was being threatened by a "silent invasion" of foreigners whose presence threatened to undermine the quality of American life. As the number of apprehensions increased, so did political pressures for the United States to curtail their numbers.

Responding to these pressures, in 1986 Congress enacted the Immigration Reform and Control Act (IRCA), which was concerned primarily with illegal immigration, but left legal immigration substantially intact. Enactment of IRCA represented a compromise among a disparate group of political interests, as well as the culmination of years of intense debate over the perceived threat of illegal immigration to American institutions. The term *control* in the bill's title was appropriate, for IRCA was designed to enable the United States once again to "take control of its borders."

IRCA prohibited the employment of illegal immigrants and required that employers verify—through documents such as Social Security cards, birth certificates, drivers' licenses, and passports—that new employees were either U.S. citizens or aliens legally authorized to work. Because *all* new employees are required to verify their citizenship or immigration status under the law, it has directly affected more Americans than any other piece of immigration legislation in American history. To enforce its provisions, IRCA established fines and jail terms for employers who knowingly hired illegal aliens. However, employers were not responsible for verifying the authenticity of the documents, but only to have in good faith determined that they were valid.

During the lengthy debate over IRCA between 1982 and 1986, one of the most frequent objections to employer sanctions was that citizens or resident aliens, especially Hispanics, who "appeared foreign" to employers would encounter discrimination. Consequently, strong antidiscrimination provisions were included in the bill; however, President Ronald Reagan's statements on signing the bill that in essence discouraged individuals from filing discrimination claims, diminished the force of these provisions.

On the other hand, IRCA provided amnesty—a grant of permanent legal residence—for illegal aliens who could prove that they had lived continuously in the United States since before 1982. It also included provisions for an agricultural guest-worker program that was intended to relieve shortages of agricultural—primarily migrant—labor.

The most controversial provision of IRCA was the offer of amnesty—legal status—to illegal aliens who had lived in the United State continuously since before January 1, 1982. Three million applications were filed, and those who did so had to undertake several additional steps to obtain permanent residency; in addition to proving that they had lived in the United States continuously since before 1982, they had to have no serious police record, prove financial responsibility, and demonstrate a knowledge of English and of American history. The impact of the IRCA on the volume of American immigration became apparent in 1989, when nearly half-a-million resident aliens were amnestied. By 1991 the number granted amnesty through the IRCA provisions exceeded one million, making the total number of immigrants admitted in that year—1.8 million—the highest for any year in American history.

Four years later, in 1990, Congress once again amended American immigration policy, increasing the numbers of immigrants admitted annually from 500,000 to 700,000. It also eliminated most of the social and political restrictions (against Communists and homosexuals, for example) adopted during the McCarthy era of the 1950s. Finally, while it retained the priority on the reunification of immediate family members, it substantially increased opportunities for highly skilled workers—scientists, artists, athletes, inventors, and professionals—as well as entrepreneurs willing to invest in businesses in the United States.

As was the case early in the twentieth century, the increasing number and variety of immigrants have created a sense of alarm among many native-born Americans that these immigrants will have a negative impact on American society, dramatically increasing population growth, draining economic resources, taking jobs from American citizens, and transforming (and for some undermining) American culture and social institutions. Immigration restrictionist sentiments have historically increased during and been aggravated by periods of economic recession and anxiety, and this relationship has recently been apparent in California, where immigrants account for nearly one-quarter (24.8 percent) of the population. In 1994, during a recession greatly influenced by substantial reductions in military spending, Californians overwhelmingly supported Proposition 187, a ballot referendum that denies state-supported health and educational services to illegal immigrants and their children.

The success of California's Proposition 187 galvanized restrictionist advocates throughout the country to demand that the United States "take control of its borders." In response, the Clinton Administration has devoted more money and political attention to immigration than any other recent administration has; it increased the Border Patrol budget, and Border Patrol agents substantially expanded enforcement of existing immigration law, particularly in their efforts to reduce border crossings of undocumented aliens from Mexico (Schmitt 1996:A1). In addition, in 1996 Congress passed new legislation directed primarily at illegal immigration, by increasing the number of Border Patrol agents, providing much more sophisticated technology with which to apprehend illegal immigrants, and authorizing enhanced barriers along the Southwest border. The law also called for new efforts to reduce the employment of unauthorized workers by establishing more effective means of verifying worker eligibility, and it substantially curtailed opportunities for people to claim asylum or refugee status. Finally, the law placed substantial restrictions on benefits for noncitizens (such as denying them Social Security or requiring foreign students attending American high schools to pay tuition). When coupled with the 1996 Welfare Reform Bill, which permitted states to deny welfare and Medicaid to *legal* immigrants, the effects were especially disastrous for elderly and disabled people. Because many legal immigrants stood to lose welfare benefits that they had worked years to establish, one of the consequences of these policies has been a dramatic increase in applications from legal immigrants for citizenship (Dugger 1997:A1).

One of the most bitterly contested and long-standing issues in the debate over immigration deals with the impact of immigrants on the domestic economy: do immigrants contribute to economic growth and income, or are they a drain on the country's economic resources generally and on native employment and earnings in particular? Among the voluminous studies on the economic impact of immigration, it is possible to find support for practically any position. However, the most recent report on the subject, a comprehensive five-hundred-page study released by the National Academy of Sciences, concluded that immigrants contribute substantial overall benefits—as much as $10 billion yearly—to the U.S. economy. However, the economic impact of immigration was not uniform; its effects were felt differently at the federal, state, and local levels. Because a substantial portion of the taxes that immigrants pay go to the federal government, immigration provided a boost to the national economy. But because state and local governments have fewer tax resources and are more likely to bear the costs (health, education, and so forth) of immigrants, they have "a negative fiscal impact at the state and local level" (Smith and Edmonston, 1997). Moreover, because immigrants are geographically concentrated in a small number of states, these costs and benefits are not felt uniformly throughout the United States; in several states, such as California, where immigrants are geographically concentrated, the tax burden to the state may be greater than the benefit from the jobs that immigrants create and the state taxes that they pay. In addition, the study found that although the overall impact of immigrants was positive, some categories of native (and earlier immigrant) workers—primarily low-skilled—were hurt by competition from immigrant labor (Smith and Edmonston 1997; Pear 1997:1; McDonnell 1997).

In addition to skilled immigrants and those being reunited with their families, since 1965 the number of immigrants entering the United States claiming refugee and asylum status has increased dramatically. Determining who can enter the country as a refugee is essentially a political judgment that is made by the federal government. Given that under the government's definition, there are an estimated 18.5 million political and economic refugees in the world today, the moral and political pressures to admit refugees are considerable. Although refugees from more than one hundred different nations have been admitted, official government policy has given special treatment to those fleeing Communism, and the vast majority of refugees to enter the United States during the 1970s and 1980s were from Cuba and Vietnam. By 1988 nearly one million Cubans and more than 500,000 Vietnamese had been admitted—both groups coming from nations where American-supported governments had been supplanted by Communist regimes. But the refugee quotas established under the 1965 law and its subsequent revisions proved inadequate to respond either to the global refugee pressures or to the specific pressures represented by groups such as the Cubans and the Vietnamese. In some instances, such as the Vietnamese, special laws were passed to enable the president to respond to emergency situations. In others, such as the case of the Cuban "Freedom Flotilla" in 1980, the political power of the Cuban American community and the propaganda value of thousands fleeing Fidel Castro's regime permitted a de facto circumvention of the law.

However, as indicated by the cases of the Haitians and the Salvadoreans, whose plight was less widely publicized, the admission of refugees for political reasons did not apply to non-Communist regimes, even those that were equally oppressive. Thus in 1984 the Reagan administration planned to offer legal status and citizenship opportunities to more than 100,000 Cubans who entered the United States during the Freedom Flotilla but failed to extend the same privileges to 7,200 Haitian refugees who had fled their nation in small boats at approximately the same time (Pear 1984:1). There was no similar groundswell of support for those fleeing government-sponsored terror in El Salvador, nor for the Haitians seeking to escape the nation's poverty and its political repression.

Sources of Migration Pressures

The growing influx of immigration to the United States in the past quarter century has been affected not only by American immigration laws, but more significantly by broader changes in the global economy. It has become increasingly apparent that American racial and ethnic relations and the adaptation of different ethnic groups to American society must be conceptualized from within the framework of a rapidly changing global economy and of the modes of incorporation of different nations and regions within it. As Saskia Sassen (Article 24), Roger Rouse (Article 26), and numerous other writers (e.g., Massey [1981a], Portes [1979], Piore [1979]) suggest, the dynamics of American immigration reflect the emergence of a broader international pattern of migration between low- and high-income countries that started in the 1960s. This pattern has contributed to the rise in legal immigration to the United States, but it has had a particular impact on illegal immigration, especially from Mexico and the Caribbean.

Conceptualizing the dynamics of contemporary immigration to the United States within a framework of globalization raises questions about the appropriateness of comparisons with previous migration waves. Traditionally, historians and social scientists have used a dualistic, "push-pull" model to explain immigration to the United States (Archdeacon 1983; Bodnar 1985; Handlin 1951; Jones 1960; Taylor 1971; Seller 1977; Dinnerstein and Reimers 1987). They have identified numerous "push" factors, such as population increases, economic deprivation, and religious and political repression, that impel people to leave their homelands. They have also identified "pull" factors, such as economic opportunity and abundance, and freedom of religious and political expression, that have lured immigrants to the United States.

A widespread assumption concerning the newest immigrant wave is that, as in the past, migration pressures—the push factors—are internal to those countries. In the past, the United States has been perceived to influence these migration pressures only to the extent that it offers a beacon of hope for emigrants to escape lives of economic impoverishment or political repression. Thus, the push factors that have impelled people to emigrate have been the consequence of policies, practices, and social arrangements that the United States has been relatively powerless to control or influence.

This traditional push-pull model is inadequate to explain forces stimulating immigration today. Pull factors, though greatly influenced by the pervasiveness of the mass media in even the remotest corners of the world, remain *qualitatively* the same as ever: the United States remains the epitome of economic abundance, affluence, and opportunity in the minds of people around the world. However, starting after World War II, the push factors that were producing immigration no longer lay largely outside U.S. influence. In the last half of the twentieth century, the United States has emerged as the world's dominant economic, political, and military power. This transformation has not only reshaped international relations but has also expanded U.S. influence on the internal affairs of many of the world's states. The major difference between immigration today and in the past, then, is the economic and political impact of the United States in those countries that have been among the major sources of immigration; that is, American policies and practices—economic, social, cultural, and political—have created or contributed to the conditions that have led to the uprooting of people in many societies, a number of whom have immigrated to the United States as a result. In other words, the increased numbers of immigrants entering the United States are an indirect—and sometimes direct—consequence of American policies and practices. Thus, as Saskia Sassen points out in "America's Immigration 'Problem' " (Article 24), the economic, political, social, and cultural impacts of immigration that many Americans define as "problems," are in many respects self-induced—a consequence of America's own policies and practices in the global economy. "By focusing narrowly on immigrants and the immigration process itself, U.S. policy makers ignored the broader international forces, many of them generated or at least encouraged by the United States, that have helped give rise to migration flows."

Accordingly, Sassen focuses on the operation of broad transnational, macrostructural factors in the global economy that affect migration. She contends that direct

American foreign investment in production for export is the critical factor linking the United States and emigrant-exporting nations today. She seeks to explain why foreign investment, which has produced rapid economic growth—and thus presumably diminishing emigration pressures—in fact contributes to high emigration levels. She focuses on the impact of foreign investment on the economic and occupational structure of developing countries, which typically involves the disruption of traditional social patterns, especially of work structures and the roles of women, who are heavily recruited into jobs in new industrial zones. The entry of women workers increases labor pools, contributing to male unemployment. Moreover, given high turnover in the export production labor market, many workers are left unemployed. Thus foreign investment not only undermines the traditional work structure and creates a pool of potential emigrants; it also promotes emigration through economic, cultural, and ideological linkages—that is, the westernization of taste and mentality—with the United States.

However, Sassen contends that, while the penetration of foreign investment into developing countries may have been instrumental in *initiating* migration to the United States, its *continuation* at record levels is a consequence of the structural transformation of the American economy in the last two decades. Thus the shift from manufacturing to service occupations has had a profound effect not only on native workers, but upon opportunities for immigrant laborers as well. Because the manufacturing sector is being transformed and dramatically diminished, job prospects for foreign workers are becoming primarily low-wage and relatively unskilled. They are also found primarily in the nation's largest cities, to which a disproportionate share of recent immigrants have been drawn. Moreover, immigrants are also widely used in the low-wage end of the service sector, many of them working in occupations (e.g., hotel workers, child-care providers, and so forth) that "service the lifestyles and consumption requirements of the growing high-income professional and managerial class."

While Sassen adopts a general model of the relationship between American policies and practices and recent increases in immigration, Alejandro Portes has applied a similar explanation to the continuing influx of Mexican workers to the United States. Portes (1979) has argued that, paradoxically, it is Third World economic *development*, not underdevelopment, that has contributed significantly to the growing pressures for emigration. The American model of economic development, with its emphasis on consumerism and consumption, and American economic forces have transformed the social structures of many developing societies. Simultaneously unemployment, underemployment, and income inequalities preclude access by the majority of the population of developing countries to these consumer goods. "In the eyes of the Mexican worker," Portes writes, "the United States stands as the place where the benefits of an advanced economy, promised but not delivered by the present national development strategy, can be turned into reality." Thus, ironically, the very forces generated by the American economic system and exported extensively to the economic life of Third World societies, have been instrumental in attracting the massive influx of immigrants to the United States.

However, both Sassen and Portes focus primarily on broad macrostructural dimensions—the migration pressures—that induce people to migrate from one country to another. On the other hand, although writers such as Massey (1987) and Roger Rouse (Article 26) recognize the formative role of macro factors in initiating Mexican migration to the United States, they also emphasize the critical role that micro factors—migrant social networks—play in sustaining it. The origins of Mexican migration to the United States are located in the imbalance between Mexican and American economic and social structures and policies, but once the process of migration has begun, it becomes self-perpetuating and is maintained through networks of individuals that sustain and expand the process itself.

Massey and his colleagues (1987) emphasize the *social* dimensions of the process of Mexican migration to the United States. They document the critical importance of social networks involving relatives, friends, and *paisonos* (community members) that link sending communities in Mexico with work sites in the United States. The roots of temporary and undocumented immigration from Mexico were firmly established earlier in the twentieth century, in response to American policies that encouraged migration. Most apparent was the bracero program, which was designed to alleviate labor shortages during World War II, but also provided a legal basis for the traditional patterns of Mexican migration. As a result of these patterns as well as the social networks in which they are enmeshed, temporary migration from Mexico to the United States has become institutionalized and "is now an integral part of economic strategies in households throughout [western Mexico] and has become a common event in the family life cycle" (Massey 1987:103).

Thus, it is not simply population pressures, under- or unemployment in Mexico, or even the general lure of economic opportunity in the United States that contributes to the continuation of undocumented migration. Rather, out-migration is directed to the United States because of the social networks that American policies and practices were instrumental in establishing. As a consequence, Mexican immigration today has now become a firmly established and self-sustaining process.

The pressures of undocumented Mexican migration to the United States has also been influenced by American involvement in the economic development of Mexican border communities, which was organized to fill the void created when the bracero program was unilaterally canceled in 1964 (Sklair 1989). Integral to the development strategies developed in northern Mexico was the *maquiladora*, assembly plants built on the Mexican side of the U.S.-Mexican border by American corporations. Here American-made parts are assembled into consumer goods (e.g., televisions, refrigerators, clothing, toys) by Mexican workers and returned virtually duty-free. For years Mexican *maquila* workers received wages that ranged from one-fifth to one-seventh of those paid to American industrial workers, and recent devaluations of the Mexican peso have reduced those figures to as little as one-fifteenth of their American counterparts (Cockcroft 1986:110). Critics of the *maquiladoras* point out that, no matter how contented workers may be in their *maquila* jobs, these factories serve as a magnet to encourage migration to Mexican border cities (Kopinak 1996; Uchitelle 1993; Ruiz and Tiano 1987). By 1974, one-third of the people on the Mexican side of the border were migrants, but only 3 percent were employed in *maquiladoras* (Cockcroft 1986:109). Therefore, as the population of Mexican border cities increased after the introduction of the *maquiladoras,* so did unemployment and underemployment rates, which, in turn, contributed to the flow of illegal immigrants to the United States. Therefore, rather than easing the pressures of illegal migration to the United States by providing jobs in Mexico, the presence of the *maquilas* has actually increased them.

Two implications can be drawn from this interpretation. First, given the thrust of the modernization process and the impact of American political and economic power throughout the world, the United States will continue to attract immigrants—legal and illegal—from Third World sources. This continuation of immigration for the foreseeable future will likely reinforce and recreate the ethnic diversity that has characterized American society almost from its founding. Second, although migration pressures are manifested in different ways in different countries, they frequently derive their impetus from American economic and political power abroad. Thus, comprehension of the dynamics of American immigration today cannot begin at America's borders. Rather, it must also examine the impact of the American presence in sending countries.

So the dynamics of American immigration today must be conceptualized more broadly as an integral component and consequence of a modern global economy that is characterized by dramatic inequalities between societies. Given the interdependent nature of a global economy characterized by inequalities between rich and poor countries, it is probable that, even as internal political opposition to immigration increases within the United States, the global presence of the United States and other Western nations throughout the world will continue to generate emigration pressures from less-developed countries, thus reinforcing the clamor at America's gates.

The Coalescing of "White" America

The "new immigrant wave" became a significant phenomenon just when ethnicity and the celebration of America's ethnic diversity became more fashionable than ever before. The main theme of the "ethnic revival" of the 1970s was the rediscovery and reassertion of the importance and value of cultural pluralism and a simultaneous rejection of Anglo-conformity and the melting pot, which envision an ideal society as culturally homogeneous rather than culturally diverse. African Americans, Chicanos, Puerto Ricans, American Indians, and Asians each asserted their cultural distinctiveness and rejected what they perceived as efforts to impose on them the culture of the white middle class.

Each of these assertions of cultural identity and distinctiveness can be seen as an effort at ethnic mobilization—"the process by which a group organizes along ethnic lines in pursuit of collective political ends" (Nagel and Olzak 1982:127). In Article 2, "Constructing Ethnicity," Joane Nagel provides an explanation for the emergence of recent tribal, pantribal, and pan-Indian movements. She sees such movements as responses to external stimuli—in particular, to policies of the American federal government that control resources available to Indians.

However, a critical impetus for the ethnic revival came from the descendants of southern and eastern European peoples, whose metamorphosis from "inbetween" peoples (see Barrett and Roediger, Article 6) to "white ethnics" reflected both their social mobility in the post–World War II era and their progressive incorporation into the category of "white." Michael Novak, grandson of Slovakian immigrants and author of *The Rise of the Unmeltable Ethnics* (1971), was one of the foremost proponents of the new ethnicity. He identified two basic elements in the movement: a sensitivity to and appreciation of the importance of ethnic pluralism; and a self-conscious examination of one's own cultural heritage (Novak 1971:17). Another prominent spokesman, Andrew Greeley, the Irish-American sociologist, priest, and novelist, noted several ways in which this ethnic "consciousness raising" was expressed: increased interest in the literary, intellectual, and artistic culture of one's ethnic background; visits to one's ancestral homeland; and increased use of one's ancestral language (Greeley 1975:149-151).

The case for a broadly based ethnic revival was supported by considerable impressionistic evidence. In 1969, for the first time, the Census Bureau asked Americans about their ethnic backgrounds. Those interviewed were given seven choices from which to select: German, English, Irish, Spanish, Polish, Italian, and Russian (and "mixed" or "other"). Thirty-eight percent of the respondents (equivalent to 75 million Americans) placed themselves in one of the seven categories. Three years later, when the Census Bureau conducted a similar survey, Americans appeared much more conscious of, or willing to indicate, their affiliation with an ethnic group. This time nearly 50 percent (equivalent to 102 million) identified with a specific national group. Moreover, during the late 1960s and early 1970s, numerous ethnic groups developed organizations, such as the Italian-American Civil Rights League, that were designed to combat negative perceptions of their group. Such self-consciously ethnic organizations also mobilized to obtain financial resources from the federal government and private foundations in order to fund activities to rekindle or awaken ethnic consciousness. In 1972 the Ethnic Heritage Studies Act gave federal government sanction to the ethnic revival by providing financial assistance to promote ethnic studies. The Act gave, in the words of one of its sponsors, "official recognition to ethnicity as a positive constructive force in our society today" (quoted in Polenberg 1980:246).

The notion of an ethnic revival was also reflected in increased academic attention to ethnicity. History, literature, and sociology courses that had focused almost exclusively on African Americans during the 1960s broadened their scope to include other ethnic groups in the 1970s. Indeed, student enrollments declined in black studies courses, and there were instances in which ethnic courses supplanted race courses completely. The increasing salience of ethnicity was also symbolized by the founding of several journals devoted to its analysis: *Ethnicity* (1974), *Journal of Ethnic Studies* (1974), *Ethnic and Racial Studies* (1978), *MELUS (Multiethnic Literature in the United States;* 1975), and the *Journal of American Ethnic History* (1981). Finally, one of the most salient indices of the rediscovery of ethnicity was the publication in 1980 of the *Harvard Encyclopedia of American Ethnic Groups,* the most comprehensive resource available on the subject today (Thernstrom 1980). Publication of the *Encyclopedia* under the aegis of the nation's most prestigious university press reflects the primacy that ethnicity has been accorded over the last three decades.

What are the reasons for this resurgence of ethnicity? Foremost was the impact that the Black Protest Movement had on the self-definition of other ethnic groups, in particular white ethnics. On the one hand, the emphasis on black pride and on understanding African American culture, stimulated by the civil rights movement of the late 1950s and 1960s, led many white ethnics to consider their own heritages more closely. Moreover, the "roots phenomenon" emerged among white ethnics that both reflected and was stimulated by the celebrated television saga "Roots," which was based on Alex Haley's attempt to trace and construct his ancestral origins in Africa.

More critical, however, were the structural contexts within which the "white ethnic" revival occurred. In Article 23 Massey points out that the economic "ethnic miracle" that European immigrants and their descendants experienced in the post–World War II era resulted from the confluence of several unique factors. First, the post-1920s hiatus in immigration from Europe effectively curtailed the infusion of "old country" cultural patterns into immigrant communities. "The cutting off of immigration from Europe eliminated the supply of raw materials for the grist mill of ethnicity in the United States, ensuring that whatever ethnic identities existed would be predominantly a consequence of events and processes occurring within the U.S." Second, the assimilation of second- and third-generation, "new" immigrant European Americans was greatly facilitated by the extraordinary post–World War II economic boom, which produced a period of economic prosperity unparalleled in American history. During the quarter of a century between 1948 and 1973, real median family income doubled. As a consequence, "first- and second-generation immigrants from southern and eastern Europe rode this wave of prosperity to achieve full economic parity with northern and western Europeans by 1980."

This economic prosperity greatly facilitated the adaptation of white ethnic groups to American society. Richard Alba (Article 15 and 1990) has shown how the experience of ethnicity among southern and eastern Europeans is affected by age and cohort. Older cohorts were far more likely to have been raised in homes in which a language other than English was spoken, to have had both parents from the same ethnic background, and not to have attended college. Members of younger cohorts, on the other hand, were much more likely to have grown up in homes in which only English was spoken, to have had ethnically mixed ancestry, and to have attended college. Moreover, members of younger cohorts were much more likely to have married spouses from different ethnic and religious backgrounds and to have switched religious affiliations than were members of the older cohorts. By the 1970s the fourth generation of the southern and eastern European immigrants was entering adulthood. As the distance from their ancestral roots increased, their identification with them weakened. The decline of the ancestral language, the dispersion of ethnic neighborhoods, the decreasing participation in and identification with the traditional religious community primarily among Catholics, especially those under thirty years of age, and the increased rates of ethnic and religious intermarriage contributed to the dwindling of a meaningful "white ethnic" identity.

Thus, white ethnics' economic, educational, and occupational mobility, as well as their geographical dispersion to ethnically undifferentiated suburbs and patterns of increased intermarriage, indicate that they have moved into the "white" mainstream, where their identification with their ethnic origins has become increasingly remote.

Moreover, there is considerable evidence that ethnicity as a source of social cohesion is decreasing, especially among the third and fourth generations. In Article 22, "Symbolic Ethnicity," Herbert Gans disputes the notion of an enduring ethnic revival, arguing that both cultural and social assimilation continue to take place in American society. Ethnicity is no longer rooted in group membership or cultural patterns but instead has become symbolic, a matter of choice, an ethnicity of "last resort." In his study of an Italian-American community in Boston in the 1960s, Gans did not find a sense of ethnic identity to be increasing. Instead, he found a straight-line decline in ethnicity over three generations. That is, ethnicity was less significant in each succeeding generation (Gans 1962). Similarly, a study by Sandberg showed a constant decline in ethnic consciousness, identification, and cohesion among Polish-Americans in Los Angeles; by the fourth generation, ethnicity had ceased to play an important role in their lives (Sandberg 1974). Finally, these findings are reinforced by increased rates of ethnic and religious intermarriage, which were discussed in Part 3.

Thus, paradoxically, at precisely the moment that white ethnics have become the most fully assimilated into American society, culturally and socially, their interest in and identification with their ethnic roots has also become the most pronounced. In *The Ethnic Myth* Stephen Steinberg argued that ". . . the impulse to recapture the ethnic past is a belated realization that ethnicity is rapidly diminishing as a significant factor in American life" (Steinberg 1981:73).

Although neither is especially sympathetic to the notion of an ethnic revival, both Irving Howe (1977) and Herbert Gans (Article 22, "Symbolic Ethnicity") suggest another source of the surge of interest in things ethnic. In an interpretation reminiscent of Herberg's (1955) explanation of the surge of religiosity a generation earlier, they find that ethnicity provides a fashionable, socially acceptable source of personal identity in an increasingly homogenized America. In Howe's words,

> We are all aware that our ties with the European past grow increasingly feeble. Yet we feel uneasy before the prospect of becoming "just Americans." We feel uneasy before the prospect of becoming as indistinguishable from one another as our motel rooms are, or as flavorless and mass-produced as the bread many of us eat. (Howe 1977:18)

Thus, although there appears to be widespread interest today among many European Americans in retrieving or maintaining a sense of ethnic identity (what Gans called *symbolic ethnicity*), precisely how deep and enduring such identities are remains problematic (for a similar interpretation, see Hirschman 1983).

Finally, Stanley Lieberson (1985) has suggested that a substantial number of white Americans have no sense of ethnic group identity other than a general notion that they are "American." The European origins of these "unhyphenated whites," as Lieberson dubs them, are either so remote or so mixed that they are able to define themselves only as "American." Lieberson's interpretation, which is reinforced by those of Doane, Alba, Gans, and Massey, suggests that increasingly ethnic identities of peoples of European descent have coalesced into an inclusive "white" category, which has emerged in response to the increasing national (as opposed to Southern regional) presence of a racial "other"—African Americans—against which to define themselves.

The Racial "Other": African Americans and the Changing Nature of Race in America

Near the end of World War II, Gunnar Myrdal, a Swedish economist and later a Nobel Prize winner, published *An American Dilemma* (1944), a massive two-volume study of American race relations that he had conducted with the financial support of the Carnegie Corporation. The book examined in greater depth than any previous study the subordinate political, economic, and social status of African Americans and the prospects for change of that status. The book's title reflected Myrdal's basic premise that American race relations were essentially a moral problem in the hearts and minds of Americans—that the caste status that constrained African Americans in virtually every aspect of their lives represented a violation of what he called the "American creed" of equality and brotherhood. The book became an immediate classic, influencing an entire generation of academics, students, clergy, and social workers, and providing the intellectual backdrop for the attack upon segregation during the 1950s and 1960s. The influence extended to the Supreme Court, which cited it in the historic 1954 *Brown* v. *Board of Education of Topeka* decision.

The pace of change in American race relations in the years following publication of *An American Dilemma* was more rapid than even Myrdal had anticipated. During the next two decades, resolution of the glaring contradiction between American ideals and African Americans' second-class citizenship became the nation's most prominent domestic political issue. Reflecting this focus, in 1965, in an introduction written for a series of essays entitled "The Negro American" in the scholarly journal *Daedalus,* President Lyndon Johnson wrote, "Nothing is of greater significance to the welfare and vitality of this nation than the movement to secure equal rights for Negro Americans" (*Daedalus* 1965:743). Johnson's crucial role in achieving passage of the landmark 1964 Civil Rights Act and the 1965 Voting Rights Act and his War on Poverty program are ample evidence that his support was not merely rhetorical.

Johnson wrote these words at the zenith of personal and national attention to the status of African Americans. However, reflecting the unrest created by their continued exclusion from mainstream American life, a wave of urban uprisings by blacks swept American cities during the mid-1960s. These uprisings claimed a toll of over one hundred lives and millions of dollars in property damage. President Johnson responded by appointing a blue-ribbon commission to investigate the causes of the civil disorders and to recommend ways in which the conditions that triggered them might be addressed. In 1968 the National Commission on Civil Disorders (popularly known as the Kerner Commission, after its chair, Illinois Governor Otto Kerner) attributed the primary responsibility for the outbreaks to "white racism" and warned that American society was moving toward "two societies, one black, one white—separate and unequal." It concluded that "there can be no higher claim on the Nation's conscience" than to eliminate "deepening racial division" by a "compassionate, massive, and sustained" commitment of resources and energy (National Advisory Commission on Civil Disorders 1968).

Johnson, by that time preoccupied with the escalation of the war in Vietnam, ignored the commission's recommendations, just as his successor, Richard Nixon, disputed its basic conclusions. Subsequently, despite several significant private and governmental efforts to implement programs to achieve racial equality, the status of African Americans no longer occupied the prominence in the American consciousness that it had done in 1965. By 1981 the editors of an issue of *Daedalus* devoted to American racial minorities would write, "It is a measure of the distance we have traveled in sixteen years that is almost unthinkable to imagine any white politician today making such a statement as Johnson's in 1965, giving such primacy to the issue of racial equality" (*Daedalus* 1981:vi).

Three decades after the Kerner Commission sounded its alarm that the nation was being divided into two societies, whether and to what extent the gap that separates black and white America has been narrowed has become the focus of intense national debate. Some observers, such as Abigail and Stephan Thernstrom (1997), have emphasized the substantial progress that African Americans have made. On the other hand, a 1998 report coauthored by Fred Harris, a former senator from Oklahoma and member of the original Kerner Commission, challenged such optimistic views, contending that "the rich are getting richer, the poor are getting poorer, and minorities are suffering disproportionately" (Eisenhower Foundation, 1998). In the section below, we will examine some of the continuities and changes in the status of African Americans since the 1960s.

There can be little doubt that the rise of black militancy was one of the most momentous developments of the turbulent 1960s. Each year during that decade, the scale of racial conflict and violence escalated. In retrospect, the beginnings appear relatively subdued. In 1960 the most dramatic events involved drugstore sit-ins in Greensboro, North Carolina, a tactic that quickly spread throughout the South. In the following years, the pace and intensity of protest increased dramatically. Civil disorders engulfed cities throughout the country, with great loss of property and lives. In the heated climate of those years, four of the most important figures in the movement for African American equality were the victims of assassins' bullets. Two of them, Malcolm X and Martin Luther King, Jr., were black; the other two, John F. Kennedy and Robert Kennedy, were white.

Between 1960 and 1970, the goals and means of the Black Protest Movement underwent substantial changes. As is characteristic of much social change, yesterday's radicalism became today's moderation. Many ideologies and tactics that came to be defined as moderate would have appeared unthinkably radical to concerned individuals—black and white—a decade earlier. Joseph C. Hough, Jr., has characterized this change as the "stretching of the extremism spectrum":

> About 1953 I had my first conversation with [a friend in the South] about race relations, and he and I agreed that while the Negro deserved a better chance in America, we must be careful to oppose two kinds of extremists—the NAACP and the Ku Klux Klan. In 1955, we had another conversation and again we agreed that Negroes ought to be able to attend desegregated public schools, but that we should oppose two kinds of extremes—White Citizens Councils and Martin Luther King. In 1966, this same friend said to me, "If we could get the good whites and the good Negroes to support Martin Luther King, perhaps we could put the brakes on these SNCC and CORE people and also put a stop to this ridiculous revival of the Ku Klux Klan. (Hough 1968:224–225)

By the late 1960s, the forms and direction of African American protest had shifted from the moderate civil rights movement to a more militant black power movement. The civil rights movement of the 1950s and early 1960s had been based essentially on an order model of society; the primary goal had been integration into the mainstream of the dominant society, and the primary means were nonviolent. As Skolnick (1969) has pointed out, the civil rights movement "operated for the most part on the implicit premise that racism was a localized malignancy within a relatively healthy political and social order; it was a move to force American morality and American institutions to root out the last vestiges of the 'disease' " (Skolnick 1969:31).

The fundamental ideological thrust of the black power movement, on the other hand, derived from a conflict model of societal functioning. In response to the intransigence and unresponsiveness of white America, articulate African American spokespersons increasingly questioned the capacity of traditional goals and means to ensure the dignity and autonomy of black people in a white society. After the Kerner Commission's report was published in 1968, militancy among African Americans, particularly among the young, increased even further. Perhaps the most important shift in attitudes among African Americans was the growing recognition that the racial problems were national and could not be confined to the South; that nonviolence was merely a *tactic* in a power struggle and in many instances was useless to obtain black equality and autonomy; and that racism was rooted in the society's institutions. Consequently, the primary efforts of the black power movement were to obtain a more equitable distribution of power in the many institutional spheres of American life and to search for new ideological forms, or cultural alternatives to those of white America.

For African Americans, however, the 1960s was a decade of progress: during this period, blacks experienced their greatest gains since their emancipation in 1865. These gains were brought about by the unprecedented efforts of federal, state, and local governments and private organizations to remove inequalities and redress injustices that had for years relegated African Americans to second-class citizenship.

Most visible and dramatic were the legal changes made by the federal government. For the first time in American history, the three branches of the federal government acted in concert on behalf of African Americans. The Supreme Court, whose *Brown* v. *Board of Education* decision had outlawed segregated schools in 1954, substantially extended the implications of the *Brown* decision, and symbolized the beginning of a new era for blacks. It outlawed state laws prohibiting racial intermarriage and racial discrimination in the rental and sale of private and public property. Moreover, the Court decisively rejected efforts by local school districts to evade its desegregation rulings, and it unanimously supported school busing as one means of achieving that goal. President Lyndon Johnson, a Southerner, provided the most unequivocal moral and political support of African American aspirations of any president in American history. Through his leadership, the Congress enacted legislation that outlawed discrimination in public accommodations, employment, housing, voting, and education. In addition, his Great Society economic programs provided federal funds to enhance occupational and educational opportunities for blacks.

By the end of the 1960s, African Americans, particularly the better educated and more highly skilled, had made substantial gains, both economically and educationally. One of the best indices of these changes was black median family income, which in 1959 was only half of that for whites. By 1964 black family income had risen to 54 percent of white income, and by 1969, reflecting the economic expansion and prosperity that characterized the decade, as well as national efforts to reduce black inequalities, it had risen to 61 percent. Thus, although problems remained acute for poorly educated and unskilled African Americans, the efforts of the 1960s had clearly produced some impressive advances.

However, the civil rights movement, which during the 1960s had generally displayed consensus concerning both goals and tactics despite internal differences, was now in disarray. Part of the reason was the movement's very success in achieving impressive legislative and judicial victories in the 1960s. The disarray also reflected the fact that for many African Americans, the optimism of the early 1960s had been shattered by the failure of these legislative changes to institute meaningful changes in their lives. It became increasingly apparent that the abolition of legal barriers to public accommodations and suburban housing, for example, did not address the essential problems of a substantial portion of the African American population. The erosion of the fragile consensus among African Americans was symbolized by the outbreaks of the civil disorders of the late 1960s, which did little to allay conscious and unconscious white anxieties concerning African American demands for substantial changes in the status quo. As many whites grew weary of what they perceived as government support for lawlessness and became tired of the constant media attention to blacks, the conservative mood of the country increased, contributing to the 1968 election of Richard Nixon to the presidency.

By the early 1970s, the impetus and fervor of the black power movement was spent. The frequency of mass social unrest dramatically declined during the decade. American involvement in Indochina formally ended, and the civil disorders that rent many American cities during the 1960s did not recur on an equally massive scale. The sense of concern for social justice that had inspired many white Americans was replaced by an indifference, even an aversion, to the problems of racial minority groups in the country. Indeed, the activism of the so-called concerned generation of the 1960s was replaced by a stance of "benign neglect." Compared with the progress achieved during the 1960s and throughout the 1970s, 1980s, and early 1990s, the rate of African American advance slowed appreciably; at worst, it was a time of retrogression and retrenchment.

Many of the most dramatic advances for African Americans since the 1960s have been in the political arena. The tactics of public confrontations, boycotts, and demonstrations, which in the late 1950s and early 1960s had been successful in effecting social change, were supplanted in the 1970s by more traditional political activity. "Politics is the civil-rights movement of the 1970s," said Maynard Jackson, the black mayor of Atlanta (Sitkoff 1981:229). Such a stance was possible because of the increase in African American political strength brought about by the Voting Rights Act of 1965, which provided federal protection for black efforts to register and vote in states throughout the South. The percentage of Southern blacks registered to vote increased from 35 percent in 1964 to 65 percent in 1969. In Alabama, the increase was from 19 to 61 percent; in Mississippi, from 7 to 67 percent; and in Georgia, from 27 to 60 percent (Polenberg 1980:192).

The increases in African American voters throughout the South substantially increased their political representation. In 1964 of all the nearly half-million elected officials in the entire country (ranging from local school-board member to President of the United States), only 103 blacks held elected offices. By 1970 this number of elected officials had increased to 1,400, and by 1994 stood at more than 8,400, more than two-thirds of them in the South. Moreover, the number of African American mayors increased from *none* in 1964 to more than 416 in 1996. Since 1964, African Americans have been elected mayor in each of the nation's five largest cities—New York, Los Angeles, Chicago, Houston, and Philadelphia; in 1998 Baltimore, Seattle, St. Louis, Kansas City, Detroit, Atlanta, Denver, San Francisco, and Washington, D.C., all had black mayors. Finally, by 1998 the Congressional Black Caucus, composed of Democratic African American members of the House of Representatives, claimed a membership of 38 out of the 435 seats.

Because of their strategic location in the major metropolitan areas of key industrial states, the combined voting strength of African Americans could swing close elections. This power was demonstrated first in 1960, when John F. Kennedy's narrow victory over Richard Nixon was due to the substantial margin that he obtained from black voters in the industrial Northeast and Midwest. It was even more noteworthy in the 1976 election, when over 90 percent of more than six-and-one-half million black voters voted for Jimmy Carter, who owed his victory margin in most of the Southern as well as several Northern states—and thus his election as a whole—directly to the overwhelming support of African American voters. Finally, the increasing significance of African American political power was made abundantly clear by Jesse Jackson's presidential campaigns in 1988 and 1991. His candidacy not only electrified the black community (and was instrumental in registering thousands of new black voters), but he gained the support of a substantial number of white voters as well.

Despite these highly visible changes, by 1994 African Americans remained less than 2 percent of all elected officials in the country, a percentage not even closely approximating their nearly 13 percent of the total population. In the South, where blacks comprise more than 20 percent of the population, only 3 percent of the elected officials were black. Moreover, in many instances the political power that black elected officials have today is limited by the fact that they are politically isolated. Finally, given the exodus of white middle-class residents and businesses to the suburbs, African Americans often find they have gained political power without the financial resources with which to provide the jobs and services (educational, medical, police and fire protection) that their constituents most urgently need.

During the 1950s, 1960s, and early 1970s, African Americans achieved substantial gains in education. In 1957 the proportion of whites aged 25–29 who had completed high school (63.3 percent) was double the proportion of blacks (31.6 percent), but by 1976 the proportions of each racial group who were high-school graduates were nearly the same (U.S. Bureau of the Census 1988a:75–76). In the late 1960s and early 1970s a steadily increasing percent of blacks began attending college, so that by 1976 the percentage of black high-school graduates enrolled in college was virtually equal to that of whites, a dramatic change when compared to the college attendance rates of blacks as late as the mid-1960s (Jones 1981).

However, between 1976 and 1985, the educational gains of the 1960s and early 1970s eroded, threatening to reverse the movement toward educational equality. The college participation rate for black high-school graduates declined dramatically, while the white participation rate remained virtually unchanged. Moreover, black college completion rates declined, as did the proportion of black students enrolled at four-year colleges and in graduate and professional schools (Carter and Wilson 1997).

However, from the mid-1980s through the 1990s, African American educational attainments have steadily improved; by 1995 the rates of high-school completion for 25–29-year-old blacks was similar (87 percent) to whites. Moreover, the college participation rates for both whites and blacks increased; the rates for both races stood at all-time highs in 1995. The white participation rate increased from 29 percent in 1985 to 34 percent in 1994, while the increase for blacks—from 20 to 27 percent—was slightly larger. After declining from 1976 to 1985, it took until 1992 for the percentage of bachelor's degrees earned by African Americans to return to the 1976 level of 6.4 percent. By 1994 the percentage of bachelor's degrees awarded to blacks stood at 7.2 percent— an all-time high (Carter and Wilson 1997).

Similarly, there was a dramatic decline in the number and percentage of graduate and professional degrees awarded to African Americans between 1976 and the mid-1980s. In 1976 blacks were awarded 6.6 percent of the nation's master's degrees, but by 1989 this figure had declined to 4.6 percent. During the 1990s, however, the percentage of master's degrees awarded to African Americans steadily increased, to 5.7 percent in 1994—still well below the 1976 figure. The number of doctoral degrees awarded to African Americans declined from 1,445 in 1980 to 771 in 1987, but it has steadily risen since then, reaching 1,287 in 1995. The greatest gains occurred in the category of professional degrees; whereas in 1976 African Americans were awarded 2,694 professional degrees, or 4.3 percent of the total, in 1994 they were awarded 4,444, or 5.9 percent of the total (Carter and Wilson 1997).

However, the somewhat dramatic educational gains during the late 1980s and early 1990s by minority students generally, and by African American students in particular, have recently slowed. The most disquieting feature of these declines is that they occurred *before* legal challenges to affirmative action programs in states such as California and Texas reduced the number of African American and Hispanic undergraduate and post-graduate students even further. After a Federal court decision that eliminated the affirmative action admissions program at the University of Texas Law School, the number of black and Mexican American students admitted dropped precipitously; five black and eighteen Mexican American students were admitted to the Law School in 1997 in contrast to sixty-five blacks and seventy Mexican Americans the previous year (Carter and Wilson 1997; Applebome 1997a:A9). Similarly, in 1998, undergraduate admissions of American Indians, African Americans and Latinos at the University of California, Berkeley, and the University of California, Los Angeles, dropped precipitously—by 45 percent at Berkeley and by 36 percent at UCLA—after the universities implemented policies based on the requirements of the 1996 California Proposition 209, which banned the use of race as a factor in considering admissions to California public colleges and universities (Bronner 1998).

However, these statistics obscure substantial qualitative differences in African American educational achievement. During the early 1990s, as a consequence of court decisions that made it easier for school districts to abandon desegregation plans that the courts had previously mandated, the nation's schools were resegregating at a faster rate than at any time since the Supreme Court's 1954 *Brown* v. *Board of Education* decision—that is, the isolation of black and Hispanic students in schools that are predominantly minority and poor was more pronounced than at any time since the 1950s, recreating the pattern of "separate and *unequal*" that the Supreme Court had ruled against in 1954 (Orfield et al. 1997; Applebome 1997b:A8). Since the 1970s, black students in the South have been more likely to attend racially integrated elementary and secondary schools than are black students in other regions of the country. However, the desegregation achieved during the 1960s and 1970s in the South has substantially eroded during the late 1980s and 1990s, coming much more closely to resemble the patterns of educational racial isolation that characterize other regions of the country. Because of the patterns of residential segregation in most American cities, two-thirds of black children attend schools that are composed predominantly of minority children. Whereas black children in rural areas, small and medium-sized towns, and suburbs are most likely to attend racially integrated schools, educational racial isolation is most acute in the central city school districts of the nation's largest cities. In 1994–1995, the ten largest central city school districts accounted for 18 percent of all black students (and 23 percent of Latino students), but only 2 percent of white students. "About a fifth of black and Latino students depend on districts that do not matter to 98 percent of white families" (Orfield et al. 1997:23). Most important, racially segregated schools tend also to be segregated by poverty. In other words, minority children—blacks and Hispanics in particular—are much more likely than whites to be disadvantaged because they attend schools with high poverty concentrations. Thus, although there have been significant educational advances for African Americans during the past two decades, the question as to whether these gains are enduring and can be translated into higher economic status remains problematic.

Thus the trends in both the political and educational areas indicate qualified improvements for African Americans. However, no such progress has taken place in the economic sphere, perhaps the most important institutional category. The economic gains of the 1960s were eroded by inflation, two recessions, and substantial reductions in federal, state, and local governmental commitments to racial progress. The economic recovery championed by the Reagan and Bush administrations during the 1980s did little to enhance the economic status of African Americans, which, until 1994, showed little improvement since the early 1970s. Although many blacks have experienced socioeconomic mobility, African Americans remain underrepresented in high-status professional, technical, and managerial positions, and overrepresented in service occupations, traditionally recognized as low-status jobs in American society (Farley and Allen 1987). During the 1970s, 1980s, and early 1990s, the income gap separating blacks and whites widened. Black median family income, which rose substantially during the 1960s—from 50 percent of white median family income in 1959 to 61 percent in 1970—began to decline in the mid-1970s and remained virtually stagnant (between 55 and 58 percent of white income) throughout the 1980s and the early 1990s. Finally, in 1995, black median family income rose to match the 61 percent it had achieved a quarter of a century earlier, but it declined once again in 1996 (see Figure 1).

However, measures of *income* inequality alone do not adequately measure the disparities between blacks and whites in economic status; indeed, the focus of many analyses of racial inequality on income understates the substantial economic black-white inequality. To obtain a more accurate picture of the racial distribution of economic resources, it is necessary to examine disparities in the distribution of wealth. *Income* refers to the economic resources that people receive during a specified period of time (usually a year), but *wealth* includes savings, investments, homes, and property; that is, wealth represents accumulated assets or stored-up purchasing power.

Most studies of the distribution of wealth in American society have relied on measures of *net worth*, which refers to the difference between a household's assets and its liabilities. In 1993 the median net worth of white households ($45,740) was more than ten times the median net worth of black households ($4,418). Or, to put it another way, in 1993 black median family income was 54.8 percent of white income, but the median net worth of black families was only 9.6 percent of white families (U.S. Bureau of the Census 1997a).

However, the net worth of many Americans who have accumulated some wealth is held almost exclusively in the equity that they have in their homes and automobiles. Oliver and Shapiro (1989a; 1989b; 1995) have therefore argued that the most accurate measures of the concentration of wealth in the United States should exclude equity in homes and vehicles, because these assets can seldom be converted to other purposes (such as financing a college education, establishing or expanding a business,

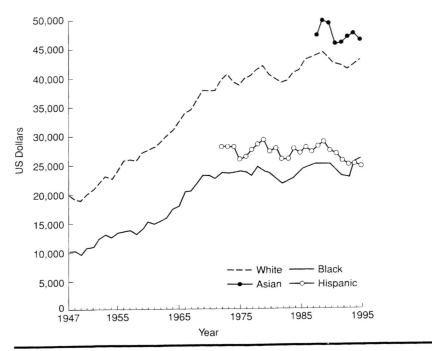

FIGURE 1   *Median Family Income, 1947–1995 (in 1995 dollars)*

or paying for emergency medical expenses). They suggest that a more appropriate measure of wealth is *net financial assets,* which refers to household wealth after the equity in homes and vehicles has been deducted. If this measure (rather than net worth) is used, figures on the overall wealth of American households and inequalities in the distribution of wealth in American society change dramatically; net financial assets tend to be much more heavily concentrated among the very wealthy. "Whereas the top 20 percent of American households earn over 43 percent of all income, the same 20 percent holds 67 percent of net worth and nearly 90 percent of net financial assets" (Oliver and Shapiro 1989a).

The disparities in net financial assets between black and white are even more pronounced than those for net worth. Oliver and Shapiro have shown that in 1988, white households had a median net worth of $43,800, but median net financial assets of only $6,999 (Oliver and Shapiro 1995:86). Black households, on the other hand, had a median net worth of $3,700, but *no* median net financial assets at all. Oliver and Shapiro conclude that blacks are therefore much more disadvantaged than whites when measures of wealth—especially net financial assets—rather than income, are used.

With the exception of three years during the 1970s, the annual black unemployment rate has been at least double that for whites since 1954, and during the

1980s, the gap between white and black unemployment rates actually increased. In 1997 black unemployment stood at nearly 10 percent of the black labor force, standing at nearly 2½ times the rate for whites (U.S. Bureau of the Census 1998). Unemployment was most acute for black teenagers. Despite declines in unemployment among all categories of workers since 1983, nearly one-fourth (22.6 percent) of black teenagers were unemployed in 1997, a figure also 2½ times higher than that for white teenagers (9.6 percent). Moreover, the National Urban League, whose research division annually surveys African American households, contends that the official unemployment rate substantially underrepresents real unemployment because it does not include discouraged workers who have dropped out of the labor force entirely. They also note that the unemployment data just cited are national averages, so they obscure the variations among different cities; the Urban League estimates that in some cities, the jobless rate for black teenagers during the 1980s may have risen to as high as 80 percent. Thus the overall economic status of African Americans appears to have made only limited gains at best during the economic boom of the 1990s.

However, William Julius Wilson (Articles 7 and 19; 1987; 1996b) has contended that this deterioration in economic status has not been felt uniformly throughout the black community. During the 1970s, middle-class blacks made impressive economic advances. The number of blacks in professional and managerial positions increased to 2½ times what it had been in 1965. Indeed, between 1975 and 1980, the largest gains in black employment were in higher-status occupations. During this period, the number of African Americans employed increased by 1.3 million, over half of them in managerial, professional, and craft jobs (Hill 1981:22). Moreover, Wilson notes that prior to 1960, the ratio of black to white income actually decreased as educational attainment increased, but that this pattern has now been reversed: the higher the black educational level, the more closely incomes approximate those of comparably educated whites.

Nevertheless, Wilson argues that because of macrostructural changes in the American economy, a growing division has emerged among African Americans between the middle class and a steadily increasing underclass—the nation's most impoverished social category, many of whom live in persistent poverty. Found predominantly in the nation's inner cities, the underclass is characterized by high rates of unemployment, out-of-wedlock births, female-headed families, welfare dependence, homelessness, and serious crime. Although those included in the underclass include some whites and, increasingly, Hispanics, its existence is most pronounced and most visible in the black ghettos of northern cities in the United States.

The nature and causes of the growing underclass have been the subject of considerable controversy. In an insightful analysis of the underclass phenomenon in the 1980s, Maxine Baca Zinn (1989) distinguishes between two broad ideologies or models—the cultural deficiency and the macrostructural—that correspond roughly to the "internal" and "external" explanations of ethnic group attainment developed in the Introduction to Part 3. These models, she argues, have been used both by social scientists and by laypeople to explain the underclass phenomenon. The cultural deficiency model emphasizes shortcomings either in the minority's culture or family system or in a welfare system believed to encourage personal traits that prevent people from pulling themselves out of poverty. The cultural deficiency model locates the explanation for the underclass in the cultural or psychological characteristics of each specific class level.

A macrostructural explanation of the underclass, on the other hand, focuses on the decline of opportunity structures. As noted in Part 3, William Julius Wilson has been one of the most prominent and articulate spokespersons for this perspective. In *The Truly Disadvantaged* (1987) and *When Work Disappears* (1996), Wilson argued that the growth of the urban underclass has resulted from major structural changes in the American economy that have caused extremely high levels of inner-city unemployment. As Wilson writes in "Work," (Article 19), "The disappearance of jobs . . . [is a critical factor in explaining] the catastrophic descent of America's ghettos into ever-deeper poverty and misery."

Earlier in the twentieth century, relatively uneducated and unskilled native and immigrant workers were able to find stable employment and income in the manufacturing sector of the economy. In the past quarter century, however, the process of deindustrialization has contributed to an economic mismatch between the available jobs and the qualifications of inner-city residents. On the one hand, most of the nation's major manufacturing centers in the industrial states of the North and Midwest have experienced dramatic declines in manufacturing—such jobs, which in the past did not require highly technical skills, have moved from the inner cities to the suburbs, the sun belt, or overseas, or have been eliminated by the introduction of more efficient technologies. On the other hand, the jobs being created in the cities demand highly technical credentials that most inner-city residents do not have. Because the African American urban poor lack the educational and occupational skills necessary for today's highly technological jobs, economic opportunities for them are rapidly diminishing. The result is disastrously high levels of unemployment.

These broad structural changes have triggered a process of "hyperghettoization," in which the urban poor are disproportionately concentrated and socially and economically isolated. As many stable working- and middle-class residents with job qualifications have moved from the inner-city neighborhoods, the stability of inner-city social institutions (churches, schools, newspapers, recreational facilities, and small businesses) has been undermined, and the social fabric of community life has deteriorated. Those remaining in such neighborhoods, increasingly the "most marginal and oppressed of the black community," have become increasingly socially isolated. "A neighborhood in which people are poor but employed," Wilson writes, "is different from a neighborhood in which people are poor and jobless" (Article 19).

Whereas Wilson's analyses have focused primarily on the black underclass, other writers (Zinn 1989; Moore and Pinderhughes 1993) argue that similar macrostructural conditions have affected Hispanics, especially Puerto Ricans and Mexicans. Increases in Hispanic poverty have been most pronounced in those regions (such as the Northeast and Midwest) in which broad structural changes in the economy have occurred. "The association between national economic shifts and high rates of social dislocation among Hispanics provides further evidence for the structural argument that economic conditions rather than culture create distinctive forms of racial poverty" (Zinn 1989).

Therefore, the major thrust of Wilson's argument is that, although both the African American and Hispanic underclass reflect a legacy of racial discrimination, class factors have become critical in sustaining the underclass today. Lacking the necessary training and job skills for positions in the modern economy, members of the underclass are instead the victims of broad economic and technological changes in American society. Even if all racial prejudice and discrimination were eliminated, African American and Hispanic members of the underclass would still lack the necessary qualifications with which to participate in the mainstream of the economy and would continue to be found primarily in the low-paying, unskilled sector where unemployment is extremely high. In the economic sphere, institutional, not attitudinal, discrimination has become critical to sustaining African American and Hispanic inequalities.

Thus the economic problems confronting African Americans are those of institutional discrimination. The thrust of Wilson's thesis is that major attention must be directed not only to the removal of racial barriers (which he acknowledges still confront African Americans in education, politics, and especially in housing) but also to the very structure of the American economy and its inability to provide opportunity for the substantial segment of its population. The challenge for American society in the next decade, therefore, is not only to ensure that the barriers of racial discrimination are dismantled, but also to make certain that class barriers now precluding minority access to economic opportunities are eliminated.

Wilson's emphasis on the structural factors contributing to black inequalities, especially his model of the effects of deindustrialization and joblessness on the creation and perpetuation of the ghetto underclass, has elicited numerous critiques. One of the most penetrating is Roger Waldinger's analysis of the changing occupational dynamics in New York City (Article 27). Waldinger argues that the shift to a post-industrial global economy has transformed the ethnic division of labor in America's major urban centers. His analysis focuses on the economic and social changes that have accompanied the decline of manufacturing and the rise of a service-oriented economy in New York City, the nation's largest and historically most ethnically diverse city. Waldinger disputes the "mismatch" hypothesis upon which much of Wilson's analysis lies. Instead, he argues that the substantial decline since 1950 in jobs previously held by whites actually provided opportunities for ethnic occupational realignment—for nonwhites to replace whites in the city's labor force. However, what was distinctive about the manner in which nonwhites succeeded whites was the salience of distinct economic niches in which different ethnic groups were concentrated. For example, blacks tended to concentrate in public-sector jobs while immigrants were more likely to be found in a wide range of small, ethnically distinct businesses. Waldinger argues that ethnic-network recruiting tends to exclude nonethnics and thus to reinforce the ethnic identification of specific occupations. The tendency for ethnic enterprises to hire coethnics has an especially significant impact on native-born blacks, who are thus excluded from occupational opportunities controlled by immigrants, as well as those dominated by native-born whites. Thus he concludes that "native blacks are the big losers in the new ethnic division of labor."

Moreover, Zinn (1989) has challenged Wilson's assumptions about gender roles in explaining the emergence and persistence of black poverty and, especially, the dramatic increase in female-headed families among African Americans and Hispanics in the past quarter century. Wilson argues that the absence of stable job opportunities in the nation's major industrial areas has undermined the conception, much more widely embraced by Hispanic immigrants, of a "traditional family unit that features men as breadwinners." Zinn contends that both the cultural deficiency and the macrostructural models have similar underlying conceptions about gender and gender roles. Both models "assume that the traditional family is a key solution for eliminating racial poverty. . . . Both models rest on normative definitions of women's and men's roles . . . and traditional concepts of the family and women's and men's roles within it." Both, therefore, tend to ignore the role of gender in explaining poverty.

Zinn's critique raises important questions concerning the ways in which racial and ethnic phenomena are affected by gender. Until recently, there has been a tendency in the literature of racial and ethnic relations in the United States to generalize about these phenomena without considering gender. However, scholars have increasingly focused on the manner in which gender intersects with race and ethnicity.

For example, as Waters and Eschbach (Article 14) point out, the historical experiences of African Americans created patterns of both male and female labor-force participation different from those of European Americans. Because black men historically have confronted substantial occupational barriers to which white men have not been subject, until recently African American women have been much more likely to work outside the home than European American women. Consequently, "labor and earnings of African American women have made a much greater relative contribution to the economic survival of the African American family" (Geschwender and Carroll-Seguin 1990:289). Moreover, labor-force participation rates for European American women are highest among working-class families and decline as the husband's income increases. However, because the incomes of African American men are lower than those of European American men, more than one income is necessary for a black family to achieve comparable income levels. Therefore, the rate of labor-force participation for African American women increases as their husband's income increases. Geschwender and Carroll-Seguin conclude that whatever economic improvements two-parent African American families have made since the 1960s have occurred because African American wives "have been far more likely to work, and to work full-time. . . . Thus, the earnings of African American wives constituted a much greater percentage of family income than was the case among European Americans" (1990:298). On the other hand, Waters and Eschbach indicate that as women's presence in the labor force has grown over the past quarter century, the proportion of white women has come to exceed that of black women, and the earnings disparity between white and black women is much narrower than it is among black and white men.

Similarly, in a superb review essay, Pedraza (1991) has examined the role of women in migration processes, highlighting issues of gender that until recently have been ignored. Proposing a "gendered understanding of the social processes of migration," she contends that gender must not simply be considered as a variable, but as a central organizing principle in comprehending the dynamics of immigration and immigrant adaptation. As she notes, gender factors are central to the decision to migrate; women tend to migrate to create or reunite families, thus facilitating the networks that sustain migration chains. As a consequence, women are a central link between macro and micro factors in the migration process. Thus there are substantial gender differences in the way in which immigrants are incorporated into the receiving society. Finally, because women in most countries of origin are limited in the social roles available to them, immigration—if not more liberating for women—is at least different for women than for men; Pedraza suggests that, as a consequence, they are more reluctant to return to their homelands and are more likely to sponsor the immigration of female relatives. In "Gendered Immigration" (Article 25) Pierrette Hondagneu-Sotelo provides a textured and nuanced case study of many of these generalizations, emphasizing not only the way in which gender influences the migration process, but also how the migration process reconstructs gender relations themselves.

Multicultural America and the Future of Race and Ethnicity

At the 1963 March on Washington, Martin Luther King, Jr., delivered one of the most memorable speeches ever uttered by an American. In this address he spoke of his dream for the future:

> *I say to you today, my friends [that] even though we face difficulties of today and tomorrow, I still have a dream. It is a dream deeply rooted in the American dream. I have a dream that one day this nation will rise up and live out the true meaning of its creed that "all men are created equal." I have a dream . . . [of] that day when all God's children, black men and white men, Jews and Gentiles, Protestants and Catholics, will be able to join hands and sing in the words of that old Negro spiritual, "Free at last! Free at last! Thank God almighty, we are free at last."* (quoted in Oates 1982:255)

Within two years of his historic address, two of the most far-reaching pieces of federal legislation to help African Americans realize this dream—the 1964 Civil Rights Act and the 1965 Voting Rights Act—were enacted. Moreover, as noted before, the predominant thrust of public policy during the late 1960s was to undermine and deny the legitimacy of the forces of ethnic and racial particularism—to eliminate the formal barriers that had previously relegated certain racial and ethnic groups to second-class citizenship. These efforts were suffused with an optimism that racial and ethnic criteria would cease to be salient issues in American life, and that the dream of racial and ethnic equality of which King had so eloquently spoken would be realized.

Today, thirty-five years after King's historic address, despite the repudiation of racist ideologies and substantial changes in many facets of society, race and ethnicity remain prominent features of American life. Civil rights legislation and well-intentioned commitments on the part of many whites have not eliminated controversies over racial and ethnic matters. For example, social programs such as affirmative action, busing, and bilingual education, all of which were implemented in order to remedy the effects of past discrimination and to achieve greater equity among racial and ethnic groups, have been denounced by scholars and politicians who contend that they contravene the very goals of equality for which they were enacted. Indeed, far from withering away, debates concerning what constitutes a racially and ethnically just society, and what are the appropriate mechanisms with which to achieve it, show little sign of diminishing in intensity.

Most important, however, is that these debates creatively and dramatically be translated into public policies that imaginatively address the racial and ethnic inequalities in American life documented throughout this book. The urgency with which this goal should be considered is reflected in numerous reports, speeches, and appeals, but never more so than in one report, *One-Third of a Nation*. Prepared by a commission cochaired by former presidents Jimmy Carter and Gerald Ford, the report warned that the future prosperity of the United States was jeopardized by the nation's failures to address the problems confronted by its racial and ethnic minorities.

> *America is moving backward—not forward—in its efforts to achieve the full participation of mi-nority citizens in the life and prosperity of the nation. . . . In education, employment, income, health, longevity, and other basic measures of individual and social well-being, gaps persist—and in some cases are widening—between members of minority groups and the majority popu-lation. . . . If we allow these disparities to continue, the United States inevitably will suffer a compromised quality of life and a lower standard of living. . . . In brief, we will find ourselves unable to fulfill the promise of the American dream. (American Council on Education 1988:1)*

A decade later, a private bipartisan commission appointed by the Milton S. Eisenhower Foundation to assess changes in American race relations since the 1968 Kerner Com-mission report reached a similar conclusion: despite a substantial expansion of the African American middle class in the succeeding thirty years, the threat of "two societies—one black, one white, separate and unequal" has persisted. Today Ameri-can society is characterized by a "millenium breach"—increasing social inequality —that has dramatically and disproportionately affected African Americans and His-panics (Eisenhower Foundation 1998). The ability of the United States to respond to the challenges of these growing inequalities will, in large measure, determine the nation's future prosperity and its stature in the estimation of the world during the twenty-first century.